Lecture Notes in Computer Science   6451

Commenced Publication in 1973
Founding and Former Series Editors:
Gerhard Goos, Juris Hartmanis, and Jan van Leeuwen

Christian Scheideler (Ed.)

Algorithms for Sensor Systems

6th International Workshop on Algorithms
for Sensor Systems, Wireless Ad Hoc Networks,
and Autonomous Mobile Entities
ALGOSENSORS 2010
Bordeaux, France, July 5, 2010
Revised Selected Papers

 Springer

Volume Editor

Christian Scheideler
University of Paderborn
Department of Computer Science
Fürstenallee 11
33102 Paderborn
Germany
E-mail: scheidel@mail.uni-paderborn.de

Library of Congress Control Number: 2010938294

CR Subject Classification (1998): F.2, G.1.2, G.2.2, C.2, I.2.9, D.2, E.1

LNCS Sublibrary: SL 5 – Computer Communication Networks and
Telecommunications

ISSN	0302-9743
ISBN-10	3-642-16987-2 Springer Berlin Heidelberg New York
ISBN-13	978-3-642-16987-8 Springer Berlin Heidelberg New York

springer.com

© Springer-Verlag Berlin Heidelberg 2010
Printed in Germany

Typesetting: Camera-ready by author, data conversion by Scientific Publishing Services, Chennai, India
Printed on acid-free paper   06/3180

Preface

This volume contains the papers presented at ALGOSENSORS 2010, the 6th International Workshop on Algorithms for Sensor Systems, Wireless Ad Hoc Networks and Autonomous Mobile Entities, held on July 5, 2010 in Bordeaux, France.

There were 31 submissions. Each submission was reviewed by four Program Committee members. The committee decided to accept 15 papers, among them two brief announcements.

The Program Committee would like to thank all who submitted papers and all the external reviewers who helped us evaluate the submissions. As the Program Chair of ALGOSENSORS 2010, I would like to express my deep gratitude to the Program Committee for all of their work during the paper review process and the fruitful discussions. I would also like to thank the Workshops Chair Ralf Klasing for organizing a wonderful workshop in Bordeaux.

July 2010   Christian Scheideler

Conference Organization

Program Chair

Christian Scheideler   University of Paderborn, Germany

Program Committee

Matthew Andrews	Bell Laboratories, USA
Novella Bartolini	University of Rome "La Sapienza," Italy
Prosenjit Bose	Carleton University, Canada
Ioannis Caragiannis	University of Patras, Greece
Bogdan Chlebus	University of Colorado Denver, USA
Sándor Fekete	Braunschweig University of Technology, Germany
Hannes Frey	University of Paderborn, Germany
Jie Gao	SUNY Stony Brook, USA
Ralf Klasing	CNRS & University of Bordeaux (LaBRI) & INRIA, France
Miroslaw Korzeniowski	Wroclaw University of Technology, Poland
Pierre Leone	University of Geneva, Switzerland
Xu Li	University of Ottawa, Canada
Zvi Lotker	Ben-Gurion University of the Negev, Israel
Alberto Marchetti-Spaccamela	University of Rome "La Sapienca," Italy
Thomas Moscibroda	Microsoft Research, USA
Pekka Orponen	Aalto University, Finland
Victor Prasanna	University of Southern California, USA
Liam Roditty	Bar-Ilan University, Israel
Paolo Santi	CNR, Italy
Gabriel Scalosub	Ben-Gurion University of the Negev, Israel
Christian Schindelhauer	University of Freiburg, Germany
Stefan Schmid	Deutsche Telekom Laboratories, Germany
Berthold Vöcking	RWTH Aachen, Germany

Local Arrangements

Ralf Klasing   CNRS & University of Bordeaux (LaBRI) & INRIA, France

External Reviewers

Nicolas Bonichon

Michael Borokhovich

Shiri Chechick

Mohammad Farshi

Maciek Gabala

Lee-Ad Gottlieb

David Ilcinkas

Artur Jez

Thomas Kesselheim

Marek Klonowski

Luca Moscardelli

Animesh Pathak

Andrzej Pelc

Hanan Shpungin

Simone Silvestri

Marcin Zawada

Table of Contents

Improved Local Algorithms for Spanner Construction

Iyad A. Kanj[1] and Ge Xia[2]

[1] School of Computing, DePaul University, 243 S. Wabash Avenue,
Chicago, IL 60604, USA
ikanj@cs.depaul.edu
[2] Department of Computer Science, Acopian Engineering Center,
Lafayette College, Easton PA 18042, USA
gexia@cs.lafayette.edu

Abstract. Let S be a set of n points in the plane, let $\mathcal{E}$ be the complete Euclidean graph whose point-set is S, and let G be the Delaunay triangulation of S. We present a very simple *local* algorithm that, given G, constructs a subgraph of G of degree at most 11 that is a geometric spanner of G with stretch factor 2.86, and hence a geometric spanner of $\mathcal{E}$ with stretch factor < 7. This algorithm gives an $O(n \lg n)$ time centralized algorithm for constructing a subgraph of G that is a geometric spanner of $\mathcal{E}$ of degree at most 11 and stretch factor < 7.

The algorithm can be generalized to unit disk graphs to give a local algorithm for constructing a plane spanner of a unit disk graph of degree at most 11 and stretch factor < 7.

Keywords: spanners, Delaunay triangulations, unit disk graphs.

1 Introduction

Let S be a set of points in the plane, and let $\mathcal{E}$ be the complete Euclidean graph whose point-set is S. It is well known that the Delaunay triangulation G of S is a plane geometric (i.e., with respect to the Euclidean distance) spanner of $\mathcal{E}$ with stretch factor $C_{del} < 2.42$ [13].

In this paper we consider the problem of constructing a bounded-degree subgraph of G that is a spanner of G under the *local* model of computation. The motivation behind these requirements stems from applications in wireless ad-hoc and sensor networks. In such applications plane spanners are used as the underlying topologies for efficient unicasting, multicasting, and broadcasting (see [4,5,10,14,15,17,19]). The bounded degree requirement is important for minimizing interference among the wireless devices in the network. A suitable model of computation for such systems is the *local* model, in which the computation performed by each device only depends on the information available within its neighborhood. More formally, a *local* algorithm is a distributed algorithm that can be simulated to run in a constant number of synchronous communication rounds [18].

C. Scheideler (Ed.): ALGOSENSORS 2010, LNCS 6451, pp. 1–15, 2010.

Under the centralized model of computation, the problem of constructing a bounded-degree subgraph of G that is a spanner has received significant interest. Bose et al. [3,4] were the first to show how to extract a subgraph of G that is a spanner of $\mathcal{E}$ with degree at most 27 and stretch factor 10.02. Bose et al. [7] then improved the aforementioned result and showed how to construct a subgraph of G that is a spanner of $\mathcal{E}$ with degree at most 17 and stretch factor 23. This result was subsequently improved by Kanj and Perković [11] who presented an algorithm that constructs a subgraph of G with degree at most 14 and stretch factor 3.54 (w.r.t. $\mathcal{E}$).[1] Very recently (unpublished), Carmi and Chaitman [8] were able to improve Kanj and Perković's result further by presenting an algorithm that computes a subgraph of G with degree at most 7 and stretch factor $(1 + \sqrt{2})^2 \cdot C_{del} < 14.1$. Carmi and Chaitman's result [8] can be extended to the distributed model of computation to yield a distributed algorithm that computes a subgraph of G of degree at most 7 and stretch factor 14.1; however, their algorithm is inherently nonlocal. All the aforementioned centralized algorithms run in $O(n)$ time when G is given as input, and in time $O(n \lg n)$ otherwise $(n = |S|)$. We note that, very recently, a spanner of $\mathcal{E}$ of degree at most 6 and stretch factor 6 was given in [2]. This spanner, however, is *not* a subgraph of G.

Computing a subgraph of G of minimum degree that is a spanner is a very challenging open problem in computational geometry (for example, see the recent survey by Bose and Smid [6]). Therefore, it becomes challenging to compute a subgraph of G of "small degree" that is a spanner. The problem, of course, becomes even more challenging if we restrict ourselves to local algorithms, due to the strict limitations imposed by the local model of computation. As a matter of fact, under the local model of computation, we are only aware of Kanj and Perković's result [11], which gives the first local algorithm that computes a subgraph of G of degree at most 14 and stretch factor 3.54.

In this paper we make some progress towards solving the aforementioned problem. We present a very simple local algorithm that constructs a subgraph of G of degree at most 11 and stretch factor 2.86 with respect to G, and hence stretch factor $2.86 \cdot C_{del} < 7$ with respect to $\mathcal{E}$. The algorithm can be implemented to run in 2 synchronous communication rounds (i.e., the locality is 2). To put the result of this paper in context, this result improves the local algorithm of Kanj and Perković [11] in terms of the minimum degree bound achieved (11 versus 14). Moreover, the algorithm presented in the current paper is simpler than that in [11].

The local algorithm presented in this paper can be implemented to run in $O(n)$ time under the centralized model when G is given, and in $O(n \lg n)$ time otherwise.

We note that in wireless computing the network is often modeled as a *unit disk graph* (UDG) rather than a complete Euclidean graph. Many of the algorithms mentioned above (among others) can be modified to construct bounded-degree plane spanners of UDGs [3,4,11,12] (see also [19]). The results in this paper can

---

[1] A journal version of the results in [11] appears in [12] (with G. Xia).

be generalized to give a local algorithm for constructing a bounded-degree plane spanner of a UDG with the same upper bounds described above on the degree and the stretch factor.

2 Preliminaries

Given a set of points S in the 2-dimensional Euclidean plane, the complete Euclidean graph $\mathcal{E}$ on S is defined to be the complete graph whose point-set is S. Each edge ab connecting points a and b is assumed to be embedded in the plane as the straight line segment ab; the *weight* of ab is the Euclidean distance $|ab|$.

Let H be a subgraph of $\mathcal{E}$. The weight of a simple path $a = m_0, m_1, ..., m_r = b$ in H is $\sum_{j=0}^{r-1} |m_j m_{j+1}|$. A subgraph H' of H is said to be a *geometric spanner* of H if there is a constant ρ such that, for every two points $a, b \in H$, the weight of a shortest path from a to b in H' is at most ρ times the weight of a shortest path from a to b in H. The constant ρ is called the *stretch factor* of H' (with respect to H). The following is a well known—and obvious—fact:

Fact 1. *A subgraph H' of graph H has stretch factor ρ with respect to H if and only if for every edge $xy \in H$: the weight of a shortest path in H' from x to y is at most $\rho \cdot |xy|$.*

For three non-collinear points x, y, z in the plane we denote by $\bigcirc xyz$ the circumscribed circle of $\triangle xyz$. A *Delaunay triangulation* of S is a triangulation of S such that the circumscribed circle of every triangle in this triangulation (i.e., every triangular face) contains no point of S in its interior [9]. It is well known that if the points in S are *in general position* (no four points in S are cocircular) then the Delaunay triangulation of S is unique [9]. In this paper—as in most papers in the literature—we shall assume that the points in S are in general position; otherwise, the input can be slightly perturbed so that this condition is satisfied. The *Delaunay graph* of S is defined as the plane graph whose point-set is S and whose edges are the edges of the Delaunay triangulation of S. An alternative equivalent definition, usually referred to as the *empty circle* property, that we end up using is:

Definition 1 (The empty circle property). ([9]) An edge xy is in the Delaunay graph of S if and only if there exists a circle through points x and y whose interior contains no point in S.

It is well known that the Delaunay graph of S is a spanner of $\mathcal{E}$ with stretch factor $C_{del} \leq 4\sqrt{3}\pi/9 < 2.42$ [13].

Given integer parameter $k > 6$, the *Yao subgraph* [20] of a plane graph H is constructed by performing the following *Yao step*: For each point p in H partition the space (arbitrarily) into k cones of equal measure/size whose apex is p, thus creating k closed cones of angle $2\pi/k$ each, and choose the shortest edge in H out of p (if any) in each cone. The Yao subgraph consists of edges in H chosen by *either* endpoint. Note that the degree of a point in the Yao subgraph of H may be unbounded.

Let G be the Delaunay graph of S. Let ca and cb be edges in G. If the interior of $\triangle cab$ is devoid of points of G, then it can be easily shown using the empty circle property (see Definition 1), that the interior of $\bigcirc cab$ subtended by chord ab whose boundary contains point c, contains no points of G (for example, see Proposition 3.3 in [12]). In this case Keil and Gutwin [13] showed the following:

Lemma 1 (Lemma 1 in [13]). *If the interior of $\bigcirc abc$ subtended by chord ab whose boundary contains point c is devoid of points of S, then there exists a path from a to b in G, in the region interior to $\bigcirc abc$ subtended by chord ab whose boundary does not contain c, whose weight is at most the length of arc $\overset{\frown}{ab}$.*

Note that if $ab \in G$ then the path described in Lemma 1 is simply the edge ab.

Let ca and cb be edges in G, and suppose that the interior of $\triangle cab$ contains no points of S. Let $\mathcal{P} : (a = m_0, m_1, \ldots, m_k = b)$ be the path referred to in Lemma 1. The path $\mathcal{P}$ was called the *canonical path* between a and b in [11,12], and the following structural properties about $\mathcal{P}$ were proved:

Lemma 2 ([11,12]). *Let ca and cb be edges in G such that $\angle bca \leq \theta$.[2] The canonical path $\mathcal{P} : (a = m_0, m_1, \ldots, m_k = b)$ in G satisfies:*

(i) *There is an edge from c to m_i, for $i = 0, \ldots, k$. Hence, if $ab \notin G$ then there is no edge in G between any pair m_i and m_j lying in the closed region enclosed by ca, cb and the edges of $\mathcal{P}$, for any i and j satisfying $0 \leq i < j \leq k$.*

(ii) *Assuming that G is a triangulation, it follows from part (i) above that $\mathcal{P}$ is unique.*

(iii) *$\angle m_{i-1} m_i m_{i+1} > \pi - \angle m_{i-1} c m_{i+1} > \pi - \theta$, for $i = 1, \ldots, k-1$.*

Two edges mx, my incident to a point m in a subgraph H of $\mathcal{E}$ are said to be *consecutive* if one of the angular sectors determined by the two segments mx and my in the plane contains no neighbors of m.

The statement of the following lemma is well known and can be easily verified by the reader:

Lemma 3. *The function $\alpha / \sin(\alpha)$ is an increasing function in the interval $(0, \pi/2]$.*

Lemma 4. *Let $|\overset{\frown}{yz}|$ denote the arc facing angle $\angle yxz$ in $\bigcirc xyz$, and suppose that $\angle yxz \leq \theta$, where $\theta \in (0, \pi/2]$. Then $|\overset{\frown}{yz}|/|yz| = \angle yxz / \sin(\angle yxz) \leq \theta / \sin \theta$.*

Proof. The equality $|\overset{\frown}{yz}|/|yz| = \angle yxz / \sin(\angle yxz)$ is true by simple geometric arguments. The inequality $\angle yxz / \sin(\angle yxz) \leq \theta / \sin \theta$ follows from Lemma 3.

The *unit disk graph* (UDG) on point-set S is the subgraph of $\mathcal{E}$ consisting of all edges xy with $|xy| \leq 1$.

---

[2] All angles in this paper are measured in radians.

3   The Spanner

Let G be the Delaunay graph of S. The basic idea behind the local algorithm is that every point selects at most 11 of its incident edges in G, and edges that are selected by both endpoints are kept; this guarantees that the degree of the resulting subgraph of G is at most 11. To ensure that the resulting subgraph is a spanner of G, we first guarantee that whenever an edge $pq \in G$ is not kept in the subgraph: (1) an edge pr is kept such that $|pr| \leq |pq|$ and $\angle rpq \leq \pi/5$, and (2) all edges on the canonical path from r to q, except possibly the first and the last edges are kept in the subgraph. Second, we use an inductive proof to show that even when the first and last edges on a canonical path are not kept, a "short" path between the endpoints of each of these two edges exists in the subgraph, which then can be used to upper bound the length of a path from r to q in the subgraph. Ensuring property (1) above requires an idea that seems counterintuitive at the surface: a longer edge incident to a point is selected in favor of a shorter consecutive edge in certain cases (step 4 of the algorithm **Spanner**, given in Figure 1). This favoritism also (implicitly) allows the inductive proof to go through (induction is now applied to "shorter" edges).

We start by presenting the local algorithm that constructs the subgraph of G and prove that it has degree at most 11 in Subsection 3.1. Then we proceed to prove an upper bound on its stretch factor in Subsection 3.2. Everything is then put together in Subsection 3.3.

3.1   The Algorithm

The algorithm is presented in a way that emphasizes its locality: each point in G selects its candidate edges independently based only on its coordinates and the coordinates of its neighbors, and only edges that are selected by both their endpoints are kept in the spanner.

A sequence of three consecutive edges incident to a point p is said to be *wide* if the sum of the two angles formed by the two pairs of consecutive edges in this sequence is at least $4\pi/5$.

Every point $p \in G$ executes the algorithm **Spanner** given in Figure 1.

Definition 2. Point p *selects* an edge pq when point p selects pq in steps 1-4 of the algorithm **Spanner**. Point p *keeps* an edge pq when both p and q select pq.

Let G' be the subgraph of G consisting of the edges that are kept after the points in G have applied the algorithm **Spanner**.

Lemma 5. *Point p selects every edge of a wide sequence of edges around it.*

Proof. The statement directly follows form step 1 of the algorithm **Spanner**.

We have the following theorem whose proof is omitted for lack of space:

Theorem 2. *The subgraph G' of G has degree at most 11.*

Algorithm Spanner

1. for every wide sequence of edges around p, p selects the three edges in the sequence;

2. p partitions the remaining space around it (the space left after the sectors determined by the wide sequences are removed) into cones of apex p, each of size $\pi/5$ (note that the boundary cones might be of smaller size);

3. p selects the shortest edge in every nonempty cone, breaking ties arbitrarily;

4. for every empty cone around p, let pr and ps be the two consecutive edges incident to p such that the empty cone is contained within the sector $\angle rps$; if pr (resp. ps) has been already selected, then p selects ps (resp. pr); otherwise, p selects the longer edge between pr and ps breaking ties arbitrarily;

5. p keeps an edge pq if and only if pq is selected by both p and q;

Fig. 1. The algorithm Spanner

3.2 The Stretch Factor

For any two points p, q in S, denote by $d_{G'}(p, q)$ the weight of a shortest path between p and q in G'. To prove that the stretch factor of G', with respect to G, is at most $\rho = \frac{2\sin(2\pi/5)\cos(\pi/5)}{(2\sin(2\pi/5)\cos(\pi/5)-1)} < 2.86$, by Fact 1, it suffices to show that for every edge pq in G such that pq is not kept in G', $d_{G'}(p, q) \leq \rho|pq|$. (The choice of ρ will be justified in Proposition 1.) The proof is by induction on the rank of pq among all edges in G. The base case is when pq is the shortest edge in G. In this case if point p does not select edge pq in step 1 of the algorithm, edge pq will end up being the shortest edge in its cone, and hence will be selected in step 3 of the algorithm. Similarly, point q will also select edge pq, and hence pq is kept in G'. Therefore, $d_{G'}(p, q) = |pq| \leq \rho|pq|$. Now let pq be an edge in G, and assume by the inductive hypothesis that for every edge $xy \in G$ such that the rank of xy is smaller than that of pq, there exists a path from x to y in G' of weight at most $\rho|xy|$. We will show that there exists a path from p to q in G' of weight at most $\rho|pq|$.

If pq is kept in G', then $d_{G'}(p, q) = |pq| \leq \rho|pq|$, and we are done. Therefore, we can assume in the rest of the proof that pq is not kept in G'. From step 5 in the algorithm **Spanner**, it follows that at least one of the points p, q does not select pq. Assume, without loss of generality, that p does not select pq. By Lemma 8 (proved below), p selects an edge pr such that: $|pr| \leq |pq|$, $\angle rpq \leq \pi/5$, and pr is kept in G'. We will exhibit a path from r to q in G', which, together with edge pr, gives a path from p to q of weight at most $\rho|pq|$. The proof is divided into two cases: the interior of $\triangle pqr$ contains no points in S (Proposition 1), and the interior of $\triangle pqr$ contains points in S (Proposition 2). Before we can proceed further, we will need the following technical lemmas:

Lemma 6. *Let xy and xz be two consecutive edges such that $|xy| > |xz|$ and $\angle yxz \geq 2\pi/5$. Then point x selects xy in the algorithm* **Spanner**.

Proof. If xy is not selected by x in step 1 of the algorithm, then when x partitions the space around it into cones of apex x in step 2, at least one empty cone will be contained in the sector $\angle yxz$. This is true because each cone has size at most $\pi/5$ and $\angle yxz \geq 2\pi/5$. Since $|xy| > |xz|$, x is guaranteed to select xy in step 4 of the algorithm.

Lemma 7. *Let xy and xz be two consecutive edges such that $\angle yxz \geq 3\pi/5$. Then point x selects both xy and xz in the algorithm* **Spanner***.*

Proof. If xy and xz are not edges of a wide sequence around x, then since $\angle yxz \geq 3\pi/5$, two empty cones defined in step 2 of the algorithm must fall within $\angle yxz$. When x considers these two empty cones in step 4, it will end up selecting both xy and xz.

Lemma 8. *Let pq be an edge in G. If point p does not select pq in the algorithm* **Spanner***, then p selects an edge pr such that $|pr| \leq |pq|$ and $\angle rpq \leq \pi/5$. Moreover, edge pr is kept in G'.*

Proof. Suppose that p does not select pq. Since p does not select pq in step 1 of the algorithm, pq belongs to a cone $\mathcal{C}$ of apex p defined in step 2. Since p does not select pq in step 3, p must have selected an edge pr in $\mathcal{C}$ such that $|pr| \leq |pq|$. Since the angle of $\mathcal{C}$ is at most $\pi/5$, $\angle rpq \leq \pi/5$.

To show that $pr \in G'$, since p selects pr, it suffices to show that pr is selected by point r in the algorithm **Spanner**. Let ps be the edge consecutive to pr in $\mathcal{C}$ (note that ps might be pq). Consider $\triangle rps$, and note that since G is a triangulation and pr and ps are consecutive edges, all edges of $\triangle rps$ are edges in G. In particular, rp and rs are consecutive edges in G. If $\angle prs \geq 3\pi/5$, then by Lemma 7 applied to rp and rs, r selects rp and we are done. Assume now that $\angle prs < 3\pi/5$. Since $\angle rps \leq \angle rpq \leq \pi/5$, it follows that $\angle psr = \pi - \angle prs - \angle rps > \pi/5$, and hence $|pr| > |rs|$. Since pr is a shortest edge in $\mathcal{C}$, $|pr| \leq |ps|$, which together with $\angle rps \leq \pi/5$, implies that $\angle prs \geq (\pi - \pi/5)/2 = 2\pi/5$. Now since $|rp| > |rs|$ and $\angle prs \geq 2\pi/5$, r selects rp by Lemma 6 applied to rp and rs. It follows that pr is kept in G'.

Lemma 9. *Let pr and pq be edges in G such that $\angle rpq \leq \pi/5$ and $|pr| \leq |pq|$. If $pr \in G'$ and $d_{G'}(r,q) \leq \rho|rq|$ then $d_{G'}(p,q) \leq \rho|pq|$.*

Proof. Let $\alpha = \angle qpr$ and $\beta = \angle rqp$. Since $pr \in G'$ and $d_{G'}(r,q) \leq \rho|rq|$, we have $d_{G'}(p,q) \leq |pr| + \rho|rq|$. Therefore, it suffices to show that $|pr| + \rho|rq| \leq \rho|pq|$. We have:

$$|pr| + \rho|rq| \leq \rho|pq|$$
$$\Leftrightarrow \sin\beta + \rho\sin\alpha \leq \rho\sin(\alpha + \beta)$$
$$\Leftrightarrow \sin\beta \leq \rho(\sin(\alpha + \beta) - \sin\alpha)$$
$$\Leftrightarrow \frac{\sin\beta}{\sin(\alpha + \beta) - \sin\alpha} \leq \rho.$$

The last inequality is true because $\alpha \leq \pi/5$ and $|pq| \geq |pr|$, which together imply that $\beta \leq \pi/2 - \alpha/2$, and hence $\sin(\alpha + \beta) > \sin\alpha$. Using trigonometric identities we can derive that:

$$\frac{\sin\beta}{\sin(\alpha+\beta)-\sin\alpha}=\frac{1}{\cos\alpha-\tan(\beta/2)\sin\alpha}.$$

Since $\alpha \le \pi/5$, $\beta/2 \le \pi/4-\alpha/4$, $\cos\alpha$ is decreasing in $[0,\pi/5]$, $\sin\alpha$ is increasing in $[0,\pi/5]$, and $\tan(\beta/2)$ is increasing in $[0,\pi/2)$, we have:

$$\frac{1}{\cos\alpha-\tan(\beta/2)\sin\alpha} \le \frac{1}{\cos(\alpha)-\tan(\pi/4-\alpha/4)\sin\alpha}$$
$$=\frac{\cos(\pi/4-\alpha/4)}{\cos(\pi/4+3\alpha/4)} \le \cos(\pi/5)/\cos(2\pi/5) \le \rho.$$

The inequality before the last follows from the facts that $\alpha \le \pi/5$ and the cosine function is decreasing in $[0,\pi/2]$.

Lemma 10. *Let x,y,z be three points in S. Let $\alpha=\angle xyz$, $\beta=\angle yxz$, and $\gamma=\alpha+\beta$. If $\gamma \le \pi/5$, $d_{G'}(y,z) \le \frac{\pi}{5\sin(\pi/5)}|yz|$, and $d_{G'}(x,z) \le \rho|xz|$, then $d_{G'}(x,y) \le \rho|xy|$.*

Proof. Since $d_{G'}(x,y) \le d_{G'}(x,z)+d_{G'}(z,y)$, from the statement of the lemma it follows that $d_{G'}(x,y) \le \frac{\pi}{5\sin(\pi/5)}|yz|+\rho|xz|$. Therefore, it suffices to show that $\frac{\pi}{5\sin(\pi/5)}|yz|+\rho|xz| \le \rho|xy|$. We have:

$$\frac{\pi}{5\sin(\pi/5)}|yz|+\rho|xz| \le \rho|xy|$$

$$\Leftrightarrow \frac{\pi}{5\sin(\pi/5)}\sin\beta+\rho\sin\alpha \le \rho\sin\gamma \quad \text{(using trigonometric relations in } \triangle xyz\text{)}$$

$$\Leftrightarrow \frac{\pi}{5\sin(\pi/5)}\sin\beta \le \rho(\sin\gamma-\sin\alpha)$$

$$\Leftrightarrow \frac{\frac{\pi}{5\sin(\pi/5)}\sin\beta}{\sin\gamma-\sin\alpha} \le \rho \quad \text{(because } \sin\gamma > \sin\alpha\text{)}$$

$$\Leftrightarrow \frac{\frac{\pi}{5\sin(\pi/5)}}{\frac{\sin\gamma-\sin(\gamma-\beta)}{\sin\beta}} \le \rho$$

$$\Leftrightarrow \frac{\frac{\pi}{5\sin(\pi/5)}}{\sin\gamma(\frac{1-\cos\beta}{\sin\beta})+\cos\gamma} \le \rho$$

$$\Leftrightarrow \frac{\frac{\pi}{5\sin(\pi/5)}}{\sin\gamma\tan\frac{\beta}{2}+\cos\gamma} \le \rho.$$

Since $\sin\gamma\tan\frac{\beta}{2} \ge 0$ (both $\beta,\gamma \in [0,\pi/5]$), and since the function $\cos x$ is a decreasing function in $(0,\pi/2]$, we have $\frac{\frac{\pi}{5\sin(\pi/5)}}{\sin\gamma\tan\frac{\beta}{2}+\cos\gamma} \le \frac{\pi}{5\sin(\pi/5)\cos(\pi/5)} \le \rho$, as required.

Now we are ready for the proof. Suppose first that the interior of $\triangle prq$ contains no points of S. Consider the canonical path $\mathcal{P}:\langle m_0=r,m_1,\ldots,m_k=q\rangle$ from r to q in G, defined in Section 2. Observe the following:

Observation 1. *Every internal point on $\mathcal{P}$ selects both edges incident to it on $\mathcal{P}$. Therefore, every edge on $\mathcal{P}$, except possibly the first and the last edges, are kept in G'.*

Proof. For any internal point m_i on $\mathcal{P}$ $(0 < i < k)$, $\angle m_{i-1} m_i m_{i+1} \geq \pi - \pi/5 \geq 4\pi/5$ by part (iii) of Lemma 2. Therefore, both edges $m_{i-1} m_i$ and $m_i m_{i+1}$ are edges of a wide sequence of edges around m_i (note that $pm_i \in G$, for $i = 0, \ldots, k$, by part (i) of Lemma 2). By Lemma 5, m_i selects both edges $m_i m_{i-1}$ and $m_i m_{i+1}$.

Now for every edge on $\mathcal{P}$ other than the first and last edges, both its endpoints are internal points on $\mathcal{P}$. Therefore, both endpoints of this edge select the edge, and the edge is kept in G'.

By Observation 1, at most two edges on $\mathcal{P}$ are not kept in G'. We distinguish the following two cases: at most one edge of $\mathcal{P}$ is not kept in G', and exactly two edges of $\mathcal{P}$ are not kept in G'.

We first consider the case when at most one edge of $\mathcal{P}$ is not kept in G'. We prove a more general result that will be useful in the treatment of the other cases as well.

Lemma 11. *Let pu and pv be any two edges in G such that $\angle upv \leq \pi/5$, $|uv| < |pq|$, and the interior of $\triangle puv$ contains no points of S. Let P_{uv} be the canonical path from u to v in G. If at most one edge of P_{uv} is not kept in G' then $d_{G'}(u, v) \leq \rho|uv|$.*

Proof. The proof is by induction on the number of edges on P_{uv}, denoted $|P_{uv}|$. To distinguish the current induction from the main one used in this subsection to upper bound the stretch factor, we refer to the hypothesis of the current induction by $\mathcal{H}$.

If $|P_{uv}| = 1$, then $|P_{uv}|$ consists of edge uv, and hence $uv \in G$. Since $uv \in G$ and $|uv| < |pq|$, by the (main) inductive hypothesis, we have $d_{G'}(u, v) \leq \rho|uv|$, and we are done.

Suppose now that $|P_{uv}| > 1$. Then there exists an internal point w on P_{uv} (i.e., w is different from u and v). Among all internal points on P_{uv}, choose w so that $\angle uwv$ is maximum. By the choice of w, no point of S is interior to $\triangle uwv$. Consequently, the interior of both $\triangle puw$ and $\triangle pwv$ contain no points of S. Consider the two subpaths P_{uw} and P_{wv} of P_{uv} from u to w and from w to v, respectively. Then we have $|P_{uw}| < |P_{uv}|$ and $|P_{wv}| < |P_{uv}|$. Since $pu, pw, pv \in G$ by part (i) of Lemma 2, and by part (ii) of Lemma 2, it follows that P_{uw} is the canonical path in G from u to w, and P_{wv} is the canonical path in G from w to v. Moreover, $\angle upw \leq \angle upv \leq \pi/5$ and $\angle wpv \leq \angle upv \leq \pi/5$. Since at most one edge on P_{uv} is not kept in G', one of the two subpaths P_{uw}, P_{wv} has all its edges in G', and at most one edge of the other subpath is not in G'. Assume, without loss of generality, that all edges of P_{wv} are kept in G', and at most one edge on P_{uw} is not kept in G'; the proof is exactly the same in the other case. By Lemma 1, we have $wt(P_{wv})$ is at most the length of arc $\widehat{wv}$ facing angle $\angle wpv$ in $\bigcirc pwv$. Since $\angle wpv \leq \pi/5$, by Lemma 4, $|\widehat{wv}| \leq (\pi/(5\sin(\pi/5)))|wv|$.

Therefore, $d_{G'}(w,v) \leq (\pi/(5\sin(\pi/5)))|wv|$. On the other hand, since P_{uw} is the canonical path from u to w, $|P_{uw}| < |P_{uv}|$, and at most one edge on P_{uw} is not kept in G', by the current inductive hypothesis $\mathcal{H}$ we have $d_{G'}(u,w) \leq \rho|uw|$. Consider $\triangle uwv$, and let $\alpha = \angle uvw$, $\beta = \angle vuw$, and $\gamma = \alpha+\beta$. Since w is on the canonical path P_{uv}, and hence w is in the region of $\bigcirc puv$ subtended by chord uv, we have $\gamma = \alpha + \beta \leq \angle upv \leq \pi/5$. Now consider the three points u, w, and v. Noting the previous facts, we can apply Lemma 10 with $x = u$, $y = v$, and $z = w$ to conclude that $d_{G'}(u,v) \leq \rho|uv|$.

Corollary 1. *If at most one edge of the canonical path $\mathcal{P}$ from r to q is not kept in G' then $d_{G'}(r,q) \leq \rho|rq|$.*

Proof. Apply Lemma 11 with $u = r$ and $v = q$.

Lemma 12. *If exactly two edges of $\mathcal{P}$ are not kept in G' then $d_{G'}(r,q) \leq \rho|rq|/(\sin(2\pi/5))$.*

Proof. If two edges of $\mathcal{P}$ are not kept in G', then by Observation 1 those edges are the first and last edges rm_1 and qm_{k-1}, respectively. We refer the reader to Figure 2 for illustration.

Choose an internal point w on $\mathcal{P}$ that maximizes $\angle rwq$. As was explained in the proof of Lemma 11, from the choice of w it follows that no point of S is interior to $\triangle rwq$, and consequently, the interior of both $\triangle prw$ and $\triangle pwq$ contain no points of S. Consider the two subpaths P_{rw} and P_{wq} of $\mathcal{P}$ from r to w and from w to q, respectively. Since $pr, pw, pq \in G$ by part (i) of Lemma 2, and by part (ii) of Lemma 2, it follows that P_{rw} is the canonical path in G from r to w, and P_{wq} is the canonical path in G from w to q. Moreover, $\angle rpw \leq \angle rpq \leq \pi/5$ and $\angle wpq \leq \angle rpq \leq \pi/5$. Since edges rm_1 and qm_{k-1} are the only edges on $\mathcal{P}$ that are possibly not kept in G', at most one edge on P_{rw} is not kept in G', and at most one edge on P_{wq} is not kept in G'. After noting that $|rw| < |pq|$ and $|wq| < |pq|$ (follow from the facts that w is in the region of $\bigcirc prq$ subtended by chord rq, and hence $|rw| \leq |rq|$ and $|wq| \leq |rq|$, and that $|rq| < |pq|$), we can now apply Lemma 11 to P_{rw} and to P_{wq} to conclude that $d_{G'}(r,w) \leq \rho|rw|$ and $d_{G'}(w,q) \leq \rho|wq|$.

Now consider $\triangle rwq$ and observe that since pw is an edge in G, we have $\angle rwq \geq \pi - \pi/5 = 4\pi/5$. Under the condition that $\angle rwq \geq 4\pi/5$ in $\triangle rwq$, it follows from basic geometry that $|rw| + |wq|$ is maximum when $\angle rwq = 4\pi/5$ and $|rw| = |wq|$. In this case we have $|rw| + |wq| \leq |rq|/(\sin(2\pi/5))$. It follows that $d_{G'}(r,q) \leq d_{G'}(r,w) + d_{G'}(w,q) \leq \rho(|rw| + |wq|) \leq \rho|rq|/(\sin(2\pi/5))$.

Now we are ready to prove that $d_{G'}(p,q) \leq \rho|pq|$ in the case when $\triangle pqr$ contains no points of S.

Proposition 1. *If the interior of $\triangle pqr$ contains no points of S then $d_{G'}(p,q) \leq \rho|pq|$.*

Proof. Consider the canonical path $\mathcal{P}$ from r to q. By Observation 1, at most two edges on $\mathcal{P}$ are not kept in G'.

If at most one edge of $\mathcal{P}$ is not kept in G', then by Corollary 1, we have $d_{G'}(r, q) \le \rho|rq|$. Now $pr \in G'$, $|pr| \le |pq|$, $\angle prq \le \pi/5$, and $d_{G'}(r, q) \le \rho|rq|$, it follows from Lemma 9 that $d_{G'}(p, q) \le \rho|pq|$.

If exactly two edges of $\mathcal{P}$ are not kept in G', then by Observation 1 those edges must be rm_1 and qm_{k-1}. By Lemma 12, we have $d_{G'}(r, q) \le \rho|rq|/(\sin(2\pi/5))$. Since rm_1 and qm_{k-1} were not kept in G', and since rm_1 was selected by m_1 and qm_{k-1} was selected by m_{k-1} (Observation 1), it follows that rm_1 was not selected by r and qm_{k-1} was not selected by q, in the algorithm **Spanner**. Since rp and rm_1 are consecutive edges at r, and pq and qm_{k-1} are consecutive edges at q (implied from part (i) of Lemma 2 and the fact that G is a triangulation), by Lemma 7, it follows that each of $\angle prm_1$ and $\angle pqm_{k-1}$ is less than $3\pi/5$, which, in turn, implies that each of $\angle prq$ and $\angle pqr$ is less than $3\pi/5$. Consider $\triangle prq$. Since $|pr| \le |pq|$, $\angle rpq \le \pi/5$, and $\angle prq < 3\pi/5$, we conclude that $2\pi/5 \le \angle prq \le 3\pi/5$, and consequently, $\sin(\angle prq) \ge \sin(2\pi/5)$. Now $|rq| = (\sin(\angle rpq)/\sin(\angle prq))|pq| \le (\sin(\pi/5)/\sin(2\pi/5))|pq| = |pq|/(2\cos(\pi/5))$. Since $d_{G'}(r, q) \le \rho|rq|/(\sin(2\pi/5))$, it follows from the previous statement that $d_{G'}(r, q) \le \rho|pq|/(2\sin(2\pi/5)\cos(\pi/5))$, and $d_{G'}(p, q) \le |pr| + d_{G'}(r, q) \le |pq| + d_{G'}(r, q) \le (1 + \rho/(2\sin(2\pi/5)\cos(\pi/5)))|pq| \le \rho|pq|$. The last inequality is true if and only if $\rho \ge \frac{2\sin(2\pi/5)\cos(\pi/5)}{(2\sin(2\pi/5)\cos(\pi/5)-1)}$, which is satisfied by the chosen value of ρ.

Proposition 2. *If the interior of $\triangle pqr$ contains points of S then $d_{G'}(p, q) \le \rho|pq|$.*

Proof. Let S' be the set of points consisting of points r and q plus all points interior to $\triangle pqr$ (note that $p \notin S'$). Let $CH(S')$ be the set of points on the

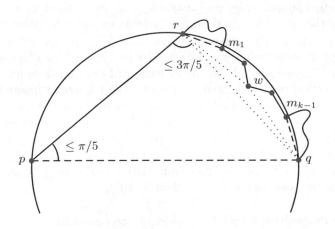

Fig. 2. Illustration for the case when both edges rm_1 and $m_{k-1}q$ are not kept in G' in the proof of Lemma 12. Dashed lines indicate edges in G and solid lines indicate edges in G that are also in G'.

convex hull of S. Then $CH(S')$ consists of points $n_0 = r$ and $n_s = q$, and some points $n_1, \ldots, n_{s-1}$ of S interior to $\triangle pqr$. Note that, by convexity, and because G is a triangulation, $pn_i \in G$, for $i = 0, \ldots, s$.

By convexity, the interior of $\triangle pn_i n_{i+1}$ contains no points of G, for $i = 0, \ldots, s-1$. Since $pn_i, pn_{i+1} \in G$, by Lemma 1 there exists a canonical path P_i from n_i to n_{i+1} in G. We argue next that at most one edge of P_i is not kept in G'.

Because n_i and n_{i+1} ($i = 0, \ldots, s-1$) are two consecutive points on $CH(S)$, and since the interior of $\triangle pqr$ is not empty, at least one of the two points n_i, n_{i+1} must be interior to $\triangle pqr$. Assume that n_i is interior to $\triangle pqr$; the proof is similar if n_{i+1} was interior (and n_i was not). If P_i consists of a single edge, then the statement that at most one edge of P_i is not kept in G' is vacuously true. Suppose now that P_i does not consist of a single edge, and consider the first point, x, after n_i on P_i. By Observation 1, at most two edges on the canonical path P_i, namely the first and the last edges (note that $\angle n_i pn_{i+1} \leq \pi/5$), are possibly not kept in G'. Therefore, to show that at most one edge on P_i is not kept in G', it suffices to show that the first edge $n_i x$ on P_i is kept in G'. Since x is an internal point on P_i, by Observation 1, x selects edge xn_i. On the other hand, n_i is a point on $CH(S)$ that is interior to $\triangle pqr$. Therefore, the angle formed by the last edge yn_i on P_{i-1} and $n_i x$ is $> \pi$. Consequently, the edges $n_i y, n_i p, n_i x$ are edges of a wide sequence around n_i (follows from part (ii) of Lemma 2), and n_i selects $n_i x$ by Lemma 5. Therefore, $n_i x \in G'$ and at most one edge on P_i is not kept in G'.

Now $pn_i, pn_{i+1} \in G$, $\angle n_i pn_{i+1} \leq \pi/5$, and at most one edge of P_i is not in G', by Lemma 11 applied to n_i and n_{i+1} after noting that $|n_i n_{i+1}| < |pq|$, we obtain $d_{G'}(n_i, n_{i+1}) \leq \rho |n_i n_{i+1}|$. It follows that $d_{G'}(r, q) = d_{G'}(n_0, n_s) \leq \sum_{i=0}^{s-1} d_{G'}(n_i, n_{i+1}) \leq \rho \sum_{i=0}^{s-1} |n_i n_{i+1}|$.

Extend rn_1 and qn_{s-1}; by convexity, rn_1 and qn_{s-1} meet at a point t inside $\triangle rpq$ (note that if $n_1 = n_s$, and hence there is exactly one point inside $\triangle pqr$, then $t = n_1 = n_{s-1}$). By convexity [1], we have $\sum_{i=0}^{s-1} |n_i n_{i+1}| \leq |rt| + |tq|$. We will now upper bound $|rt| + |tq|$. Please refer to Figure 3 for illustration.

Since $|pr| \leq |pn_1|$ and t is on the extension of rn_1, we have $|pt| \geq |pr|$. If t' is the intersection point of rt and pq, then by the triangular inequality we have $|rt| + |tq| \leq |rt'| + |t'q|$. Therefore, we may assume that t is on pq. Moreover, since $|pt| \geq |pr|$, $|rt| + |tq|$ is largest when $|pr| = |pt|$ (this corresponds to $t = t''$ in Figure 3). In this case we have $|rt| + |tq| \leq 2|pr|\sin(\pi/10) + |pq| - |pr|$ (since $|rt| \leq 2|pr|\sin(\pi/10)$). Now $d_{G'}(p, q) \leq |pr| + d_{G'}(r, q) \leq |pr| + \rho \sum_{i=0}^{s-1} |n_i n_{i+1}| \leq |pr| + \rho(|rt| + |tq|) \leq |pr| + \rho(2|pr|\sin(\pi/10) + |pq| - |pr|) \leq \rho|pq|$. The last inequality is true because $\rho \geq 1/(1 - 2\sin(\pi/10))$.

Combining Proposition 1 with Proposition 2, we conclude:

Theorem 3. *The subgraph G' is a spanner of G with stretch factor (w.r.t. G)* $\rho = \frac{2\sin(2\pi/5)\cos(\pi/5)}{(2\sin(2\pi/5)\cos(\pi/5)-1)} < 2.86$.

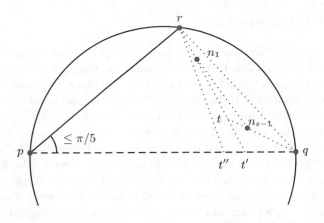

Fig. 3. Illustration for the proof of Proposition 2

3.3 Putting It Together

Combining the results in Subsection 3.1 and Subsection 3.2, we have:

Theorem 4. *The algorithm* **Spanner** *is a 2-local algorithm that, given the De-launay triangulation G of a point-set S, computes a subgraph of G of degree at most 11 that is a spanner of G with stretch factor $\rho = \frac{2\sin(2\pi/5)\cos(\pi/5)}{2\sin(2\pi/5)\cos(\pi/5)-1} < 2.86$. The processing time for each $p \in S$ in the algorithm is linear in the degree of p.*

Proof. Let G' be the subgraph of G consisting of the set of edges that are selected by both endpoints after the application of the algorithm **Spanner**. By Theorem 2, the degree of G' is at most 11. By Theorem 3, G' is a spanner of G with stretch factor (w.r.t. G) $\rho = \frac{2\sin(2\pi/5)\cos(\pi/5)}{(2\sin(2\pi/5)\cos(\pi/5)-1)} < 2.86$.

   The algorithm is a 2-local algorithm because it can be implemented in 2 synchronous communication rounds. In the first round, each point sends its co-ordinates to its neighbors. In the second round, each point p selects some edges incident on it according to steps 1-4 in the algorithm **Spanner**; then p informs each neighbor q whether it has selected edge pq or not. A point p keeps an edge pq if p has selected pq and it has received a message from its neighbor q (in the second round) indicating that q has selected pq as well. Finally, It is easy to see that the processing time at a point p is linear in the degree of p in G.

Corollary 2. *Given a set S of n points in the plane, there exists an $O(n \lg n)$ time (centralized) algorithm that computes a spanner G' of $\mathcal{E}$, such that G' is a subgraph of the Delaunay triangulation of S, G' has degree at most 11, and G' has stretch factor $\rho \cdot C_{del} < 7$ with respect to $\mathcal{E}$, where C_{del} is the stretch factor of the Delaunay triangulation of S with respect to $\mathcal{E}$.*

Proof. The algorithm starts by computing the Delaunay triangulation G of S in time $O(n \lg n)$ (see [9]), and then feeds G to the algorithm **Spanner**. Noting that the stretch factor of G (with respect to $\mathcal{E}$) is $C_{del} < 2.42$, the statement of the theorem then follows from Theorem 4.

4   Unit Disk Graphs

Unit disk graphs (UDGs) are very important in wireless computing since they have been widely used as a theoretical model for wireless networks. In particular, the problem of constructing bounded-degree plane spanners of UDGs has received a lot of interest [7,12,15,16]. In such applications the local model of computation is a suitable working model because the wireless devices have limited energy, and lack the centralized coordination.

The results in Section 3 do not directly give a local algorithm for constructing a bounded-degree plane spanner of a UDG U for two reasons. The first reason is that the Delaunay triangulation of the point-set of U cannot be computed locally, and the second reason is that not every edge in the Delaunay triangulation of the point-set of U is an edge in U (i.e., has length at most 1 unit).

To overcome the above-mentioned obstacles, Wang et al. [16] introduced a plane subgraph of U, called $LDel^{(2)}(U)$, that can be computed by a 3-local algorithm [12], and that contains all Delaunay edges of length at most 1. Moreover, they proved that the stretch factor of $LDel^{(2)}(U)$ is at most $C_{del} < 2.42$. Subsequently, $LDel^{(2)}(U)$ has been used as the underlying subgraph in several local and distributed algorithms that construct bounded-degree plane spanners of UDGs (see [12,15,16], to name a few). We can use $LDel^{(2)}(U)$ as the underlying subgraph G in the algorithm **Spanner** to obtain the following result:

Theorem 5. *There exists a 3-local algorithm that, given a connected UDG U on n points, computes a plane subgraph of U of degree at most 11 that is a spanner of the complete Euclidean graph on the point-set of U, and that has stretch factor $\rho \cdot C_{del} = \frac{2 \sin(2\pi/5) \cos(\pi/5)}{2 \sin(2\pi/5) \cos(\pi/5) - 1} \cdot C_{del} < 7$. The processing time for each $p \in U$ in the algorithm is $O(\delta_p \lg \delta_p)$, where δ_p is the degree of p in U.*

References

1. Benson, R.: Euclidean Geometry and Convexity. Mc-Graw Hill, New York (1966)
2. Bonichon, N., Gavoille, C., Hanusse, N., Perković, L.: Plane spanners of maximum degree six. In: Proceedings of the 37th International Colloquium on Automata, Languages and Programming (2010),
   http://dept-info.labri.fr/~gavoille/article/BGHP10
3. Bose, P., Gudmundsson, J., Smid, M.: Constructing plane spanners of bounded degree and low weight. In: Möhring, R.H., Raman, R. (eds.) ESA 2002. LNCS, vol. 2461, pp. 234–246. Springer, Heidelberg (2002)
4. Bose, P., Gudmundsson, J., Smid, M.: Constructing plane spanners of bounded degree and low weight. Algorithmica 42(3-4), 249–264 (2005)
5. Bose, P., Morin, P., Stojmenovic, I., Urrutia, J.: Routing with guaranteed delivery in ad hoc wireless networks. Wireless Networks 7(6), 609–616 (2001)
6. Bose, P., Smid, M.: On plane geometric spanners: A survey and open problems,
   http://dept-info.labri.fr/~gavoille/lecture-articles/BS09a
7. Bose, P., Smid, M., Xu, D.: Diamond triangulations contain spanners of bounded degree. In: Asano, T. (ed.) ISAAC 2006. LNCS, vol. 4288, pp. 173–182. Springer, Heidelberg (2006), To appear in Algorithmica

8. Carmi, P., Chaitman, L.: Bounded degree planar geometric spanner,
   http://arxiv4.library.cornell.edu/abs/1003.4963v1
9. de Berg, M., van Kreveld, M., Overmars, M., Schwarzkopf, O.: Computational
   Geometry: Algorithms and Applications, 3rd edn. Springer, Heidelberg (2008)
10. Gudmundsson, J., Levcopoulos, C., Narasimhan, G.: Fast greedy algorithms for
    constructing sparse geometric spanners. SIAM Journal on Computing 31(5), 1479–
    1500 (2002)
11. Kanj, I., Perković, L.: On geometric spanners of Euclidean and unit disk graphs.
    In: Proceedings of the 25th International Symposium on Theoretical Aspects of
    Computer Science, pp. 409–420 (2008)
12. Kanj, I., Perković, L., Xia, G.: On spanners and lightweight spanners of geometric
    graphs. SIAM Journal on Computing 39(6), 2132–2161 (2010)
13. Keil, J., Gutwin, C.: Classes of graphs which approximate the complete Euclidean
    graph. Discrete & Computational Geometry 7, 13–28 (1992)
14. Kranakis, E., Singh, H., Urrutia, J.: Compass routing on geometric networks. In:
    Proceedings of the 11th Canadian Conference on Computational Geometry, pp.
    51–54 (1999)
15. Li, X.-Y., Calinescu, G., Wan, P.-J.: Distributed construction of planar spanner
    and routing for ad hoc wireless networks. In: Proceedings of the IEEE Conference
    on Computer Communications (2002)
16. Li, X.-Y., Calinescu, G., Wan, P.-J., Wang, Y.: Localized delaunay triangulation
    with application in Ad Hoc wireless networks. IEEE Transactions on Parallel and
    Distributed Systems 14(10), 1035–1047 (2003)
17. Narasimhan, G., Smid, M.: Geometric Spanner Networks. Cambridge University
    Press, Cambridge (2007)
18. Peleg, D.: Distributed computing: A Locality-Sensitive Approach. SIAM Mono-
    graphs on Discrete Mathematis and Applications (2000)
19. Wang, Y., Li, X.-Y.: Localized construction of bounded degree and planar spanner
    for wireless ad hoc networks. Mobile Networks and Applications 11(2), 161–175
    (2006)
20. Yao, A.C.-C.: On constructing minimum spanning trees in k-dimensional spaces
    and related problems. SIAM Journal on Computing 11(4), 721–736 (1982)

Planar Hop Spanners for Unit Disk Graphs*

Nicolas Catusse, Victor Chepoi, and Yann Vaxès

Laboratoire d'Informatique Fondamentale
Université d'Aix-Marseille
Faculté des Sciences de Luminy
F-13288 Marseille Cedex 9, France
{nicolas.catusse,victor.chepoi,yann.vaxes}@lif.univ-mrs.fr

Abstract. The simplest model of a wireless network graph is the Unit Disk Graph (UDG): an edge exists in UDG if the Euclidean distance between its endpoints is ≤ 1. The problem of constructing planar spanners of Unit Disk Graphs with respect to the Euclidean distance has received considerable attention from researchers in computational geometry and ad-hoc wireless networks. In this paper, we present an algorithm that, given a set X of terminals in the plane, constructs a planar hop spanner with constant stretch factor for the Unit Disk Graph defined by X. Our algorithm improves on previous constructions in the sense that (i) it ensures the planarity of the whole spanner while previous algorithms ensure only the planarity of a backbone subgraph; (ii) the hop stretch factor of our spanner is significantly smaller.

Keywords: Planar spanner, Unit Disk Graph, Geometric Networks, Wireless Networks.

1 Introduction

The problem of constructing sparse spanners (i.e., subgraphs approximating the distances between the vertices of the original graph up to a certain stretch factor) of geometric graphs has received considerable attention in computational geometry and ad-hoc wireless networks; we refer the reader to the book by Narasimhan and Smid [10]. The simplest model of a wireless network graph is the *Unit Disk Graph* (UDG): an edge between two terminals u, v exists in this graph if the Euclidean distance between u and v is at most one. Some routing algorithms such as *Greedy Perimeter Stateless Routing* require a *planar* subgraph to route the messages through the network. Therefore, additionally to the small stretch factor, it is plausible to require that the obtained spanner is also planar.

In this paper, we design an algorithm that, given a set X of n points on the plane, constructs a planar spanner with constant hop stretch factor for the Unit Disk Graph defined by X. Contrary to the problem of constructing planar *Euclidean length* spanners, for which several algorithms provide small stretch

* This research was partly supported by the ANR grant BLAN06-1-13889 (projet OPTICOMB).

C. Scheideler (Ed.): ALGOSENSORS 2010, LNCS 6451, pp. 16–30, 2010.

factors (see [9], for instance), the problem of constructing planar *hop* spanners with constant stretch factor remained open. Some partial solutions ensuring the planarity of a certain backbone subgraph were proposed in [1,8]. Our algorithm improves on the results of [1,8] in the sense that (i) our construction ensures the planarity of the whole spanner; (ii) the hop stretch factor provided by our algorithm is significantly better. Additionally, our spanner can be constructed via a localized distributed algorithm. Planarity, low stretch factor, and localized construction constitute key ingredients to obtain efficient routing schemes for ad-hoc and wireless geometric networks.

The rest of the paper is organized as follows. In Section 2, we briefly review the literature related to geometric spanners and Unit Disk Graphs. Section 3 presents a very simple construction that provides a sparse spanner for UDG with low hop stretch factor. In general, this construction does not ensure the planarity of the spanner. Section 4 describes an algorithm that updates the spanner defined in Section 3 in order to obtain a planar spanner still preserving a small hop stretch factor. In Section 5, we prove some results necessary to prove the planarity and the hop stretch of the spanner computed by our algorithm.

2   Previous Work

We start with basic definitions. Given a connected graph $G = (V, E)$ with n vertices embedded in the Euclidean plane, the hop length of a path $\gamma(u, v)$ between two vertices u, v of G is the number of edges of $\gamma(u, v)$. The *hop distance* $d_G(u, v)$ between u and v in G is the length of a shortest path connecting u and v in G. A subgraph H of G is a *spanner* of G if there is a positive real constant t such that for any two vertices, $d_H(u, v) \leq t d_G(u, v)$. The constant t is called the *hop stretch factor* of H. If instead of number of edges in a path $\gamma(u, v)$ we consider the total Euclidean length of the edges of $\gamma(u, v)$, then we can define another distance measure on G and a corresponding notion of a spanner, which is called *Euclidean spanner* and its stretch factor is called *Euclidean stretch factor*. All results of our paper concern hop spanner of Unit Disk Graphs, therefore we often write "spanner" and "distance" instead of "hop spanner" and "hop distance".

Spanner properties of geometric graphs have been surveyed by Eppstein [5] and more recently by Bose and Smid [3]. Bose et al. [2] proved that the *Gabriel Graph* is an $\Omega(\sqrt{n})$ hop spanner and a $\Theta(\sqrt{n})$ Euclidean spanner for UDG, and that the *Relative Neighborhood Graph* is a $\Theta(n)$ and a $\Theta(n)$ Euclidean spanner for UDG. Gao et al. [8] proposed a randomized algorithm to construct an Euclidean and a hop spanner for UDG. This algorithm creates several clusters (using a method described in [7]) connected by a *Restricted Delaunay graph*. The subgraph consisting of edges between distinct clusters is planar. This construction provides a constant Euclidean stretch factor in expectation but its hop stretch factor is not given. Alzoubi et al. [1] proposed for the same problem a distributed algorithm that uses the *Local Delaunay Triangulation* defined by Li, Călinescu, and Wan in [9]. However, the hop stretch factor obtained by

[1] is huge (around 15000) and the intra-cluster edges may cross the edges of
the triangulation (and therefore does not provide a full planar hop spanner).
Chen et al. [4] presented the construction of Euclidean spanners for *Quasi-UDG*
which can be used for routing. Their construction method is similar to our approach in the sense that it also uses a regular squaregrid to partition the set
of terminals into clusters (for a similar partition of the plane used for routing,
see [11]). Recently Yan, Xiang, and Dragan [12] established a *balanced separator*
result for Unit Disk Graph which mimics the celebrated Lipton-Tarjan planar
balanced separator theorem. Based on this result, they derive a compact and low
delay routing labeling scheme for UDG. Finally, for the construction of spanner
of general disk graphs see also [6].

3   Sparse Almost Planar Spanners

Let X be a set of n points (terminals) in the plane. In this section, we describe a
very simple algorithm, namely Algorithm 1, that constructs a sparse 5-spanner
$H' = (X, E')$ of the Unit Disk Graph $G = (X, E)$ defined by X. It uses a regular
grid Γ on the plane with squares of side $\frac{\sqrt{2}}{2}$. A square of Γ is said to be *nonempty*
if it contains at least one terminal from X. For any point $x \in X$, let $\pi(x)$ denote
the square of Γ containing x. The graph $H' = (X, E')$ has two types of edges :
a subset $E'_0 \subseteq E'$ of edges connecting terminals lying in the same square and
a subset E'_1 of edges running between terminals lying in distinct squares; let
$E' = E'_0 \cup E'_1$. To define E'_0, in each nonempty square π we pick a terminal
(the *center* of π) and add to E'_0 an edge between this terminal and every other
terminal located in π. Clearly, all of them are edges of G because the distance
between two points lying in the same square of side $\frac{\sqrt{2}}{2}$ is at most 1. In E'_1 we
put exactly one edge of G running between two nonempty squares if such an
edge exists. In the sequel, with some abuse of notation, we will denote by $\pi\pi'$
the shortest edge of UDG running between two squares π and π'.

Algorithm 1. Construction of sparse spanner H'

1: For each square π, pick a terminal c_π (the *center* of π) and add to E'_0 an edge
   between c_π and every other terminal located in π.
2: For all squares π, π' connected by an edge of G, add to E'_1 the shortest edge between
   π and π'.

Proposition 1. *The graph $H' = (X, E')$ is a 5-hop spanner for G with at most*
10n edges.

Proof. For the first assertion, it suffices to prove that $d_{H'}(u, v) \le 5d_G(u, v)$ for
any two adjacent in G vertices u, v. If u and v belong to the same square π,
then they are neighbors of the center of π, hence they are connected in H' by a
path of length 2. Now, suppose that u and v belong to different squares. Since
uv is an edge of G, the graph H' must contain an edge $u'v'$ of G with $u' \in \pi(u)$

and $v' \in \pi(v)$. Therefore the terminals u and v are connected in H' by a path of length ≤ 5 consisting of two paths of length 2 passing via the centers of the clusters $\pi(u)$ and $\pi(v)$ and connecting u and v to u' and v', respectively, and the edge $u'v'$ joining these clusters. To prove the second assertion, let n_0 denote the number of non-empty squares. Then obviously $|E_0'| \leq n - n_0$. Since from each nonempty square π we can have edges of E_1' to at most 20 other such squares(see Fig. 2), and since each such edge is counted twice, we conclude that $|E_1'| \leq 10n_0$. Therefore $|E'| \leq (n - n_0) + 10n_0 \leq 10n$. $\qquad\square$

4   Planar Spanners

In this section, we describe the Algorithm 2 that builds a planar hop spanner H for a UDG graph G. We first compute a planar set of *inter-cluster edges* E_3 whose end-vertices belong to distinct squares of Γ and then, a second set of *intra-cluster edges* E_0 connecting the vertices that belong to the same square.

4.1   Computing E_3

First we define the l_1-*distance* $l_1(\pi, \pi')$ between two squares π and π' in Γ as the graph distance between π and π' in the dual grid (squares become vertices and two vertices are adjacent if their squares have a common side). The l_1-*length* $l_1(ab)$ of an edge ab of G is the l_1-distance between the squares that contain their end-vertices and the *interval* $I(x, y)$ between two terminals $x, y \in X$ consists of all squares lying on a shortest l_1-path of the dual grid between $\pi(x)$ and $\pi(y)$.

Now, we give an brief and informal description of Algorithm 2 for computing E_3. The edge set E_3 is a planar subset of the edge set E_1' defined in the previous section. We remove some edges to obtain a planar graph while preserving a bounded hop stretch factor of the resulting spanner. The principle of our algorithm is to minimize the l_1-length of preserved edges: if the end-vertices of an edge uv of E_1' are joined by a path in E_1' having the same total l_1-length as uv, then uv is removed. An edge with large l_1-length potentially crosses many squares and, as a consequence, many edges of UDG. Hence, taking such an edge in our planar spanner would exclude many other (potentially, good) edges from the spanner. For each removed edge, there is a path having a constant number of edges between its end-vertices. Therefore, after the removal of these edges, the stretch factor is still bounded by a constant. The minimization of the l_1-length is not sufficient to obtain a planar graph but we show that this operation considerably decreases the number of crossing configurations. The next step of the algorithm consists in repairing the remaining crossings. During this step, some edges are removed to ensure the planarity and some other edges are added back to preserve a small distance between the end-vertices of removed edges. Notice that our construction uses only local information and can be easily implemented as a localized distributed algorithm. Using the proof outlined below, we establish that the edge set obtained at the end of this process is indeed planar.

Algorithm 2. Construction of the spanner H

1: Let $H' = (X, E_1')$ be the inter-cluster graph returned by **Construction of Sparse Spanner**.

2: Let $G_1 = (X, E_1)$ be the graph obtained from H' by removing every edge $ab \in E_1'$ whose end-vertices are joined by a *replacement path*, i.e., a path $P \neq ab$ between $\pi(a)$ and $\pi(b)$ such that $l_1(P) = l_1(ab)$.

3: For each pair of crossing edges $xy, x'y'$ of E_1, identify the crossing configuration (according to Fig. 4) and remove the edge $x'y'$. Let $G_2 = (X, E_2)$ be the graph obtained from G_1 by removing these edges.

4: For each edge $x'y'$ removed in Step 3, unless $xy, x'y'$ form a Configuration 0 or $4'$, if there is no replacement path in G_2 for $\pi(y)\pi(y')$, then add the edge $\pi(y)\pi(y')$ (according to Fig. 4). Let $G_3 = (X, E_3)$ be the resulting graph.

5: Compute the set of intra-cluster edges E_0 as described in subsection 4.2.

6: Output the graph $H = (X, E_0 \cup E_3)$.

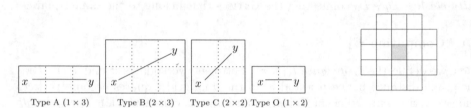

Type A (1×3) Type B (2×3) Type C (2×2) Type O (1×2)

Fig. 1. Classification of edges

Fig. 2. Twenty neighboring squares

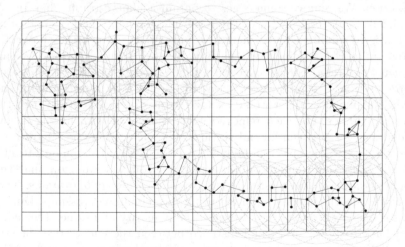

Fig. 3. Planar spanner H

Theorem 1. *The inter-cluster graph $G_3 = (X, E_3)$ is planar.*

To prove this theorem, we proceed in several steps (the proofs of Propositions 3 to 8 are postponed to the next section). We classify the edges of G according to the relative positions of the squares containing their end-vertices (see Fig. 1). Then, using this classification, we consider all possible crossing configurations between two edges of E_1. Proposition 3 analyzes these configurations and shows that in most cases one of the two crossing edges has a replacement path.

Proposition 2. *If the crossing configuration between two edges $xy, x'y' \in E_1'$ does not belong to the list of Fig. 4, then one of these edges, say xy, has a replacement path passing via $\pi(x')$ or $\pi(y')$.*

Since the edges of E_1 do not admit replacement paths, we deduce that only a few crossing configurations may occur between two edges of E_1.

Proposition 3. *For two edges of E_1, there exist only seven possible crossing configurations listed in Fig. 4.*

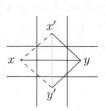
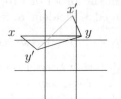

Configuration 0   Configuration 1   Configuration 2

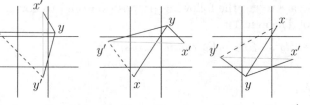

Configuration 3   Configuration 4   Configuration 4'   Configuration 5

Fig. 4. The seven remaining configurations after Step 2. The solid lines indicate the edges in E_1' and the dashed lines indicate the edges that may be or not in E_1'.

Now we consider the edges added at Step 4. To prove that the graph returned by our algorithm is planar, we will show that these new edges do not intersect each other and do not intersect the edges that survive Step 3. Let $e' \in E_3 - E_2$ be an edge added during Step 4, let $e \in E_3 \cap E_2$ be an edge crossing e' that survived Step 3. Let also $xy, x'y' \in E_1$ be the crossing edges due to which the edge $x'y'$ has been removed and the edge $e' = \pi(y)\pi(y')$ has been added. By a case analysis of all configurations listed in Fig. 4, we verify that in all cases except Configuration 0 and 4' (easily treated separately) there is a replacement path for e' in G_1 passing via $\pi(x')$. Since the edge e' is added at Step 4 only if it does not admit a replacement path in G_2, the following result excludes the existence of a replacement path for e' distinct from the path going through $\pi(x')$.

Proposition 4. *If the edge $\pi(y)\pi(y')$ from Fig. 4 has a replacement path in G_1 distinct from the path that goes through $\pi(x')$, then there is a replacement path between $\pi(y)$ and $\pi(y')$ in G_2.*

To deal with the crossing configurations formed by the edges e and e', we distinguish two cases. Then either such a configuration belongs to the list from Fig. 4 and a case analysis lead to a contradiction, or, by Proposition 2, one of these two edges admits a replacement path that passes through a square containing an end-vertex of the other edge. This edge must be e' because e was not removed during Step 2. However, as noticed above, Proposition 4 implies that this path must be the one passing through $\pi(x')$, otherwise this replacement path would survive Step 3 and e' would not be added. Since the replacement path arising in Proposition 2 passes via a square containing an end-vertex of e, the edge e must be incident to $\pi(x')$. Therefore, in the proof of Proposition 5 we analyze all possible crossings between e' and an edge incident to $\pi(x')$.

Proposition 5. *An edge from $E_3 - E_2$ cannot cross an edge from $E_3 \cap E_2$.*

Finally, we prove that the edges added during Step 4 do not cross each other. First, notice that if two edges of $E_3 - E_2$ cross, then one of them cross an edge from E_1. By Proposition 5, this edge of E_1 was removed during Step 3. Hence, we get a crossing between an edge of $E_3 - E_2$ and an edge of $E_2 - E_3$. The list of these configurations can be extracted from the proof of Proposition 5. They are analyzed case by case to get the following proposition (and to conclude the outline of the proof of Theorem 1):

Proposition 6. *The edges of $E_3 - E_2$ cannot cross.*

4.2   Computing E_0

We will consider several choices for the set of edges E_0 that interconnect the vertices lying in the same square. Let $\alpha(E_0)$ be the maximum distance in the graph $G_0 = (X, E_0)$ between two vertices belonging to the same square. In the next subsection, the hop stretch factor of our spanner is expressed as a function of $\alpha(E_0)$. A possible choice for E_0 is to set a clique or a star on terminals on each non-empty square, yielding $\alpha(E_0) = 1$ and $\alpha(E_0) = 2$, respectively. In this case, the diameter of the clusters is small but we do not get a planar spanner. The following proposition shows that an appropriate choice of E_0 ensures both planarity and constant diameter of clusters.

Proposition 7. *There exists a set of intra-cluster edges E_0 such that $H = (X, E_3 \cup E_0)$ is planar and $\alpha(E_0) \leq 44$.*

4.3 Hop Stretch Factor

Now, we analyze the hop stretch factor of H, namely we show that H is a $10\alpha(E_0)+9$ hop spanner for G. As noticed above, it suffices to prove the spanner property for two adjacent vertices of G. After Step 1, we get a spanner H' whose hop stretch factor is at most $2\alpha(E_0)+1$. Since the maximal l_1-length of an edge of a Unit Disk Graph G is 3, if an edge from E_1' is removed during Step 2, then it is replaced by a path containing at most 3 edges from E_1 for an edge of type B. Taking into account the edges from E_0, we obtain a stretch factor $\leq 4\alpha(E_0)+3$. In Step 3, again some edges are removed and replaced by paths. The following proposition asserts that the resulting length of these paths is bounded. Finally, in Step 4 edges are only added, thus the stretch factor cannot be worsened.

Proposition 8. *If an edge e of E_1 is removed during Step 3, then it is replaced in E_3 by a path containing at most $3l_1(e) \leq 9$ edges.*

Proposition 8 shows that after Step 4 an inter-cluster edge of G is replaced by at most 9 inter-cluster edges of E_3. Taking into account the edges of E_0, we get a final stretch factor equal to $10\alpha(E_0)+9$. Summarizing, here is the main result of this paper:

Theorem 2. *Given a set X of n terminals in the plane, the graph $H = (X, E_0 \cup E_3)$ computed by our algorithm is a planar spanner of the Unit Disk Graph G of X with hop stretch factor at most $10\alpha(E_0)+9$.*

5 Proof of Theorem 2

In this section, we sketch the proofs of most intermediate results necessary to establish Theorem 2. Most of these proofs consist in a case analysis of several configurations of points, which are treated using similar arguments. Due to space limitation and to the repetitive nature of most proofs, in each proof we provide a complete analysis only of some (most) representative configurations.

5.1 Preliminary Results

We start with few simple useful observations.

Lemma 1. *If $[x, y]$ and $[x', y']$ are two crossing line segments, then either $|xx'| < |xy|$ or $|yy'| < |x'y'|$.*

Proof. Let $p = [x, y] \cap [x', y']$. By applying the triangle inequality to the triplets (x, p, x') and (y, p, y'), we get $|xx'|+|yy'| < |xp|+|px'|+|yp|+|py'| = |xy|+|x'y'|$, whence at least one of the inequalities $|xx'| < |xy|$ or $|yy'| < |x'y'|$ holds.   □

Lemma 2. *If xy and $x'y'$ are two crossing edges of G, then at least one edge from xx', yy' and one edge from $xy', x'y$ belongs to G.*

Lemma 3. *If xy and $x'y'$ are two crossing edges from E_1' (i.e., shortest edges between two squares), then the vertices x, y, x', y' belong to distinct squares of Γ.*

Proof. Suppose that x and x' belong to a square π. By Lemma 1, either $|xy'| < |x'y'|$ and $x'y'$ is not the shortest edge between $\pi(x')$ and $\pi(y')$, or $|x'y| < |xy|$ and xy is not the shortest edge between $\pi(x)$ and $\pi(y)$, a contradiction with the assumption that xy and $x'y'$ belong to E_1'. $\qquad\square$

Lemma 4. *Let xy an edge of G. If a vertex z belongs to rectangle $R(xy)$ having xy as diagonal, then $xz, zy \in G$ and thus the edge xy does not belong to E_1.*

Proof. As z belongs to a right triangle having xy as hypotenuse, we get $|zx| < |xy|$ and $|zy| < |xy|$. Since $xy \in G$, we deduce that xz and zy also belong to G, yielding that xy does not belong to E_1. $\qquad\square$

Lemma 5. *If $\pi(x)\pi(x'), \pi(x')\pi(y) \in G$ and $x' \in I(x, y)$, then $xy \notin E_1$.*

Lemma 6. *If xy is an edge of type A and z a vertex in the square between $\pi(x)$ and $\pi(y)$, then z is adjacent to at least one of the end-vertices of xy.*

5.2   Proof of Proposition 3

For each type of edges, we analyze the possible crossings between an edge xy of this type and another edge $x'y'$. We specify two subsets of squares $\{\pi_i, i = 1, ..., k\}$ and $\{\pi_j', j = 1, ..., l\}$ with $x' \in \bigcup_{i=1}^{k} \pi_i$ and $y' \in \bigcup_{j=1}^{l} \pi_j'$ that cover, modulo rotations and symmetry, all possible crossing configurations (note that, by Lemma 3, the vertices x, y, x', y' must belong to distinct squares). We provide a complete analysis only for the case when the edge xy is of type A.

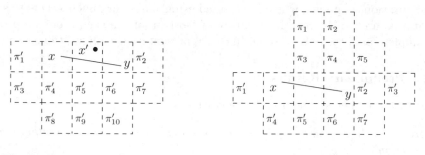

Fig. 5. Case $* \times A$: $x' \in I(x, y)$ **Fig. 6.** Case $* \times A$: $x' \notin I(x, y)$

Case 1: $x' \in I(x, y)$ (Fig. 5). In this case, we assert that exactly one edge xx' or $x'y$ belongs to G. Indeed, by Lemma 6 at least one of these edges belongs to G. If both edges belong to G, then xy has a replacement path and does not belong to E_1. Suppose without loss of generality that xx' does not belong to G. By Lemma 3, we deduce that $yy' \in G$, thus $x'y, yy' \in G$. Furthermore, since $x'y'$

belongs to E_1, by Lemma 5 y does not belong to the interval between x' and y'. Then $y' \notin \pi'_2 \cup \pi'_6 \cup \pi'_7 \cup \pi'_{10}$. Since $xx' \notin G$, necessarily $y' \notin \pi'_1 \cup \pi'_3$ because, if y' belongs to one of these squares, then either $x \in R(x'y')$ or $x' \in R(xy)$ and $xx' \in G$ by Lemma 4, a contradiction. If $y' \in \pi'_8$, then yy' does not belong to G, and by Lemma 3 $xx' \in G$, a contradiction. Finally, the cases $y' \in \pi'_4, \pi'_5$ or π'_9 correspond respectively to Configuration 1, 2 and 3 of Fig. 4.

Case 2: $x' \notin I(x, y)$ (Fig. 6). If $x' \in \pi_1 \cup \pi_2$, either $y' \in I(x, y)$ and this configuration was previously analyzed, or one end-vertex of xy belongs to $R(x'y')$ and by Lemma 4 the edge $x'y'$ does not belong to E_1. If $x' \in \pi_5$, then $y' \in \pi'_6$ and $y \in R(x'y')$, by Lemma 4 the edge $x'y'$ does not belong to E_1. For $x' \in \pi_4$, if $y' \in \pi'_6$ we get $y \in I(x', y')$ and this case was already analyzed. If $y' \in \pi'_2 \cup \pi'_3 \cup \pi'_7$, then $y \in R(x'y')$ and by Lemma 4 the edge $x'y'$ does not belong to E_1. Finally, for $x' \in \pi_3$, if $y' \in \pi'_4 \cup \pi'_6$, we obtain the same configuration as $x' \in \pi_4$ and $y' \in \pi'_5$. If $y' \in \pi'_1 \cup \pi'_2$, one end-vertex of the edge xy belongs to $R(x'y')$ and by Lemma 4 the edge $x'y'$ does not belong to E_1. The cases $(x' \in \pi_3, y' \in \pi'_5)$ and $(x' \in \pi_4, y' \in \pi'_5)$ correspond to Configuration 0, 4 and 4' of Fig. 4.

5.3 Proof of Proposition 4

For each crossing remaining after Step 2 (configurations listed in Fig. 4) such that the edge $\pi(y)\pi(y')$ admits a replacement path in G_1 that does not pass via $\pi(x')$ we will prove that such a replacement path also exists in G_2. We consider each edge of the replacement path of G_1 and show that either this edge is not removed in Step 2, or that there exists another replacement path for the edge $\pi(y)\pi(y')$ in G_2. We provide a complete analysis only for Configuration 1 of Fig. 4, all other configurations are treated analogously.

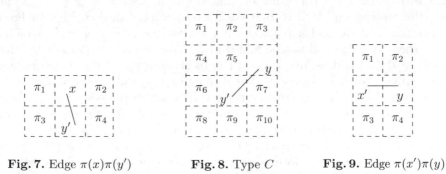

Fig. 7. Edge $\pi(x)\pi(y')$ **Fig. 8.** Type C **Fig. 9.** Edge $\pi(x')\pi(y)$

First, notice that, if the edge xy' is not crossed by another edge of E_1, then together with the edge xy it forms a replacement path for the edge $\pi(y)\pi(y')$. We assert that the edge $\pi(x)\pi(y')$ always belongs to G. Indeed, since $xy \in G$, x belongs to the right half of $\pi(x)$. The vertex x' belongs to the right half of $\pi(x')$ because otherwise xx' would belong to G, excluding, by Lemma 5, the edge xy from being in E_1. Furthermore, the vertex x is above x' and to the left of y', otherwise, either $x' \in R(xy)$ or $x \in R(x'y')$ and, by Lemma 4, either $x'y'$ or xy does not belong to E_1. We conclude that $|x'y'| > |xy'|$ and since $x'y'$ belongs to G, $\pi(x)\pi(y')$ also belongs to G. If the edge $\pi(x)\pi(y')$ is not crossed by another edge of E_1, then we are done. Otherwise, let $ab \in E_1$ be an edge crossing $\pi(x)\pi(y')$. Since we should only consider the configurations listed in Fig. 4, we can suppose that $a \in \pi_2 \cup \pi_4$ and $b \in \pi_1 \cup \pi_3$ (see Fig. 7).

First, suppose that $a \in \pi_2 = \pi(x')$. From $ab \in G$ we deduce that a belongs to the left half of $\pi(x')$. As already noticed, x belongs to the right half of $\pi(x)$ and thus $xa \in G$, by Lemma 5 we get a contradiction with $xy \in E_1$. Now if $a \in \pi_4$, from $ab, yy' \in G$, we can deduce that a belongs to left half of $\pi(a)$ and y' belongs to the right half of $\pi(y')$, then $y'a \in G$. So if $b \in \pi_1 \cup \pi_3$ by Proposition 3, ab and $x'y'$ cannot cross. Hence if $b \in \pi_1$, either $y' \in R(ab)$ or $a \in R(x'y')$ and by Lemma 5 both contradict $ab, x'y' \in E_1$. Finally, if $b \in \pi_3$, there is no edge between b and a vertex of $\pi(y')$. Indeed, by Lemma 5, such an edge would exclude ab from being in E_1. Therefore, both y' and the end-vertex z of $\pi(x)\pi(y')$ are located outside the ball of radius ab centered in b. Since ab crosses the edge $\pi(x)\pi(y')$, z is located below ab. Since $\pi(x)\pi(y')$ is a shortest edge between $\pi(x)$ and $\pi(y')$, y' cannot lie above ab. As previously noticed, ab cannot cross $x'y'$, the vertex a must belong to $R(x'y')$, by Lemma 4 a contradiction with $x'y' \in E_1$. This concludes the analysis of Configuration 1. The analysis of the six remaining configurations are analogous.

5.4   Proof of Proposition 5

We will consider the configurations listed in Fig. 4 between an edge $\pi(y)\pi(y')$ from $E_3 - E_2$ and an edge from $E_3 \cap E_2$. We will also analyze the possible crossings between $\pi(y)\pi(y')$ and an edge adjacent to $\pi(x')$. Such an edge may form with $\pi(y)\pi(y')$ a configuration that does not appear in Fig. 4 (in this case, the replacement path of that edge was corrupted during Step 3). From Proposition 4, if we find a replacement path for the edge $\pi(y)\pi(y')$ avoiding $\pi(x')$, then this edge will not be added in E_3. We denote by ab the edge that crosses $\pi(y)\pi(y')$ and assume without loss of generality that the vertices a and b are located above and below the line defined by $\pi(y)\pi(y')$, respectively.

Let $xy, x'y' \in E_1$ be the crossing edges due to which the edge $x'y'$ has been removed and the edge $e' = \pi(y)\pi(y')$ has been added. We distinguish several cases depending on the type of configuration formed by xy and $x'y'$. If xy and $x'y'$ form a Configuration 1, we never add an edge between $\pi(y)$ and $\pi(y')$ because the edges xy and $\pi(x)\pi(y')$ form a replacement path for this edge. So we provide a complete analysis for the case in which xy and $x'y'$ form a Configuration 2. Suppose that xy and $x'y'$ form this configuration. Since $xy \in E_1$ does not admit a replacement path, no edge between $\pi(x)$ and $\pi(x')$ belongs to E.

First, we show that $a \notin \pi_5$ (see Fig. 8). Suppose not; since $y'x' \in E_1$ is necessarily shorter than $y'a$ and a is outside the ball of radius 1 centered in x, the vertex a cannot be located below the edge xy. Now, by the choice of a and b, the vertex b must belong to $\pi_7 \cup \pi_9 \cup \pi_{10}$ and crosses xy otherwise either $y \in R(ab)$ or $y' \in R(ab)$ and we get a contradiction with $ab \in E_1$. If $b \in \pi_7 \cup \pi_{10}$, since $\pi(x)\pi(x') \notin E_1$ and ab crosses xy, Lemma 2 implies that $\pi(b)\pi(y) \in E_1$. So ab has a replacement path with the edges $\pi(b)\pi(y)$ and $\pi(a)\pi(y)$, and we get a contradiction. If $b \in \pi_9$, when the crossing configuration between ab and xy has been treated in Step 3, the edge ab should be removed, and we get a contradiction again. Next, we assert that b cannot belong to π_5. Indeed, otherwise a must belong to the rectangle $R(z,t)$ where z and t are the end-vertices of the edge $\pi(y)\pi(y')$. Hence, the edge $\pi(y)\pi(y')$ has a replacement path and does not belong to E_1, a contradiction. By inspecting the list of configurations from Fig. 4, one can verify that an edge of type C appears only in Configuration 1. Due to symmetry, this leads us to analyze four cases. Two of them have been already treated because the vertex a belong π_5. It remains two cases and in both of them, $b \in \pi_7$. We will consider several cases depending on the location of a. (see Fig. 8).

First suppose that $a \in \pi_3$. In this case yb does not belong to E because, otherwise, since ab has no replacement path, ya cannot belong to E and, by Lemma 2, we conclude that $y'b$ belongs to E. Together with by, this edge forms a replacement path for the edge $\pi(y)\pi(y')$ that does not pass via $\pi(x')$. The existence of such a path contradicts the presence of $\pi(y)\pi(y')$ in E_1, showing that indeed there is no edge of G between $\pi(y)$ and $\pi(b)$. In other words, all terminals of $\pi(y)$ are located outside the ball $B(b,1)$ of radius 1 centered in b. This ball contains a and thus separates $\pi(y) - B(b,1)$ into two regions: a region A located to the left of ab and another region A' located to the right of ab. Notice that since $ab \cap \pi(y')\pi(y) \neq \emptyset$, the end-vertex of $\pi(y')\pi(y)$ that belongs to $\pi(y)$ must be located in the region A' and, since $\pi(y')\pi(y)$ is a shortest edge between $\pi(y)$ and $\pi(y')$, no terminal belongs to A (it is easy to verify that any point of A is closer to $\pi(y')$ than any point of A'). In particular, the vertex y belongs to A' and thus the edges ab and xy cross. On the other hand, since $by \notin E$, Lemma 2 implies that $xa \in E$. Finally, by noticing that $x' \in R(xa)$, we deduce that the edge xx' belongs to E, which is impossible since xx' and xy form a replacement path for xy that does not pass via $\pi(x')$.

Now, suppose that $a \in \pi_6$. We assert that by' does not belong to E. Indeed, if by' belongs to E, then ay' does not belong to E otherwise ab has a replacement path via y'. By Lemma 2, we deduce that by belongs to E. This yields a replacement path for the edge $\pi(y)\pi(y')$ consisting of $y'b$ and by, that contradicts $\pi(y)\pi(y') \in E_1$ and shows that indeed $by' \notin E$. Now, note that the edge ab crosses the square $\pi(y')$ and the part of $\pi(y')$ outside the ball of radius 1 centered in b consists of one region A located above ab and one region A' located below ab. Since $\pi(y)\pi(y') \cap ab \neq \emptyset$, the end-vertex of $\pi(y)\pi(y')$ that belong to $\pi(y')$ must belong to A'. Therefore, the vertex y' must belong to A' as well, otherwise, i.e. if y' belong to A, $y'\pi(y)$ would be shorter that the edge $\pi(y)\pi(y')$. But in this case, $x'y'$ cannot belong to G. This contradicts the fact that xy and $x'y'$ are the edges due to which $\pi(y)\pi(y')$ has been added and concludes the proof for the Configuration 2. The analysis of other configurations are analogous.

5.5   Proof of Proposition 6

Assume by way of contradiction that two edges e and f of $E_3 - E_2$ cross. Since these edges have been added to restore a path between the end-vertices of an edge from E_1, one of them, say e, crosses the edge e' of E_1 because of which the edge f has been added. Therefore, to derive a contradiction and establish Proposition 6, it is sufficient to verify that the edge f added to replace the edge e' does not cross the edge e. This is actually an immediate consequence of Lemma 3 since for each possible crossing configuration between an edge $e' = x'y'$ and an edge $e = xy$ listed in Fig. 4, the edges $f = \pi(y)\pi(y')$ and $e = xy$ have an end-vertex in $\pi(y)$ and thus cannot cross.

5.6   Proof of Proposition 7

The set E_0 can be obtained as follows. First, we partition X into clusters consisting of all vertices which belong to the same non-empty square of the grid Γ. Then, we consider each non-empty square π crossed by an edge $e \in E_3$ (one can show that each square of Γ can be crossed by at most one edge) and so that the two regions R_1 and R_2 into which e partitions the square π are both non-empty. First notice that only edges of type A may define such partitions. Indeed, any edge of type O crosses only the squares containing its end-vertices while any edge of type B or C crossing a non-empty square defines a right triangle and, by Lemma 4, any terminal in this triangle yields the existence of a replacement path for this edge.

Next, we partition the terminals located in π into two subsets corresponding to the regions R_1 and R_2. We consider each pair of adjacent partitions (i.e. the partitions whose regions share a common side) and we add to a set Y the shortest edge between them if one exists. Then, for each partition, we compute a minimum spanning tree on those vertices of the partition that are connected by edges to vertices outside π (i.e., the vertices of $V(Y) \cup V(E_3)$). Finally, we connect each vertex of π that does not belong to $V(Y) \cup V(E_3)$ to its closest neighbor in the spanning tree of its partition. We claim that the two subsets arising from a square π crossed by an edge of E_3 are connected by a path passing through at most one neighboring square of π. Indeed, consider a pair of vertices x and y that belong to distinct partitions of π. Since xy and e are crossing edges of G, from Lemma 2 and the fact that e has no replacement path, we deduce that one end-vertex of e is adjacent to both x and y. This shows that indeed x and y are joined by a path passing via a single neighboring square. As already noticed in Section 3, there are at most 20 edges of E_3 (see Fig. 2) having an end-vertex in a given square. We deduce that there is a path of length at most 44 between every pair of vertices of the same square of Γ.

It remains to show that the edges of E_0 do not cross each other and do not cross the edges of E_3. First, consider an edge xy connecting two neighboring partitions (i.e., an edge of E_3 or an edge of E_0 added due to splitting of a square) and suppose that xy crosses an edge $x'y'$ of a minimum spanning tree T. One end-vertex of xy, say x, must belong to the square containing x' and y', otherwise

xy partitions this square into two non-empty regions. Since $x'y' \in E(T)$, among xx' and xy', one edge, say xx', is at least as long as $x'y'$. Hence, by Lemma 1, yy' is shorter than xy, a contradiction with the choice of xy. The proof is analogous if instead of an edge of T, we consider an edge $x'y'$ added to connect x' to its closest neighbor y' in $V(T)$ (by the choice of $x'y'$, again $|xx'| \geq |x'y'|$). Finally, if $x'y'$ connects two neighboring partitions, then the edges xy and $x'y'$ must have an end-vertex in the same square and we get a contradiction with Lemma 3. Now, it remains the case of two edges having their end-vertices in the same partition. Clearly, two edges of a minimum spanning tree cannot cross and the same holds for two edges connecting a terminal to its closest neighbor in $V(T)$. Now, suppose that x is the closest neighbor of y in $V(T)$ and that xy crosses $x'y' \in E(T)$. Since $x'y' \in E(T)$, either xx' or xy', say xx', is at least as long as $x'y'$. Hence, by Lemma 1, yy' is shorter than xy, a contradiction with the choice of xy. This concludes the proof of Proposition 7.

5.7   Proof of Proposition 8

Let us consider an edge $e = x'y'$ removed during Step 3. This proof is a corollary of two claims: (i) $\pi(x')\pi(y)$ belongs to E_3 or its deletion doesn't affect the length of the path between $\pi(x')$ and $\pi(y')$ in E_3 (ii) the edge $\pi(y)\pi(y')$ either belongs to E_3 or has a replacement path consisting of edges from E_3. Indeed, these two claims imply that the squares $\pi(x')$ and $\pi(y')$ are joined by a path whose length is at most three times the l_1-length of the edge $x'y'$. The worst case arises for Configurations 2 and 5 when the edge $\pi(x')\pi(y')$ has a replacement path of length 3 in E_3. In this case, the total length of the path joining $\pi(x')$ and $\pi(y')$ is three while the l_1-length of $x'y'$ is one.

It remains to establish claims (i) and (ii). Claim (ii) directly follows from Proposition 4 because according to this proposition a replacement path of $x'y'$, distinct from the one passing via $\pi(x')$, always survives Step 2. To establish Claim (i) we first notice that the l_1-length of $\pi(x')\pi(y)$ is 1, thus it has no replacement path. Then, we consider all crossing configurations of Fig. 4. We suppose that $\pi(x')\pi(y)$ is replaced during Step 3 and either derive a contradiction or obtain a shortcut between $\pi(x')$ and $\pi(y')$. We provide a complete analysis only for the crossing Configurations 1, 2, and 3 between xy and $x'y'$. Suppose that $\pi(x')\pi(y)$ (see Fig. 9) is removed during Step 3. Since $\pi(x')\pi(y)$ is an edge of type O, it can be replaced only if it forms with an edge $ab \in E_1$ a Configuration 2 or 5. Without loss of generality, suppose that a is located above the line defined by the edge $\pi(x')\pi(y)$ and that b is located below this line.

First we prove that in all cases ab and xy cross. Let t and z be the end-vertices of the edge $\pi(x')\pi(y)$ that belong respectively to $\pi(x')$ and $\pi(y)$. The edge $\pi(x')\pi(y)$ was replaced either by the edges $\pi(x')\pi(a)$ and $\pi(a)\pi(y)$ or by the edges $\pi(x')\pi(b)$ and $\pi(b)\pi(y)$. Assume the first assertion holds, the proof for the second one is identical (up to symmetry). In this case, if there is no edge running between $\pi(b)$ and the squares $\pi(x')$ and $\pi(y)$, we deduce that the edges xy and ab cross. Indeed, suppose the contrary and consider the two regions A and A' of the square $\pi(y)$ located respectively to the left and to the right of the ball of radius $|ab|$ centered in b. Since ab crosses $\pi(x')\pi(y)$ but not xy, the vertex z must be located in the region A' while y is located in A. In this case, it is easy to verify that y is closer to any vertex of $\pi(x')$ than z, a contradiction with the assumption that $\pi(x')\pi(y)$ is a shortest edge between $\pi(x')$ and $\pi(y)$. Hence, indeed ab and xy cross and thus both y and z are located in A'.

If ab and $\pi(x')\pi(y)$ form a Configuration 5, t is also located outside the ball of radius $|ab|$ centered in b. From their respective locations, it is again easy to verify that the distance between x and t is at most the distance between x and y. Hence, $xy \in G$ implies $xt \in G$, a contradiction with the fact that xy and $x'y'$ form a Configuration 1, 2 or 3.

Now if ab and $\pi(x')\pi(y)$ form a configuration 2, an edge of G may exist between $\pi(a)$ and an extremity of $\pi(x')\pi(y)$. If $b \in \pi_3$ and $a \in \pi_1$, if $\pi(a)\pi(y)$ and $\pi(b)\pi(y)$ belong to E_1, ab has been removed during step 3. If $\pi(a)\pi(y)$ or $\pi(b)\pi(y)$ doesn't belong to E_1, we can use the same arguments as previously when ab and $\pi(x')\pi(y)$ form a Configuration 5. Finally if $b \in \pi_4$ and $a \in \pi_2$, if $\pi(x')\pi(y)$ has been replaced by a path via π_4, we obtain a shortcut between $\pi(x')$ and $\pi(y')$ with the edges $\pi(x')\pi(b)$ and $\pi(b)\pi(y')$. Otherwise $\pi(b)\pi(y)$ doesn't belong to E_1 then $\pi(a)\pi(x)$ belongs to E_1 and $x' \in R(\pi(a), \pi(x))$. So $xx' \in G$, contradiction with the fact that xy and $x'y'$ form a Configuration 1, 2 or 3.

References

1. Alzoubi, K., Li, X., Wang, Y., Wan, P., Frieder, O.: Geometric spanners for wireless ad hoc networks. IEEE Trans. Par. Dist. Syst. 14, 408–421 (2003)
2. Bose, P., Devroye, L., Evans, W., Kirkpatrick, D.: On the spanning ratio of Gabriel graphs and β-skeletons. SIAM J. Discr. Math. 20, 412–427 (2006)
3. Bose, P., Smid, M.: On plane geometric spanners: a survey and open problems (2009) (submitted)
4. Chen, J., Jiang, A., Kanj, I.A., Xia, G., Zhang, F.: Separability and topology control of quasi unit disk graphs. In: INFOCOM 2007, pp. 2225–2233 (2007)
5. Eppstein, D.: Spanning trees and spanners. In: Sack, J.-R., Urrutia, J. (eds.) Handbook of Computational Geometry, pp. 425–461. Elsevier Science Publishers B.V., North-Holland, Amsterdam (2000)
6. Fürer, M., Kasiviswanathan, S.P.: Spanners for geometric intersection graphs. In: Dehne, F., Sack, J.-R., Zeh, N. (eds.) WADS 2007. LNCS, vol. 4619, pp. 312–324. Springer, Heidelberg (2007)
7. Gao, J., Guibas, L.J., Hershberger, J., Zhang, L., Zhu, A.: Discrete mobile centers. Discr. Comput. Geom. 30(1), 45–63 (2003)
8. Gao, J., Guibas, L., Hershberger, J., Zhang, L., Zhu, A.: Geometric spanner for routing in mobile networks. In: ACM MobiHoc 2001, pp. 45–55 (2001)
9. Li, X., Călinescu, G., Wan, P.: Distributed construction of planar spanner and routing for ad hoc wireless networks. In: INFOCOM 2002 (2002)
10. Narasimhan, G., Smid, M.: Geometric Spanner Networks. Cambridge University Press, Cambridge (2007)
11. Rührup, S.: Position-based Routing Strategies, PhD Thesis, University of Paderborn, Germany (2006)
12. Yan, C., Xiang, Y., Dragan, F.F.: Compact and low delay routing labeling scheme for unit disk graphs. In: WADS 2009, pp. 566–577 (2009)

Brief Announcement: Hierarchical Neighbor Graphs: A Sparse Connected Structure for Euclidean Point Sets

Amitabha Bagchi, Adit Madan, and Achal Premi

Indian Institute of Technology, New Delhi 110016, India
bagchi@cse.iitd.ernet.in, madanadit@gmail.com,
achalpremi@gmail.com

Abstract. In this paper we introduce a new randomized method for constructing a bounded degree connected structure on points in Euclidean space: p-hierarchical neighbor graphs. The structure has a flavor of hierarchical clustering and requires only local knowledge and minimal computation at each node to be formed and repaired. Hence it is a suitable interconnection model for an ad hoc wireless network. Our structure has expected constant degree, diameter logarithmic in the size of the set and good spanner-like properties in a probabilistic sense.

The area of topology control is primarily concerned with the question of how to construct a connected network while keeping in mind the various constraints wireless devices operate under. In this paper we propose a novel architecture for connectivity in wireless networks: Hierarchical neighbor graphs. Our structure is a randomized one that effectively combines ideas from skip list data structures [5,1] and nearest-neighbor graphs [6,4] to give a hierarchical bounded degree structure for connecting points in a plane. The structure has short paths between nodes both in terms of number of hops and the distance covered in traversing the paths. Furthermore, hierarchical neighbor graphs can be built with local information and light computation.

1 Hierarchical Neighbor Graphs: Definition

Consider a countable set of points $V \subset \mathbb{R}^2$ with the property that no finite subset of $\mathbb{R}^2$ contains an infinite number of points. We are given a function $w : V \to [1, \infty)$ such that each node $u \in V$ has battery power $w(u)$ associated with it (assuming 1 unit is the minimum battery power a node needs to operate.) Taking a parameter p such that $0 < p < 1$, we form the p-hierarchical neighbor graph on V with weight function w, denoted $\mathsf{HN}_p^w(V)$ as follows:[1]

1. We create a sequence $\{S_n : n \geq 0\}$ of subsets of V such that $S_0 = V$.
   - Deterministically, all $u \in S_{i-1}$ with $\lfloor \log_{\frac{1}{p}} \rfloor w(u) \geq i$ are put into S_i.
   - The remaining points of S_{i-1} are placed in S_i with probability p independently. We say that the *level* of u, denoted $lev_p(u)$ is i if $u \in S_i$ and $u \notin S_{i+1}$.

---

[1] We will use the notation that for $u, v \in \mathbb{R}^2$, $d(u, v)$ is the Euclidean distance between the points.

C. Scheideler (Ed.): ALGOSENSORS 2010, LNCS 6451, pp. 31–33, 2010.

2. Each point $u \in V$ grows a circle around it which stops growing the first time a point $v \in V$ with $lev_p(v) > lev_p(u)$ is encountered. u makes connections to all nodes w with $lev_p(w) = lev_p(u)$ that lie within this circle and to the node(s) of $S_{lev_p(u)+1}$ that lie on the circumference of the circle.

From an algorithmic point of view we note that all connections are made through local interactions i.e. the structure can be constructed (and repaired) in a fully distributed manner.

2   Properties of Hierarchical Neighbor Graphs

Bounded degree: An important property of hierarchical neighbor graphs is that the expected degree of a node is bounded in terms of p and w and does not depend on the total number of nodes. We can show the following theorem:

Theorem 1. *The expected degree of any point $v \in V$ in $\mathsf{HN}_p^w(V)$ constructed with parameter p on an arbitrary point set $V \subset \mathbb{R}^2$ is at most*

$$\frac{1}{p} + \frac{6}{p} \cdot \left(\log_{\frac{1}{p}} w(v) + \frac{1}{1-p} \right).$$

For the case where all the weights are 1 and the point sets are generated by a Poisson point process we show a better bound of $\theta(\frac{1}{p})$. We note that it is quite expected that the degree bound does not contain the intensity of the point process λ in it, since $\mathsf{HN}_p^w(V)$ is essentially a nearest neighbor model.

Number of hops: To bound communication delay in networks, we need to construct a topology with a small hop-stretch factor. In order to do this we introduce the notation $ht(\mathsf{HN}_p^W(V)) = \max_{u \in V} lev_p(u)$. For finite point sets, we claim the following theorem, that follows easily from standard skip list analysis.

Theorem 2. *For $\mathsf{HN}_p^w(V)$ constructed on a finite set V, define let the total weight of V be $W(V) = \sum_{u \in V} w(u)$. Then*

$$P(ht(\mathsf{HN}_p^w(V) \geq k) \leq W \cdot p^k,$$

for $k \geq \max_{u \in V} \log_{\frac{1}{p}} w(u)$.

From this theorem it is easy to deduce that the number of hops between any two points is $\theta(\log W(V))$ with high probability (i.e. with probability at least $1 - 1/(W(V))$ since two times the highest level in the structure is a natural upper bound on the number of hops between any two points.

Bounding the stretch: A major concern of topology control mechanisms is that the graph be a spanner i.e. given a point set V and a interconnection structure G, if we denote the shortest distance between points $u, v \in V$ along the edges of G by $d_G(u, v)$, the ratio $\delta_G = \max_{u,v \in V} \frac{d_G(u,v)}{d(u,v)}$, known as the *distance stretch* of G should be low.

We believe that hierarchical neighbor graphs are spanners in a probabilistic sense i.e. there is very low probability that the distance between two nodes is large compared to their Euclidean distance. To this end we are currently able to show the following weak result:

Theorem 3. *Given parameters p and λ s.t. $0 < p < 1$ and $\lambda > 0$, the graph $\mathsf{HN}_p(V)$ built on a set of points V generated by a Poisson point process with intensity λ has the property that for any two points $u, v \in V$ such that $d(u, v) = l$, there are positive constants c_1 and $c_2 < 1$ depending only on p and λ such that for $0 < \theta < \frac{\pi}{3}$,*

$$P\left(d_p(u, v) > \frac{l}{1 - 2\sin\left(\frac{\theta}{2}\right)}\right) \leq \exp\left\{-\frac{c_1}{l^4 \cdot \left(1 - c_2 \cdot \frac{\theta}{\pi}\right)}\right\}.$$

One way of interpreting this theorem is that given a large integer M, the probability that two points that are at least $\ell = \log M$ units apart have their distance stretched to ℓ^5 is at most $1/M$.

A fuller version of this paper can be found at [2]. For a detailed discussion of hierarchical neighbor graphs as a topology control mechanism for data collection is sensor networks, please see [3].

References

1. Bagchi, A., Buchsbaum, A., Goodrich, M.T.: Biased skip lists. Algorithmica 42(1), 31–48 (2005)
2. Bagchi, A., Madan, A., Premi, A.: Hierarchical neighbor graphs: An energy-efficient bounded degree connected structure for wireless sensor networks (July 2009), arXiv:0903.0742v3 [cs.NI]
3. Bagchi, A., Madan, A., Premi, A.: Hierarchical neighbor graphs: A fully distributed topology for data collection in wireless sensor networks (2010),
   http://www.cse.iitd.ernet.in/~bagchi
4. Ballister, P., Bollobás, B., Sarkar, A., Walters, M.: Connectivity of random k-nearest-neighbour graphs. Adv. Appl. Prob (SGSA) 37, 1–24 (2005)
5. Pugh, W.: Skip lists: A probabilistic alternative to balanced trees. Commun. ACM 33(6), 668–676 (1990)
6. Xue, F., Kumar, P.R.: The number of neighbors needed for the connectivity of wireless networks. Wirel. Netw. 10, 169–181 (2004)

Minimum Energy Broadcast on Rectangular Grid Wireless Networks

Atsushi Murata[1] and Akira Matsubayashi[2]

[1] Division of Electrical and Computer Engineering, Kanazawa University,
Kanazawa 920-1192, Japan
[2] Division of Electrical Engineering and Computer Science, Kanazawa University,
Kanazawa 920-1192, Japan
mbayashi@t.kanazawa-u.ac.jp

Abstract. The minimum energy broadcast problem is to assign a transmission range to each node in an ad hoc wireless network to construct a spanning tree rooted at a given source node such that any non-root node resides within the transmission range of its parent. The objective is to minimize the total energy consumption, i.e., the sum of the δth powers of a transmission range ($\delta \geq 1$). In this paper, we consider the case that $\delta = 2$, and that nodes are located on a 2-dimensional rectangular grid. We prove that the minimum energy consumption for an n-node $k \times l$-grid with $n = kl$ and $k \leq l$ is at most $\frac{n}{\pi} + O(\frac{n}{k^{0.68}})$ and at least $\frac{n}{\pi} + \Omega(\frac{n}{k}) - O(k)$. Our bounds close the previously known gap of upper and lower bounds for square grids. Moreover, our lower bound is $\frac{n}{3} - O(1)$ for $3 \leq k \leq 18$, which matches a naive upper bound within a constant term for $k \equiv 0 \pmod 3$.

1 Introduction

In ad hoc wireless networks, communication is established via a sequence of wireless connections between neighboring nodes. It is well known that a transmission power at least $\gamma \cdot \text{dist}(u, v)^\delta$ is necessary for a node u to directly transmit a data message to a node v, where $\text{dist}(u, v)$ is the distance between u and v, and $\gamma \geq 1$ and $\delta \geq 1$ are the transmission-quality parameter and the distance-power gradient, respectively, which depend on environment [9]. In what follows, we fix $\gamma = 1$ and assume that nodes are located on the Euclidean plane.

It is important to save energy consumption in ad hoc wireless networks because wireless nodes are often driven by batteries. The *minimum energy broadcast problem*, i.e., the problem of transferring a data message to all nodes in an ad hoc network with the minimum total energy consumption has extensively been studied. Formally, this problem is to assign a transmission range $r_u \geq 0$ to each node u so that there exists a spanning tree rooted at a given source node and satisfying $\text{dist}(u, v) \leq r_u$ for any node u and its child v, and that the cost $\sum_u r_u^\delta$ is minimized.

It is known that the minimum energy broadcast problem is NP-hard for any $\delta > 1$ [6]. Approximation ratios for this problem have been proved in [10,7,8,1].

C. Scheideler (Ed.): ALGOSENSORS 2010, LNCS 6451, pp. 34–46, 2010.

The best known algorithm achieving the approximation ratio of 4.2 for any $\delta \geq 2$ on the Euclidean plane was presented in [5]. Calamoneri, Clementi, Ianni, Lauria, Monti, and Silvestri considered the case that $\delta = 2$, and that n nodes are located on a square grid with side length $\sqrt{n} - 1$ [4]. They proved that the minimum cost is between $\frac{n}{\pi} - O(\sqrt{n})$ and $1.01013\frac{n}{\pi} + O(\sqrt{n})$. They also conjectured that a broadcast on the square grid based on a circle packing called the Apollonian gasket would achieve a cost matching the lower bound asymptotically.

In this paper, we demonstrate that a simple application of early results on the Apollonian gasket answers the conjecture. Specifically, we prove that a broadcast on an n-node square grid based on Apollonian gaskets achieves a cost of $\frac{n}{\pi} + O(n^{\frac{S}{2}+\epsilon})$, where S is the Hausdorff dimension of an Apollonian gasket. Because it is well known that $S < 1.314534$ [2], our upper bound matches the lower bound of [4] within an $o(n)$ term. We also generalize these results to rectangular grids. The upper bound on square grids is extended to $\frac{n}{\pi} + O(k^{S-2+\epsilon}n)$ for any $k \times l$-grid with $n = kl$ and $k \leq l$. Moreover, we present a lower bound of $\frac{n}{\pi} + \Omega(\frac{n}{k}) - O(k)$. Thus, we can obtain upper and lower bounds matching within an $o(n)$ term as long as $k = \omega(1)$. Although we do not know a tight factor of n for all $k = O(1)$, our lower bound is $\frac{n}{3} - O(1)$ for $3 \leq k \leq 18$, which matches a naive upper bound of $\frac{n}{3} + O(k)$ for $k \equiv 0 \pmod 3$.

Our upper bounds can be obtained by polynomial time algorithms. Moreover, we prove our lower bounds using a refined technique of the proof of [4].

2   Apollonian Gasket

Let $T(a, b, c)$ be the range bounded by the curvilinear triangle of three mutually tangent disks of curvatures (i.e., reciprocals of a radius) a, b, and c, where $a, b, c \geq 0$, and at most one of a, b, and c equals 0. The *Apollonian gasket* of $T(a, b, c)$ is a set of infinite disks $\{D_i\}_{i \geq 1}$ such that D_i has the maximal radius of all the disks contained in $T(a, b, c) \setminus \bigcup_{j=1}^{i-1} D_j$. D_1 is said to be of level 1. D_i $(i \geq 2)$ is said to be of level j if it is tangent to a disk of level $j - 1$ but not to a disk of a higher level than $j - 1$. For any disk D of level $j \geq 2$, we call the unique disk of level $j - 1$ tangent to D the parent of D. The *exponent* of $\{D_i\}$ is defined as $S := \inf\{t \mid \sum_{i=1}^{\infty} r_i^t < \infty\} = \sup\{t \mid \sum_{i=1}^{\infty} r_i^t = \infty\}$, where r_i is the radius of D_i. It is well known that S does not depend on a, b, or c, and that S is equal to the Hausdorff dimension of an Apollonian Gasket [3]. Currently best provable bounds on S were presented by Boyd:

Theorem A ([2]). $1.300197 < S < 1.314534$.

We denote $\sigma(a, b, c, t) := \sum_{i=1}^{\infty} r_i^t$, which is finite for any $t > S$.

3   Broadcast on Square Grids

In this section, we assume that $n = m^2$ nodes are located on points with coordinates (x, y) of integers $0 \leq x, y < m$.

Our algorithm to construct a broadcast on an $m \times m$-grid is based on a natural generalization of an Apollonian Gasket to a circle packing of the square Q with side length $m - 1$ bounding the grid. Specifically, the algorithm, called AGBS, is defined as follows:

1. Locate a maximal disk D_1 of level 1 contained in Q.
2. For $j \geq 2$, we have $4 \cdot 3^{j-2}$ ranges in $Q \backslash$ (union of disks of lower level than j). Locate a maximal disk of level j in each range if such a disk has radius at least 1. Repeat this step until we have no range to locate a maximal disk of radius at least 1.
3. Let $\mathcal{D} := \{D_i\}_{i \geq 1}$ be the set of located disks. For each $i \geq 1$, let r_i be the radius of D_i. For each $i \geq 2$, let t_i be the tangency point of D_i and the parent of D_i.
4. For each $i \geq 1$, move and enlarge D_i so that it is centered at a nearest node c_i to the original center and has radius $r'_i := r_i + 1 + \frac{3\sqrt{2}}{2}$.
5. Locate disks of radius 1 centered at grid points on the line segments from (x, y) to (x', y) and from (x', y) to (x', y'), where (x, y) and (x', y') are the coordinates of a source node s and c_1, respectively.
6. For each $i \geq 2$, locate disks of radius 1 centered at grid points on the line segments from (x, y) to (x', y) and from (x', y) to (x', y'), where (x, y) and (x', y') are the coordinates of a nearest node t'_i to t_i and c_i, respectively.
7. Assign each node v the maximum radius of a disk centered at v if such a disk exists, 0 otherwise.

Figure 1 illustrates a broadcast constructed by AGBS.

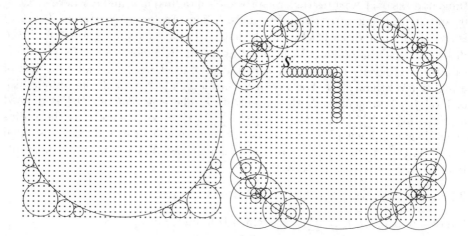

Fig. 1. A broadcast on a 40×40-grid constructed by AGBS: disks located after Step 2 (left) and the completed broadcast (right)

Lemma 1. *AGBS constructs a broadcast.*

Proof. After Step 2, any range T bounded by a curvilinear triangle in $Q \setminus \bigcup_i D_i$ cannot contain a disk of radius 1. If $T = T(a, b, c)$ with $a \geq 0$ and $b, c > 0$, then any point p in T can be covered by a disk of radius less than 1 that is contained in T and tangent to a disk D of curvature b or c. Thus, p is covered by D by increasing the radius of D by 2. If T is a curvilinear triangle with one curve of a disk D and two line segments of Q, then T is covered by D by increasing the radius of D by $1 + \sqrt{2}$. Therefore, Q is covered by $\bigcup_i D_i$ by increasing all the radii by $1 + \sqrt{2}$. Moreover, t_i' is covered by the parent of D_i after the increase of its radius because $\mathrm{dist}(t_i, t_i') \leq \frac{\sqrt{2}}{2}$. Because the distance of c_i and the original center of D_i is at most $\frac{\sqrt{2}}{2}$, after Step 4, Q is covered by D_is centered at grid points. Steps 5 and 6 guarantee that a data message from s is transferred to all the nodes covered by $\bigcup_i D_i$. Thus, AGBS constructs a broadcast. $\square$

Let $\mathcal{C}$ be the set of disks located in Steps 5 and 6. Then, the cost of AGBS is $\mathsf{cost} = \sum_i r_i'^2 + |\mathcal{C}|$.

Lemma 2. $|\mathcal{C}| \leq \sum_i (\sqrt{2}\, r_i + 2) + m$.

Proof. Suppose $i \geq 2$. Because $\mathrm{dist}(t_i, t_i') \leq \frac{\sqrt{2}}{2}$ and the distance of c_i and the original center of D_i is at most $\frac{\sqrt{2}}{2}$, it follows that $\mathrm{dist}(t_i', c_i) \leq r_i + \sqrt{2}$. This means that the number of disks located in Step 6 from t_i' to c_i is at most $\sqrt{2}\, r_i + 2$. The number of disks located in Step 5 is obviously at most $2\lceil (m-1)/2 \rceil \leq m$. $\square$

Lemma 3. *For any $\epsilon > 0$, it follows that $\sum_i r_i = O(m^{S+\epsilon})$.*

Proof. Consider disks after Step 2. Let $I_1 := D_1$ and I_2 be one of the four disks of level 2. Then, for $j \geq 3$, let I_j be the disk tangent to I_{j-1} and to two line segments of Q. For $j \geq 1$, let T_j be a range bounded by the curvilinear triangle of I_j, I_{j+1}, and Q (Fig. 2), and let $\mathcal{T}_j$ be the set of disks contained in T_j. It follows that $\sum_i r_i \leq 4\sum_j (\text{radius of } I_j) + 8\sum_j \sum_{D_i \in \mathcal{T}_j} r_i$. We can observe that $\sum_j (\text{radius of } I_j) \leq \frac{\sqrt{2}}{2} m$ and that for $j \geq 2$, T_j is similar to T_{j-1} with the shrink factor of $3 - 2\sqrt{2}$. Thus, we have

$$\sum_i r_i \leq 2\sqrt{2}\, m + \frac{8}{1 - (3 - 2\sqrt{2})} \sum_{D_i \in \mathcal{T}_1} r_i = 2\sqrt{2}\, m + 4(\sqrt{2} + 1) \sum_{D_i \in \mathcal{T}_1} r_i. \quad (1)$$

Because $T_1 = T(0, \frac{2}{m-1}, \frac{2(3+\sqrt{2})}{m-1})$ is similar to $T(0, 2, 2(3 + \sqrt{2}))$ with the scale factor of $m - 1$, and because every disk in $\mathcal{T}_1$ has radius at least 1, it follows that

$$\sum_{D_i \in \mathcal{T}_1} r_i \leq \sum_{D_i \in \mathcal{T}_1} r_i^{S+\epsilon} \leq \sigma\left(0, \frac{2}{m-1}, \frac{2(3+\sqrt{2})}{m-1}, S + \epsilon\right) \quad (2)$$
$$< \sigma(0, 2, 2(3 + \sqrt{2}), S + \epsilon) m^{S+\epsilon}.$$

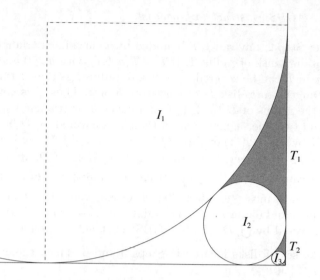

Fig. 2. I_j and T_j

Because $\sigma(0, 2, 2(3 + \sqrt{2}), S + \epsilon)$ is a finite value[1] independent of m, by (1) and (2), we have the lemma. □

Theorem 1. *For any $\epsilon > 0$, AGBS has a cost of $\frac{n}{\pi} + O(n^{\frac{S}{2}+\epsilon})$.*

Proof. Because $\pi \sum_i r_i^2 \le (m-1)^2 < m^2$, it follows from Lemmas 2 and 3 that $\mathsf{cost} = \sum_i r_i'^2 + |\mathcal{C}| = \sum_i r_i^2 + O(\sum_i r_i) + m < \frac{m^2}{\pi} + O(m^{S+\epsilon}) = \frac{n}{\pi} + O(n^{\frac{S}{2}+\epsilon})$. □

By Lemmas 2 and 3, the running time of AGBS is $n + O(|\mathcal{D}| + |\mathcal{C}|) = n + O(\sum_i r_i + m) = n + O(n^{\frac{S}{2}+\epsilon}) = O(n)$.

4   Broadcast on Rectangular Grids

In this section, we assume that $n = kl$ nodes ($k \le l$) are located on points with coordinates (x, y) of integers $0 \le x < l$ and $0 \le y < k$.

4.1   Upper Bounds

Our broadcast algorithm on rectangular grids is based on a simple application of AGBS to maximal square grids contained in a given rectangular grid. Specifically, the algorithm, called AGBR, is defined as follows:

---

[1] In fact, we can guarantee $\sigma(0, 2, 2(3 + \sqrt{2}), S + \epsilon)$ to be reasonably small if we are allowed to have a certain ϵ. For example, we can estimate $\sigma(0, 2, 2(3+\sqrt{2}), 1.4) \le 0.97$ using the recurrence presented in [2].

1. Let $k_0 := l$ and $k_1 := k$. For each $i \geq 1$ with $k_i > 0$, recursively define $k_{i+1} := k_{i-1} \bmod k_i$, $l_i := k_{i-1} - k_{i+1}$, and $n_i := k_i l_i$.
2. Let G_1 be a $k_1 \times k_0$-grid and s be a source node. For each $i \geq 1$ with $k_i > 0$, repeat (a) and (b).
   (a) Divide G_i into a $k_i \times l_i$-grid G_i' and a $k_{i+1} \times k_i$-grid G_{i+1}.
   (b) Divide G_i' into l_i/k_i square grids, and apply AGBS on each square grid with setting a nearest node to s as the source node.
3. For each square grid Q appeared in Step 2(b) and not containing s, the nearest node to s is adjacent to a node v of another square grid Q' closer to s. Locate a disk of radius 1 centered at v, so that a broadcast message from s is transferred to Q via Q'.
4. Assign each node v the maximum radius of a disk located centered at v if such a disk exists, 0 otherwise.

Figure 3 illustrates a broadcast constructed by AGBR.

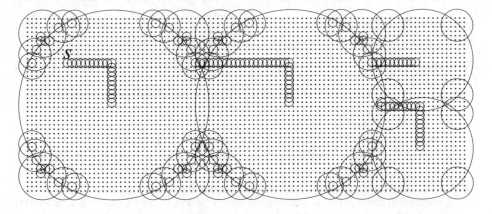

Fig. 3. A broadcast on a 40×100-grid constructed by AGBR

Theorem 2. *For any $\epsilon > 0$, AGBR has a cost of is $\frac{n}{\pi} + O(k^{S-2+\epsilon}n)$.*

Proof. Let $\mathcal{C}$ be the set of disks located in Step 3. Then, by Theorem 1, the cost of AGBR is

$$\text{cost} \leq \sum_{i \geq 1} \left(\frac{k_i^2}{\pi} + O(k_i^t) \right) \frac{l_i}{k_i} + |\mathcal{C}| = \frac{n}{\pi} + O(\sum_{i \geq 1} k_i^{t-1} l_i) + |\mathcal{C}|, \qquad (3)$$

where $t := S + \epsilon$. We can observe that $k_{i+1} < k_i \leq l_i = k_{i-1} - k_{i+1} \leq k_{i-1}$ for any $i \geq 1$. Therefore, it follows that for $i \geq 3$,

$$k_i^{t-1} l_i \leq k_i^{t-1} k_{i-1} \leq k_i^{t-1}(k_{i-2} - k_i) \leq \frac{(t-1)^{t-1}}{t^t} k_{i-2}^t \leq \frac{(t-1)^{t-1}}{t^t} k_{i-2}^{t-1} l_{i-2}. \qquad (4)$$

Here, we have used the fact that $x^\alpha(\beta - x)$ with $\alpha, \beta > 0$ is maximized at $x = \frac{\alpha\beta}{1+\alpha}$. It follows from (4) that

$$\sum_{i \geq 1} k_i^{t-1} l_i = \sum_{i \geq 1} (k_{2i-1}^{t-1} l_{2i-1} + k_{2i}^{t-1} l_{2i}) \tag{5}$$
$$= O(k_1^{t-1} l_1 + k_2^{t-1} l_2) = O(k^{t-1} l) = O(k^{t-2} n).$$

Moreover,

$$|\mathcal{C}| \leq \sum_{i \geq 1} \frac{l_i}{k_i} \leq \sum_{i \geq 1} l_i = l + k = \frac{n}{k} + 1. \tag{6}$$

By (3), (5), and (6), we have the theorem.   □

Because the running time of AGBS is $O(n)$, the running time of AGBR is $n + \sum_{i \geq 1} O(k_i^2) + |\mathcal{C}| = O(n)$.

Theorem 2 is not useful to bound a factor of n for the case $k = O(1)$. The following theorem is simple but provides an explicit factor of n for any $k \geq 3$.

Theorem 3. *For a $k \times l$-grid with $n = kl$ and $k \geq 3$, the minimum cost is at most $\frac{n}{3} + \frac{2}{3}k - 1$ if $k \bmod 3 = 0$, $(1 + \frac{1}{k})\frac{n}{3} + \frac{2}{3}k - \frac{1}{3}$ otherwise.*

Proof. It can easily be verified that the following algorithm constructs a desired broadcast:

1. Locate a disk of radius 1 centered at every (x, y) with $0 \leq x \leq l - 2$, $0 \leq y \leq k - 2$, and $y \bmod 3 = 1$.
2. Locate a disk of radius 1 centered at every $(l - 1, y)$ with $1 \leq y \leq k - 2$.
3. If $k \bmod 3 \geq 1$, then locate a disk of radius 1 centered at every $(x, k - 1 - i)$ with $1 \leq x \leq l - 2$, $x \bmod 3 = 1$, and $0 \leq i \leq k \bmod 3$.
4. Locate a disk of radius 1 centered at a source node.
5. Assign each node v the transmission range of 1 if there exists a disk centered at v, 0 otherwise.

□

Figure 4 illustrates a broadcast of Theorem 3. The running time of the algorithm of Theorem 3 is obviously $O(n)$.

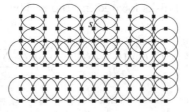

Fig. 4. A broadcast on a 8×13-grid based on Theorem 3

4.2 Lower Bounds

Proof Sketch. Let $R := \{1, \sqrt{2}, 2, \sqrt{5}, 2\sqrt{2}, 3, \sqrt{10}, \ldots\}$ be the set of radii of disks centered at a node and having at least one node on the boundary. Suppose that $\mathcal{D} := \{D_i\}_{i \geq 1}$ is a broadcast on a $k \times l$-grid with the minimum cost denoted by cost, and that D_1 is centered at a source node s. It should be noted that any D_i has a radius $r_i \in R$. The proof of the lower bound for square grids in [4] is as follows: For any $D_i \in \mathcal{D}$ not covering s, there exists a sequence $\mathcal{H}_i$ of disks *activating* D_i, i.e., transferring a data message from the outside of D_i to the center c_i of D_i. We can observe that $n \leq \sum_i N(r_i) - \sum_{D_i \not\ni s} M(r_i)$, where $N(r_i)$ and $M(r_i)$ are the numbers of nodes in D_i and $D_i \cap \bigcup_{A \in \mathcal{H}_i} A$, respectively. Moreover, the following inequalities are proved in [4]:

$$N(r) < \pi r^2 + 2\sqrt{2}\, r - 5 \text{ for any } r \in R \text{ with } r > \sqrt{10}, \qquad (7)$$

$$\sum_{D_i \ni s} r_i = O(r_{\max}), \text{ and} \qquad (8)$$

$$M(r) \geq 2\sqrt{2}\, r - 5 \text{ for any } r \in R.$$

Here, $r_{\max} := \max_i\{r_i\}$, which is $O(\sqrt{n})$ on a square grid. Thus, we have $n \leq \sum_{D_i \ni s} N(r_i) + \sum_{D_i \not\ni s}(N(r_i) - M(r_i)) = \pi \sum_i r_i^2 + O(\sqrt{n}) = \pi \cdot \text{cost} + O(\sqrt{n})$. To obtain a lower bound of $\frac{n}{\alpha}$ with $\alpha < \pi$ by this proof, we need to improve bounds of $N(r)$ and/or $M(r)$ so that $N(r) - M(r) \leq \alpha r^2$. However, there is no effective room for such improvement. Our key idea is to estimate the overlap of D_i and $\mathcal{H}_i$ by the cost instead of by $M(r_i)$. If $\text{dist}(v, c_i) \geq a_i$ for every node v covered by the first disk $\tilde{D}_i$ in $\mathcal{H}_i$, then the total cost of disks in $\mathcal{H}_i \setminus \{\tilde{D}_i\}$ is at least a_i. Therefore, if we can choose $\mathcal{Z} \subset \mathcal{D}$ such that $D_i \in \mathcal{Z}$ implies $\mathcal{H}_i \cap \mathcal{Z} = \{\tilde{D}_i\}$, and that any $A \notin \mathcal{Z}$ activates a unique disk of $\mathcal{Z}$, then we have $\text{cost} \geq \sum_{D_i \ni s} r_i^2 + \sum_{s \notin D_i \in \mathcal{Z}}(r_i^2 + a_i)$. From this observation, we can obtain a sufficient condition $N(r_i) - L(a_i, r_i) \leq \alpha(r_i^2 + a_i)$ for the lower bound of $\frac{n}{\alpha}$, where $L(a_i, r_i)$ is the number of nodes covered by $D_i \cap \tilde{D}_i$. Because $L(a_i, r_i) + \alpha a_i$ is minimized at $a_i \simeq r_i$, by (7) and $r_{\max} = O(k)$, we can prove that the sufficient condition is satisfied with $\alpha = \pi - \Omega(k^{-1})$.

Now we describe our formal proof. Let $\mathcal{T} := (\mathcal{D}, \mathcal{E})$ be a spanning tree rooted at D_1, where $\mathcal{E}$ is a set of pairs (D, D') such that D covers the center of D'. For each $D_i \in \mathcal{D}$, let $\tilde{D}_i^{\mathcal{T}}$ be the nearest ancestor to D_i that covers a node not covered by D_i if such an ancestor exists, D_1 otherwise. It should be noted that if $\mathcal{A}_i^{\mathcal{T}}$ is the set of disks between $\tilde{D}_i^{\mathcal{T}}$ and D_i on $\mathcal{T}$ (excluding both $\tilde{D}_i^{\mathcal{T}}$ and D_i), then every node covered by $A \in \mathcal{A}_i^{\mathcal{T}}$ is covered also by D_i. Therefore, $\tilde{D}_i^{\mathcal{T}}$ covers also a node in D_i. Let $\mathcal{Z}^{\mathcal{T}}$ be the set of disks $D \in \mathcal{D}$ such that there exists a sequence of disks $Z_1, \ldots, Z_h \in \mathcal{D}$, where $Z_1 = D$, $Z_j = \tilde{Z}_{j+1}^{\mathcal{T}}$ for $1 \leq j < h$, and Z_h is a leaf of $\mathcal{T}$. It should be noted that $D_1 \in \mathcal{Z}^{\mathcal{T}}$.

Lemma 4. $\bigcup_i D_i = D_1 \cup \bigcup_{D \in \mathcal{Z}^{\mathcal{T}} \setminus \{D_1\}} (D \setminus \tilde{D}^{\mathcal{T}})$.

Proof. For any disk $D' \notin \mathcal{Z}^{\mathcal{T}}$, there exists $D \in \mathcal{Z}^{\mathcal{T}}$ covering every node covered by D'. Therefore, it follows that $\bigcup_i D_i = \bigcup_{D \in \mathcal{Z}^{\mathcal{T}}} D$. Moreover, by the definition of $\mathcal{Z}^{\mathcal{T}}$, $D \in \mathcal{Z}^{\mathcal{T}} \setminus \{D_1\}$ implies that $\tilde{D}^{\mathcal{T}} \in \mathcal{Z}^{\mathcal{T}}$, and that there is no sequence $Z_1, \ldots, Z_h = D$ such that $Z_j = \tilde{Z}_{j+1}^{\mathcal{T}}$ for $1 \le j < h$ and $Z_h = \tilde{Z}_1^{\mathcal{T}}$. Therefore, for each node $v \in D \cap \tilde{D}^{\mathcal{T}}$, there exists an ancestor $A \in \mathcal{Z}^{\mathcal{T}}$ of D such that $v \in A \setminus \tilde{A}^{\mathcal{T}}$, or $v \in D_1$. Thus, the lemma holds.   □

Lemma 5. *For any spanning tree $\mathcal{T}$ associated with $\mathcal{D}$ and rooted by D_1, and for any leaves Y_p and Z_q of $\mathcal{T}$, let $\mathcal{Z}^{\mathcal{T}}(Y_p) := \{Y_1, \ldots, Y_p\}$ and $\mathcal{Z}^{\mathcal{T}}(Z_q) := \{Z_1, \ldots, Z_q\}$, where $Y_1 = Z_1 = D_1$, $Y_j = \tilde{Y}_{j+1}^{\mathcal{T}}$ for $1 \le j < p$, and $Z_j = \tilde{Z}_{j+1}^{\mathcal{T}}$ for $1 \le j < q$. Then, there exists $\mathcal{T}$ satisfying the following conditions for any pair of leaves Y_p and Z_q of $\mathcal{T}$:*

1. *The nearest common ancestor A to Y_p and Z_q in $\mathcal{T}$ is contained in $\mathcal{Z}^{\mathcal{T}}(Y_p) \cap \mathcal{Z}^{\mathcal{T}}(Z_q)$.*
2. *There exists $1 \le a \le \min\{p, q\}$ such that $Y_j = Z_j$ for $1 \le j < a$, and that $Y_a = Z_a = A$.*

Proof. It should be noted that Condition 2 is implied by Condition 1 because $Y_1, \ldots, Y_{a-1}$ ($Z_1, \ldots, Z_{a-1}$, resp.) are uniquely determined by Y_a (Z_a, resp.) and $\mathcal{T}$. Therefore, we prove that we can obtain $\mathcal{T}$ satisfying Condition 1 for any pair of leaves Y_p and Z_q of $\mathcal{T}$.

Fix Y_p and Z_q, and assume $A \notin \mathcal{Z}^{\mathcal{T}}(Y_p)$ and $A \in \mathcal{A}_i^{\mathcal{T}}$ for some $D_i \in \mathcal{Z}^{\mathcal{T}}(Y_p)$. Let $(A, D) \in \mathcal{E}$ such that D is on the path between A and Z_q in $\mathcal{T}$. Because every node covered by A is covered also by D_i, we can obtain another spanning tree $\mathcal{T}' = (\mathcal{D}, \mathcal{E}')$ from $\mathcal{T}$ by replacing (A, D) with (D_i, D), so that D_i becomes the nearest common ancestor to Y_p and Z_q in $\mathcal{T}'$. If Y_p is not a leaf of $\mathcal{T}'$, or if $D_i \in \mathcal{Z}^{\mathcal{T}'}(Z_q)$, then $\mathcal{T}'$ satisfies Condition 1 with respect to Y_p and Z_q fixed here.

Otherwise, assume $D_i \notin \mathcal{Z}^{\mathcal{T}'}(Z_q)$ and $D_i \in \mathcal{A}_j^{\mathcal{T}'}$ for some $D_j \in \mathcal{Z}^{\mathcal{T}'}(Z_q)$. Let $(D_i, D') \in \mathcal{E}'$ such that D' is on the path between D_i and Y_p in $\mathcal{T}'$. Because every node covered by D_i is covered also by D_j, we can obtain another spanning tree $\mathcal{T}''$ from $\mathcal{T}'$ by replacing (D_i, D') by (D_j, D'), so that D_j becomes the nearest common ancestor to Y_p and Z_q in $\mathcal{T}''$. Let $D_h \in \mathcal{Z}^{\mathcal{T}'}(Y_p)$ with $\tilde{D}_h^{\mathcal{T}'} = D_i$. It should be noted that $D_h \in \mathcal{Z}^{\mathcal{T}''}(Y_p)$, and that if Z_q is a leaf of $\mathcal{T}''$, then $D_j \in \mathcal{Z}^{\mathcal{T}''}(Z_q)$. Moreover, $\tilde{D}_h^{\mathcal{T}''} = D_j$ holds. This is because any disk from D' to D_h on $\mathcal{T}'$ is contained in $\mathcal{A}_h^{\mathcal{T}'}$, and hence, in $\mathcal{A}_h^{\mathcal{T}''}$, and because every node covered by D_i is covered by D_j, which means that D_j covers a node not covered by D_h. Thus, $D_j \in \mathcal{Z}^{\mathcal{T}''}(Y_p) \cup \mathcal{Z}^{\mathcal{T}''}(Z_q)$ if Z_q is a leaf of $\mathcal{T}''$.

By repeating the above argument for every pair of leaves, we will obtain a desired spanning tree.   □

In what follows, we fix a spanning tree $\mathcal{T} = (\mathcal{D}, \mathcal{E})$ satisfying the conditions of Lemma 5 and omit the superscript $\mathcal{T}$ from each symbol.

Definition 1. *For any $r \ge 1$ and an integer $a \ge 0$, let $L(a, r)$ be the minimum number of grid points of an infinitely large grid that is covered by two disks D of radius r and $\tilde{D}$ satisfying the following conditions:*

1. D and $\tilde{D}$ are centered at grid points,
2. $\tilde{D}$ covers a grid point not covered by D, and a grid point of coordinates (x, y) such that D covers (x, y), $(x, y \pm 1)$, and $(x \pm 1, y)$.
3. The shortest Manhattan distance between a node in $D \cap \tilde{D}$ and the center of D is a.

Let $N(r)$ be the number of grid points of an infinitely large grid that is covered by a disk of radius r centered at a grid point. We define $X(a, r) := \frac{N(r) - L(a, r)}{r^2 + a}$, which can be used to estimate a lower bound of cost as follows:

Lemma 6. If $N(r) \leq \alpha r^2 + \beta r$ and $X(a, r) \leq \alpha$ for any $r \in R$ with $r \leq r_{\max}$ and any $a \geq 0$, then $\mathsf{cost} \geq \frac{n}{\alpha} - O(\frac{\beta}{\alpha} r_{\max})$.

Proof. For each $D_i \in \mathcal{Z} \setminus \{D_1\}$, let a_i be the shortest Manhattan distance between a node in $D_i \cap \tilde{D}_i$ and the center of D_i. Because $\mathcal{A}_i \cap (\mathcal{A}_j \cup \{D_j, \tilde{D}_j\}) = \emptyset$ for any $D_j \in \mathcal{Z} \setminus \{D_i\}$ by Lemma 5, $\mathcal{A}_i$ plays only a role of transferring a data message from $\tilde{D}_i$ to D_i, which requires a cost at least the cost of a_i disks of radius 1. Thus, we have $\mathsf{cost} \geq r_1^2 + \sum_{D_i \in \mathcal{Z} \setminus \{D_1\}} (r_i^2 + \dot{a}_i)$. Moreover, if D is a disk with $(\tilde{D}_i, D) \in \mathcal{E}$ and $D \in \mathcal{A}_i \cup \{D_i\}$, then the center (x, y) of D is covered by $\tilde{D}_i$, and (x, y), $(x, y \pm 1)$, and $(x \pm 1, y)$ are covered by D_i. Thus, (\# nodes in D_i) $-$ (\# nodes in $D_i \cap \tilde{D}_i$) is at most $X(a_i, r_i) \cdot (r_i^2 + a_i)$ if $s \notin D_i$. It should be noted that this holds even if D_i covers fewer than $N(r_i)$ nodes due to its location close to the boundary of the underlying $k \times l$-grid. Thus, it follows from (8) and Lemma 4 that

$$n \leq N(r_1) + \sum_{D_i \in \mathcal{Z} \setminus \{D_1\}} \left((\text{\# nodes in } D_i) - (\text{\# nodes in } D_i \cap \tilde{D}_i) \right)$$

$$\leq \sum_{D_i \ni s} (\alpha r_i^2 + \beta r_i) + \sum_{s \notin D_i \in \mathcal{Z}} X(a_i, r_i) \cdot (r_i^2 + a_i) \leq \alpha \cdot \mathsf{cost} + O(\beta r_{\max}),$$

by which we obtain the lemma. $\qquad \square$

We bound $X(a, r)$ and $r_{\max}$ from above by the following lemmas. We can easily verify the following lemma by (7) and simple calculation.

Lemma 7. For any $r \in R \setminus \{1\}$, it follows that $N(r) < \pi(r^2 + r - c)$, where $c := \sqrt{2} - \frac{2}{\pi} \approx 0.778$. $\qquad \square$

For any $r > 0$, let $N'(r)$ be the minimum number of nodes of an infinitely large grid that is covered by a disk of radius r centered at any point (i.e., not necessarily a grid point) on the Euclidean plane.

Lemma 8. For any $r \geq \frac{\sqrt{2}}{2}$, it follows that $N'(r) \geq \pi(r - \frac{\sqrt{2}}{2})^2$.

Proof. Let D be a disk of radius r and centered at a point v. If we locate a square of side length 1 centered at each grid point covered by D, then $N'(r)$ equals the total area of these squares. Because the squares contain the disk of radius $r - \frac{\sqrt{2}}{2}$ centered at v, the lemma holds. $\qquad \square$

Lemma 9. *For any* $r \geq 1$, $X(a, r)$ *is maximized in the case that* $a \leq \lfloor r \rfloor - 1$.

Proof. Suppose that disks D and $\tilde{D}$ satisfies the conditions of Definition 1. Then, there exists a grid point of coordinates (x, y) such that D covers (x, y), $(x, y \pm 1)$, and $(x \pm 1, y)$. We may assume without loss of generality that $y \leq x$ and that D is centered at (w, z) with $w \leq x$ and $z \leq y$. Because $(x + 1, y)$ is covered by D and $(x - w) + (y - z) \geq a$, if $a \geq \lfloor r \rfloor$, then $y > z$. Hence, eight points $(x + p, y + q)$ with $(p, q) \in \{-1, 0, 1\} \times \{-1, 0, 1\} \setminus \{(1, 1)\}$ are covered by D. Thus, at any grid point $\tilde{D}$ is centered, at least three of the eight points are covered by $D \cap \tilde{D}$. This yields $X(a, r) \leq \frac{N(r) - 3}{r^2 + \lfloor r \rfloor}$ for any $a \geq \lfloor r \rfloor$.

On the other hand, if $\tilde{D}$ has radius 1 and is centered at $(w + \lfloor r \rfloor, z)$, then at most four points $(w + \lfloor r \rfloor - 1, z)$, $(w + \lfloor r \rfloor, z)$, and $(w + \lfloor r \rfloor, z \pm 1)$ are covered by $D \cap \tilde{D}$. This means that $X(\lfloor r \rfloor - 1, r) \geq \frac{N(r) - 4}{r^2 + \lfloor r \rfloor - 1} > \frac{N(r) - 3}{r^2 + \lfloor r \rfloor}$. The last inequality holds because we can easily observe that $N(r) \geq r^2 + \lfloor r \rfloor + 3$ for any $r \geq 1$. □

Lemma 10. *For any* $r \in R \setminus \{1\}$ *and any* $a \geq 0$, *it follows that* $X(a, r) < \frac{N(r)}{r^2 + r - c}$.

Proof. By Lemma 9, we may assume $a \leq \lfloor r \rfloor - 1$. By Lemma 7, we can observe that for any $r \in R \setminus \{1\}$, $\frac{N(r) - L(a, r)}{r^2 + a} < \frac{N(r)}{r^2 + r - c}$ holds if $L(a, r) \geq \pi(b - c)$, where $b := r - a$.

For any pair of disks D and $\tilde{D}$ satisfying the conditions of Definition 1, a disk of radius $b/2$ is contained in $D \cap \tilde{D}$. Therefore, it follows from Lemma 8 that for $b \geq \sqrt{2}$, $L(a, r) \geq \frac{\pi}{4}(b - \sqrt{2})^2$, which is larger than $\pi(b - c)$ for any $b \geq 6$.

Assume $1 \leq b < 6$. Let $\lambda(b) := L(0, b')$, where $b' \in R$ is the largest value with $b' \leq b$. By the definition of $L(a, r)$, we can observe that $L(a, r) \geq L(a - i, r - i)$ for any integer i with $0 \leq i \leq a$, and that $L(0, r) \geq L(0, r')$ for any $1 \leq r' \leq r$. Therefore, $\lambda(b)$ is a lower bound of $L(a, r)$ and a non-decreasing function, and hence, we have the lemma if $\lambda(b) \geq \pi(b - c)$ for $1 \leq b < 6$. This can be verified by evaluating $L(0, b)$ for each $b \in R$ with $b \leq 4$ and observing $L(0, 4) = 17 > \pi(6 - c) \approx 16.4$ as shown in Fig. 5. □

Lemma 11. *For any* $r \in R$ *with* $r \leq \sqrt{202}$ *and any* $a \geq 0$, *it follows that* $X(a, r) \leq 3$.

Proof. We can verify by numerical computation that $\frac{N(r)}{r^2 + r - c} < 3$ for any $r \in R \setminus \{1, \sqrt{2}, \sqrt{5}\}$ with $r \leq \sqrt{202}$. Thus, by Lemma 10, we have the lemma for such r. For $r \in \{1, \sqrt{2}, \sqrt{5}\}$, we can verify $\frac{N(r) - L(a, r)}{r^2 + a} \leq 3$ by evaluating $L(a, r)$ for every possible combination of a and r, i.e., $N(1) = 5$, $N(\sqrt{2}) = 9$, $N(\sqrt{5}) = 21$, $L(0, 1) = 2$, $L(0, \sqrt{2}) = 4$, $L(0, \sqrt{5}) = 7$, and $L(1, \sqrt{5}) = 4$. □

Lemma 12. *For any* $k \geq 3$, *it follows that* $r_{\max} \leq \frac{2}{3}k + \frac{13}{6}$.

Proof. On a $k \times l$-grid, a disk D of radius $r_{\max}$ centered at a node v covers at most $(2r_{\max} + 1)k$ nodes of a $k \times (2r_{\max} + 1)$-grid. By Theorem 3, there exists a broadcast on the $k \times (2r_{\max} + 1)$-grid with a cost at most $\frac{(2r_{\max} + 1)k}{3} + \frac{2r_{\max} + 1}{3} +$

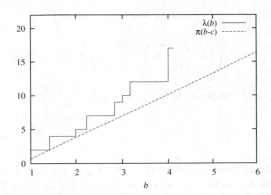

Fig. 5. Plots of $\lambda(b)$ and $\pi(b - c)$

$\frac{2}{3}k - \frac{1}{3} = \frac{2}{3}(k+1)r_{\max} + k$. This cost cannot be larger than $r_{\max}^2$, for otherwise, we can obtain a broadcast on the $k \times l$-grid with a cost less than cost by replacing D with the broadcast of Theorem 3. Thus, we have

$$r_{\max} \leq \frac{k+1}{3} + \sqrt{\left(\frac{k+1}{3}\right)^2 + k} < \frac{2}{3}k + \frac{13}{6}.$$

$\square$

Theorem 4. $\mathsf{cost} \geq \frac{n}{\pi} + \Omega(\frac{n}{k}) - O(k)$. *In particular,* $\mathsf{cost} \geq \frac{n}{3} - O(1)$ *if* $3 \leq k \leq 18$.

Proof. By Lemmas 6 and 10–12, it suffices to prove the following claims:

1. There exist α with $\alpha^{-1} = \pi^{-1} + \Omega(k^{-1})$ and $\beta = O(1)$ such that for any $r \in R$ with $\sqrt{202} < r \leq r_{\max}$, $N(r) \leq \alpha r^2 + \beta r$ and $X(a, r) \leq \alpha$.
2. There exists $\beta = O(1)$ such that for any $r \in R$ with $r \leq \sqrt{202}$, $N(r) \leq 3r^2 + \beta r$.
3. $r_{\max} \leq \sqrt{202}$ if $k \leq 18$.

The second claim is immediate because $r = O(1)$. Moreover, the third claim can be verified simply by applying Lemma 12. As for the first claim, it follows from (7) and Lemma 10 that for $r \in R$ with $\sqrt{202} < r \leq r_{\max}$,

$$X(a, r) \leq \frac{\pi r^2 + 2\sqrt{2}\, r - 5}{r^2 + r - c} = \pi - \frac{(\pi - 2\sqrt{2})r + (5 - \pi c)}{r^2 + r - c}$$

$$< \pi - \frac{\pi - 2\sqrt{2}}{r} \leq \pi - \frac{\pi - 2\sqrt{2}}{r_{\max}}. \tag{9}$$

If we set $\alpha := \pi - \frac{\pi - 2\sqrt{2}}{r_{\max}}$ and $\beta := \pi$, then it follows that

$$N(r) - (\alpha r^2 + \beta r) \leq \pi r^2 + 2\sqrt{2}\, r - 5 - (\alpha r^2 + \beta r)$$

$$< \frac{\pi - 2\sqrt{2}}{r_{\max}} r^2 - (\pi - 2\sqrt{2})r \leq 0. \tag{10}$$

Moreover, it follows from Lemma 12 that

$$\alpha^{-1} = \pi^{-1}\left(1 + \frac{\pi - 2\sqrt{2}}{\pi r_{\max} - \pi + 2\sqrt{2}}\right) = \pi^{-1} + \Omega(k^{-1}). \tag{11}$$

By (9)–(11), we have the first claim.   □

References

1. Ambühl, C.: An optimal bound for the MST algorithm to compute energy efficient broadcast trees in wireless networks. In: Caires, L., Italiano, G.F., Monteiro, L., Palamidessi, C., Yung, M. (eds.) ICALP 2005. LNCS, vol. 3580, pp. 1139–1150. Springer, Heidelberg (2005)
2. Boyd, D.W.: Improved bounds for the disk-packing constant. Aequationes Math. 9, 99–106 (1973)
3. Boyd, D.W.: The residual set dimension of the Apollonian packing. Mathematika 20, 170–174 (1973)
4. Calamoneri, T., Clementi, A., Ianni, M.D., Lauria, M., Monti, A., Silvestri, R.: Minimum-energy broadcast and disk cover in grid wireless networks. Theoret. Comput. Sci. 399, 38–53 (2008)
5. Caragiannis, I., Flammini, M., Moscardelli, L.: An exponential improvement on the MST heuristic for minimum energy broadcasting in ad hoc wireless networks. In: Arge, L., Cachin, C., Jurdziński, T., Tarlecki, A. (eds.) ICALP 2007. LNCS, vol. 4596, pp. 447–458. Springer, Heidelberg (2007)
6. Clementi, A., Crescenzi, P., Penna, P., Rossi, G., Vocca, P.: On the complexity of computing minimum energy consumption broadcast subgraphs. In: Ferreira, A., Reichel, H. (eds.) STACS 2001. LNCS, vol. 2010, pp. 121–131. Springer, Heidelberg (2001)
7. Flammini, M., Klasing, R., Navarra, A., Perennes, S.: Improved approximation results for the minimum energy broadcasting problem. Algorithmica 49, 318–336 (2007)
8. Flammini, M., Klasing, R., Navarra, A., Perennes, S.: Tightening the upper bound for the minimum energy broadcasting. Wireless Networks 14, 659–669 (2008)
9. Pahlavan, K., Levesque, A.H.: Wireless Information Networks, 2nd edn. Wiley-Interscience, Hoboken (2005)
10. Wan, P.J., Călinescu, G., Li, X.Y., Frieder, O.: Minimum-energy broadcasting in static ad hoc wireless networks. Wireless Networks 8, 607–617 (2002)

Scheduling Multicast Transmissions under SINR Constraints

Thomas Erlebach and Tom Grant

Dept. of Computer Science, University of Leicester
{te17,tg53}@mcs.le.ac.uk

Abstract. The problem of scheduling wireless transmissions under signal to interference-plus-noise ratio (SINR) constraints has received increasing attention recently. While previous work has considered the unicast case where each transmission has one sender and one receiver, we consider the setting of multicast requests where each transmission has one sender and a set of receivers. A set of multicast transmissions can be scheduled in the same round if the SINR at all receivers is above a certain threshold. The goal is to minimise the number of rounds. Building on the relationship between SINR scheduling and unit disk graph colouring established by Halldórsson (ESA 2009), we present an $\mathcal{O}(\log \Gamma)$-approximation algorithm for multicast scheduling in the SINR model, where Γ is the ratio of the longest to the shortest link length, considering only the longest link of each multicast request. The algorithm uses uniform power assignment and can be implemented online. We also compare the model of atomic multicasts (where all receivers of a multicast must receive the transmission in the same round) to the model of splittable multicasts (where a multicast sender can transmit in several rounds, each time serving a subset of its receivers). Furthermore, we consider the throughput maximisation problem and obtain an $\mathcal{O}(\log \Gamma)$-competitive randomised online algorithm and show that every deterministic algorithm, even for unicast links and using arbitrary power assignments, has competitive ratio $\Omega(\log \Gamma)$.

1 Introduction

Wireless ad-hoc networks allow a set of wireless nodes to form a network without any pre-existing infrastructure. Such networks are very versatile, but there are limitations. To receive a transmission successfully, the reception strength of the signal must be greater than the sum of other transmissions in the network with the addition of any background noise. In other words, the signal to interference-plus-noise ratio (SINR) must be above a certain threshold. This is an important feature of wireless networks, especially in situations where nodes have close proximity to each other or where the network has a high level of traffic. Such scenarios can reduce the capacity and impair the performance of wireless networks. Therefore, it is essential that scheduling schemes take into account interference constraints, otherwise they may suffer a considerable amount of transmission errors such as corrupted or lost packets.

C. Scheideler (Ed.): ALGOSENSORS 2010, LNCS 6451, pp. 47–61, 2010.
© Springer-Verlag Berlin Heidelberg 2010

In earlier theoretical studies of wireless networks, interference was typically modelled in a simplistic way, e.g., by assuming that a transmission can be received by any node that is at distance at most r_1 from the sender, and the transmission creates interference at any node that is at distance at most $r_2 > r_1$ from the sender. One of the shortcomings of such models is that the cumulative effects of interference are neglected. To address this and other shortcomings, it has been proposed that the SINR model, also called the physical model, be used for theoretical worst-case analysis as well [14], and that model has now been widely adopted, see, e.g., [11,4,1,6,2,10].

Given a set of transmission requests, each requesting a direct transmission from a sender to a receiver, a fundamental problem is to compute a shortest schedule for completing the requests. A schedule proceeds in rounds, and each round consists of a set of transmissions that can take place simultaneously without violating SINR constraints. The length of a schedule is the number of rounds. Another natural optimisation problem, called the throughput problem, is to maximise the number of transmissions that can be scheduled simultaneously in one round.

An important aspect of a wireless transmission schedule is the power that is assigned to the nodes for their transmissions. The simplest approach is to use a *uniform* power assignment where all nodes use the same transmission power. Uniform power assignments may be preferred due to the simpler implementation and must be used in homogeneous networks where power control is not available due to hardware constraints. Other power assignments that have been considered in the literature are *oblivious* power assignments, where the power assigned to the sender of a transmission is a function of the distance to the receiver, and *arbitrary* power assignments, where the power assigned to a sender can be set arbitrarily (for example, depending on the interference caused by simultaneous transmissions by other senders).

Previous work on transmission scheduling under SINR constraints has considered unicast transmissions, i.e., the case where each transmission has one sender and one receiver. However, a fundamental property of wireless transmissions is that a single transmission can be received by several nodes that are within the sender's transmission range. Furthermore, there are many scenarios where nodes of the network may want to transmit the same message to a set of other nodes, e.g., in the exchange of routing information between neighbours in a virtual topology maintained on top of the physical network or in the flooding of information across the network. Therefore, in this paper we consider the wireless transmission scheduling problem for multicast requests. Our aim is to investigate how existing methods developed for the unicast setting can be adapted to the multicast setting. We consider algorithms that use uniform power assignment. Although the lack of power control has been shown to be sub-optimal by a factor logarithmic in the maximum power used [14,2], we argue that it is meaningful to study uniform power schedules. The predominant reason for this is that solutions based on uniform power are simpler for implementation, both in hardware and software. Thus, such methods are more likely to be adopted and utilised by practitioners. A similar justification has also been given in [2,10]. Furthermore, we measure the approximation ratio of our algorithms compared to optimal solutions with arbitrary power assignment.

The unicast case of both the scheduling and the throughput problem was proved $\mathcal{NP}$-complete by Goussevskaia et al. [8] for uniform power. As the unicast case is a special case of the multicast case, the multicast version is also $\mathcal{NP}$-complete for scheduling and throughput with uniform power. Andrews and Dinitz [1] prove that the throughput problem is $\mathcal{NP}$-hard for arbitrary power. These results provide motivation for studying approximation algorithms for these problems.

1.1   Related Work

Most of the related work that we are aware of and that we discuss in this section has been for unicast transmissions. A starting point for the theoretical analysis of the capacity of wireless networks was the seminal work by Gupta and Kumar [9] that studied the throughput in a setting where the nodes are distributed uniformly at random. More recently, there has been an extensive study of offline scheduling and throughput problems in the SINR model with respect to arbitrary networks and with a focus on worst-case analysis and approximation algorithms [14,13,5,11,4,1,6,2,10]. The uniform power variant has also been under intense scrutiny especially due to its appeal to both theoreticians and applied researchers, leading to constant-factor approximation algorithms for scheduling and throughput (compared to the optimal solution with uniform power) [6,11]. The difference between uniform and non-uniform power assignments was first investigated by Moscibroda and Wattenhofer [14].

Halldórsson [10] considers the wireless scheduling problem in comparison with the optimal solution that uses an arbitrary power assignment. He shows that the scheduling problem can be related to the colouring of unit disk graphs at a constant-factor loss of approximation ratio in the case of links of similar length. This yields simple online algorithms with uniform power that achieve ratio $\mathcal{O}(1)$ for links of similar lengths and ratio $\mathcal{O}(\log \Gamma)$ for arbitrary links, where Γ is the ratio between the maximum and minimum link lengths. Our results for the multicast setting build on these results. Furthermore, in [10] Halldórsson also presents an $\mathcal{O}(\log n \cdot \log \log \Gamma)$-approximation algorithm using an oblivious power assignment, the so-called *square-root assignment* [5]. This is the first approximation algorithm with ratio polylogarithmic in the size of the input. He complements this result by a lower bound construction showing that any oblivious power assignment cannot achieve a better ratio than $\Omega(\log \log \Gamma)$ in the worst case. Furthermore, he mentions that the results also hold for the throughput problem.

We note that broadcast transmissions, which can be considered as an extreme case of multicast transmissions, were studied in [7] and [15]. Additionally the online version of the wireless throughput problem has also been studied very recently by Fanghänel et al. [3]. They assume that requests can have a duration in the interval $[1, T]$. They show that no deterministic algorithm with oblivious power assignment can achieve competitive ratio better than $\Omega(T \cdot \Gamma^{d/2})$. Furthermore, they present an $\mathcal{O}(T \cdot \Gamma^{(d/2)+\varepsilon})$-competitive deterministic online algorithm and a randomised $\mathcal{O}(\log \Gamma \cdot \log T)$-competitive online algorithm. They also consider a generalisation of the problem where requests have to be assigned to one of k channels.

1.2 Our Results

We consider the scheduling problem for multicast requests under SINR constraints, assuming that the nodes are points in the two-dimensional Euclidean plane and the received signal strength is proportional to the power of the transmitted signal divided by the distance to the power of α, where α is the path loss exponent and assumed to be a constant greater than 2 (in practice, α is typically assumed to be between 2 and 6). We consider multicast transmissions to be *atomic*, which is to say that in a given multicast group, all receivers must successfully receive the transmission in the same round. Building on Halldórsson's [10] results for the unicast case, we present an $\mathcal{O}(\log \Gamma)$-approximation algorithm for multicast scheduling under SINR constraints. In the multicast case, Γ denotes the ratio of the longest to the shortest link length, considering only the longest link of each multicast request. Note that Γ can be much smaller than the ratio of the longest to the shortest link among all unicast links that are part of a multicast request. As our algorithm is based on partitioning the requests into length classes and using unit disk graph colouring to schedule each length class, it can also be used as a simple online algorithm.

We also discuss the relationship between schedules for such atomic multicasts and schedules for splittable multicasts, where the sender of a multicast can transmit in several rounds, serving a subset of its receivers in each round.

As with previous work, we show that our approach is also applicable to the case of throughput maximisation. Moreover, we present a lower bound showing that every deterministic online algorithm has competitive ratio $\Omega(\log \Gamma)$ even for the unicast version of the throughput problem. This complements previous lower bounds where the algorithm was restricted to oblivious power assignments.

2 Preliminaries

We assume that senders and receivers are points in two-dimensional Euclidean space, and we use $\delta(p, q)$ to denote the Euclidean distance between two points p and q. For a given undirected graph $G = (V, E)$, $\Delta(G)$ denotes the maximum degree of any vertex in V. Note that any graph G can be coloured with $\mathcal{O}(\Delta(G))$ colours using any greedy colouring algorithm. A graph $G = (V, E)$ is a *unit disk graph* (for disks with radius r) if each vertex $v \in V$ can be associated with a disk of radius r centred at a point p_v in the plane such that two vertices $u, v \in V$ are adjacent if and only if the corresponding disks intersect (or, equivalently, if the distance between p_u and p_v is at most $2r$). We note the following simple property of unit disk graphs.

Lemma 1. *If a unit disk graph with disks of radius r has maximum degree $k \geq 1$, increasing the radius of the disks from r to cr for some $c > 1$ increases the maximum degree to at most $\mathcal{O}(kc^2)$.*

In the following, we first discuss notation for unicast requests and multicast requests and then define the problems we are considering. As we are presenting adaptations of previous work, in particular [10], we strive to keep similar notation for clarity.

2.1 Unicast Requests

A unicast request ℓ_v is a transmission request from a single sender s_v to a single receiver r_v. We also interchangeably refer to requests as *links*, as is common practice in the literature.

We override notation when the context is clear and denote the *length* of a link ℓ_v by $\ell_v = \delta(s_v, r_v)$. Additionally, we use the shorthand δ_{uv} to refer to the distance $\delta(s_u, r_v)$ between the sender s_u of a link ℓ_u and the receiver r_v of another link ℓ_v. A set L of links is *nearly equilength* if the lengths of the links in L are within a factor of 2 of each other. When discussing a set of nearly equilength links, we let D be a value such that the lengths of all links lie in the interval $[D, 2D]$.

For a set L of nearly equilength unicast links with lengths in $[D, 2D]$, as in [10] $G'_q(L)$ denotes the unit disk graph formed by disks with radius $qD/2$ and with the unicast receivers as centres.

For a given set L of unicast links, we denote by Γ the ratio $\max_v \ell_v / \min_u \ell_u$ of the maximum link length to the minimum link length.

We denote the power assigned to a sender s_v as $\mathcal{P}_v$. For all our algorithms we assume that all senders are assigned the same power and that there is no constraint on the maximum power level.

To model the degradation of a transmitted signal over distance, we let α be the path loss exponent and adopt the common assumption that $2 < \alpha \leq 6$. The received signal strength of a transmission on link ℓ_v from s_v to r_v is $\mathcal{P}_v / \ell_v^\alpha$.

Let $\mathcal{S}_v$ be the set of senders that are transmitting concurrently with a sender s_v and let N represent the background noise in the network. We use the SINR model of interference, which is interchangeably termed the *physical model*. A unicast transmission ℓ_u from s_u to r_u is successfully received if the following constraint is satisfied:

$$\frac{\mathcal{P}_u/\ell_u^\alpha}{N + \displaystyle\sum_{s_v \in \mathcal{S}_u \setminus \{s_u\}} \mathcal{P}_v/\delta_{vu}^\alpha} > \beta \tag{1}$$

Here, $\beta \geq 1$ denotes the minimum SINR required for a successful reception. As in previous work, we assume throughout the paper without loss of generality that $N = 0$. This assumption can be justified by noting that the effect of noise can be made arbitrarily small by scaling up the power of all senders. Furthermore, one sometimes considers the case $\beta = 1$ for simplicity, as by Lemma 6 any constant $\beta > 1$ can be achieved losing only a constant factor in the approximation ratio.

2.2   Multicast Requests

A *multicast request* or *multicast group* is a set of unicast links with a common sender. A multicast group m_v is represented as a pair (s_v, R_v) where s_v is the sender and $R_v = \{r_{v_1}, r_{v_2} \ldots r_{v_{k_v}}\}$ is a set of $k_v \geq 1$ receivers. Intuitively, a multicast request (s_v, R_v) asks for a single transmission by the sender s_v that is successfully received by all receivers in R_v simultaneously. For $1 \leq i \leq k_v$, we use ℓ_{v_i} to refer to the link with sender s_v and receiver r_{v_i}. Again, we override notation and also use ℓ_{v_i} to refer to the length of that link. Without loss of generality, we assume that the receiver with index 1 is a receiver that is furthest from the sender of m_v, i.e., $\ell_{v_1} = \max_{1 \leq i \leq k_v} \ell_{v_i}$. The distance between the sender of multicast group m_u to a given receiver r_{v_i} in multicast group m_v is denoted by $\delta_{uv_i} = \delta(s_u, r_{v_i})$.

For a given set M of multicast groups, we denote by Γ the ratio of the maximum link length to the minimum link length amongst all longest links of the multicast groups in M, i.e., the value $\max_v \ell_{v_1} / \min_u \ell_{u_1}$.

A set M of multicast links is *nearly equilength* if the lengths of the longest links in each group are within a factor of 2 of each other, i.e., there is a D such that $\ell_{v_1} \in [D, 2D]$ for all $m_v \in M$.

A multicast transmission from s_u to R_u is successfully received if for all receivers $r_{u_i} \in R_u$ inequality (1) holds.

A *schedule* for a set M of multicast links is a partition of M into subsets, called *rounds* or *slots*, and an assignment of powers to all senders of requests in M, such that the multicast transmissions assigned to the same slot are successfully received by all their receivers.

Halldórsson [10] defines the affectance on the receiver r_v of a unicast link ℓ_v to be the ratio of the interference received from concurrent transmissions by other senders to the received signal strength at r_v from s_v. In the multicast context we define the affectance on a receiver r_{v_i} in a multicast group m_v to be the ratio of the interference received from concurrent transmissions by other senders to the received signal strength at r_{v_i} from s_v. Note that a receiver r_{v_i} successfully receives a transmission from s_v if and only if the affectance of concurrent transmissions on r_{v_i} is at most $1/\beta$.

For $p \geq 1$, a *p-signal* schedule is a schedule for which the affectance on any receiver of any multicast request is at most $1/p$. (Equivalently, the SINR at every multicast receiver is at least p.) A *p-signal slot* or *p-signal set* is one round of a p-signal schedule.

2.3   Problem Definitions

We are concerned with the following two optimisation problems. The multicast scheduling problem, denoted by M-SCHEDULING, is to compute, for a given set M of multicast requests, a p-signal schedule with a minimum number of rounds. The multicast throughput problem, denoted by M-THROUGHPUT, is to compute, for a given set M of multicast requests, a largest subset of M that forms a p-signal slot. The corresponding problems for unicast requests are called SCHEDULING and THROUGHPUT.

An algorithm for one of these problems is called a ρ-approximation algorithm, and has approximation ratio ρ, if it runs in polynomial time and always outputs a solution that is at most a factor of ρ away from the optimum.

In the online versions of these problems, the requests are presented to the algorithm one by one, and the algorithm must process each request without knowledge of future requests. In the scheduling problems, this means that the algorithm must assign a round and a power to the request, and in the throughput problem, the algorithm must accept or reject the request and, if accepted, assign a power to the sender. In both problems, decisions of the algorithm are irrevocable, and the solution must be feasible at all times. In the online version, we compare the quality of the solution produced by an algorithm with the quality of an optimal offline solution for the same input. An online algorithm is *ρ-competitive*, or has *competitive ratio* ρ, if it always produces a solution that is within a factor ρ of the optimum.

Even though our algorithms use uniform power assignments, we compare their solutions with an optimal solution that can use arbitrary power assignments. This strengthens the approximation results. For a given set R of unicast or multicast links, we denote an optimal solution by $\text{OPT}_p(R)$. For convenience, when discussing the scheduling problem, we may also use $\text{OPT}_p(R)$ to refer to the length of the optimal schedule. If $p = 1$, we also write OPT for OPT_p.

So far we have assumed that multicast requests are *atomic*, i.e., the sender of a multicast request can transmit only once and all its receivers must successfully receive the transmission in the same round. One can also consider a variant of the scheduling problem with *splittable* multicast requests. In that variant, the sender of a multicast request can transmit in several rounds, and each of its receivers must successfully receive the transmission in at least one of those rounds. It is clear that the optimal splittable schedule cannot be longer than the optimal atomic schedule.

3   Algorithm for Multicast Scheduling

We present an $\mathcal{O}(\log \Gamma)$-approximation algorithm for M-SCHEDULING. We follow the approach of Halldórsson [10] and show that a constant-factor approximation for nearly equilength multicast groups can be achieved by a greedy colouring of a suitably defined unit disk graph. The difficulty is that a set of nearly equilength multicast groups may contain unicast links that are much shorter than the longest links of the groups, and hence it is not enough to argue about nearly equilength unicast links. We recapitulate some results by Halldórsson [10] which we require.

As in [10], two unicast links ℓ_u and ℓ_v are called *q-independent* if they satisfy

$$\delta_{uv} \cdot \delta_{vu} \geq q^2 \cdot \ell_v \ell_u . \tag{2}$$

A set of links is q-independent if any pair of links in the set is q-independent.

For a given set L of unicast requests, the *link graph* $G_q(L)$ is a graph with a vertex for each request in L and an edge between two vertices if the corresponding requests are not q-independent.

Recall that $G'_q(L)$ denotes the unit disk graph with a disk of radius $qD/2$ centred at each receiver of a link in L.

Halldórsson shows that there is a close relationship between link graphs $G_q(L)$ and unit disk graphs $G'_{q'}(L)$ for the same set of unicast links.

Lemma 2. [10] *For any $q \geq 1$ and any set L of nearly equilength unicast links, $G'_q(L) \subseteq G_{q+1}(L)$ and $G_q(L) \subseteq G'_{2(q+1)}(L)$.*

Halldórsson shows that unicast links that belong to the same q^α-signal slot are q-independent, and he establishes a slightly weaker version of the converse statement as stated in the following lemma.

Lemma 3. [10] *Let S be a z-independent set of nearly equilength unicast links. Then, with uniform power assignment, S is an $\Omega(z^\alpha)$-signal set.*

Furthermore, Halldórsson gives the following lower bound on OPT for nearly equilength links.

Lemma 4. [10] *Let L be a set of nearly equilength unicast links and q be any constant. Then $\mathrm{OPT}(L) = \Omega(\Delta(G_q(L)))$.*

Halldórsson combines the above statements to show that a constant factor approximation for scheduling a set L of nearly equilength unicast links can be obtained by greedily colouring either $G_q(L)$ or $G'_{q'}(L)$, for suitably chosen constants q and q'. The results listed above can be combined to derive the statement of Theorem 1.

Theorem 1. [10] *Let $p \geq 1$ be an arbitrary constant. Then there is a $q = q(p) \geq 1$ such that for any set L of nearly equilength unicast links, any colouring of $G'_q(L)$ with $\mathcal{O}(\Delta(G'_q(L)))$ colours gives a p-signal schedule with uniform power that is within a constant factor of the optimal p-signal schedule for L.*

Proof. By Lemma 3, for every p there is a z such that any z-independent set of nearly equilength links is a p-signal set (with uniform power). Let $q = 2(z + 1)$. By Lemma 2, $G_z(L) \subseteq G'_q(L)$, and hence any independent set in $G'_q(L)$ is z-independent and therefore a p-signal slot. Thus, any colouring of $G'_q(L)$ constitutes a p-signal schedule. By Lemma 4, the optimal 1-signal schedule for L, and therefore also the optimal p-signal schedule for L, has length $\Omega(\Delta(G_{q+1}(L)))$ and thus, by Lemma 2, length $\Omega(\Delta(G'_q(L)))$. □

Consider Algorithm 1 for scheduling a set of nearly equilength multicast groups. It creates a unit disk graph H that has one disk for every multicast group, centred at the receiver of the longest link in that multicast group. The radius is set to $(q/2+4)D$, where q is chosen according to Theorem 1. Then a greedy colouring of that unit disk graph is returned as the schedule, i.e., we schedule each multicast group in the round given by the colour assigned to the corresponding disk, and assign uniform power to all senders.

For a set M of multicast groups, let L_M be the set of unicast links obtained by taking the longest link ℓ_{v_1} from every multicast group $m_v \in M$.

Data: a set M of multicast requests with longest link lengths in $[D, 2D]$
Result: a p-signal schedule S_M for M with uniform power

1 let $q = q(p)$ be the value from Theorem 1;
2 construct the unit disk graph H with disks of radius $(q/2 + 4)D$ centred at the receivers r_{v_1} of all $m_v \in M$;
3 greedily colour H with $\mathcal{O}(\Delta(H))$ colours;
4 return the colouring of H as a p-signal schedule S_M with uniform power;

Algorithm 1. Algorithm for nearly equilength multicast requests

Lemma 5. *Let M be a set of nearly equilength multicast groups. For any constant $p \geq 1$, any greedy colouring of the unit disk graph H constructed by Algorithm 1 gives a p-signal schedule for M whose length is at most a constant factor longer than the optimal p-signal schedule for L_M.*

Proof. Let D be such that the length of the longest link in each multicast group lies in the interval $[D, 2D]$.

The algorithm chooses $q = q(p) \geq 1$ according to Theorem 1. Hence we have that any colouring of $G'_q(L_M)$ with $\mathcal{O}(\Delta(G'_q(L_M)))$ colours gives a p-signal schedule with uniform power for L_M that is within a constant factor of $\text{OPT}_p(L_M)$.

The unit disk graph H constructed by the algorithm is the unit disk graph obtained from $G'_q(L_M)$ by increasing the radius of the disks from $qD/2$ to $(q/2 + 4)D$. As $q \geq 1$, this increases the radius of the disks by at most a factor of 9, so by Lemma 1 the maximum degree of H is within a constant factor of the maximum degree of $G'_q(L_M)$. Hence, a greedy colouring of H with $\mathcal{O}(\Delta(H))$ colours uses only $\mathcal{O}(\Delta(G'_q(L_M)))$ colours. Note that any greedy colouring of H is also a colouring of $G'_q(L_M)$ with $\mathcal{O}(\Delta(G'_q(L_M)))$ colours and thus, by Theorem 1, constitutes a p-signal schedule S_{L_M} for L_M that is a constant-factor approximation of $\text{OPT}_p(L_M)$.

Observe that for any multicast group m_v, the disk in H with centre r_{v_1} contains the disks with radius $qD/2$ centred at any receiver r_{v_j} of the multicast group m_v, as the distance between two receivers of the same multicast group is at most $4D$ by the triangle inequality (using that each unicast link in m_v has length at most $2D$).

We claim that a greedy colouring of H gives a p-signal schedule S_M for M with uniform power that is within a constant factor of $\text{OPT}_p(L_M)$. Since the maximum degree of H is within a constant factor of the maximum degree of $G'_q(L_M)$, the number of colours in any greedy colouring of H is a constant-factor approximation of $\text{OPT}_p(L_M)$. It remains to show that the schedule S_M derived from any greedy colouring of H constitutes a p-signal schedule. Consider an arbitrary link ℓ_{v_i} of a multicast group m_v. Let U be the set of all multicast groups $m_u \neq m_v$ that are scheduled in the same round as m_v in S_M. If $i = 1$, i.e., if ℓ_{v_i} is the longest link of m_v, we can simply argue as follows: The received signal strength from s_v at r_{v_1} and the total strength of interfering signals received at r_{v_1} are the same in S_M and in S_{L_M}, so the affectance at r_{v_1} is at most $1/p$ in

S_M. If $i \neq 1$, we need a more elaborate argument. Let s'_v be an arbitrary point in the plane that has distance $2D$ from r_{v_i}, and let ℓ'_v be the unicast link with sender s'_v and receiver r_{v_i}. Consider the unit disks of radius $qD/2$ centred at r_{v_i} and at all r_{u_1} for $m_u \in U$. Observe that these unit disks are the disks that constitute $G'_q(L')$, where L' is the set of unicast links containing the link ℓ'_v and the links ℓ_{u_1} for all $m_u \in U$. Furthermore, these unit disks are disjoint since they are contained in the respective disks of radius $(q/2 + 4)D$ that have received the same colour in H. By Theorem 1, the links in L' constitute a p-signal set $S_{L'}$. In the round in which m_v is scheduled in S_M, the received signal strength from s_v at r_{v_i} is at least as large as the received signal strength from s'_v at r_{v_i} in $S_{L'}$, and the total strength of interfering signals received at r_{v_i} is the same in S_M and in $S_{L'}$. Therefore, the affectance at r_{v_i} is at most $1/p$ in S_M. □

As any p-signal schedule for M is also a p-signal schedule for L_M, it is clear that $\mathrm{OPT}_p(L_M)$ cannot be larger than $\mathrm{OPT}_p(M)$. Thus, we obtain the following corollary.

Corollary 1. *For any constant $p \geq 1$, Algorithm 1 is a constant-factor approximation algorithm for* M-SCHEDULING *with nearly equilength multicast groups.*

We can now tackle arbitrary sets M of multicast requests using the standard approach of partitioning the requests into a logarithmic number of length classes. Assume without loss of generality that the lengths of the longest links of all multicast groups lie in the interval $[1, \Gamma]$. Partition the set M of multicast groups into $\lceil \log \Gamma \rceil$ classes M_i where M_i consists of all multicast groups with a longest link of length in $[2^i, 2^{i+1})$. Apply Algorithm 1 to each class M_i separately and obtain a schedule for M by concatenating the schedules for the classes M_i. As the schedule for each class M_i is a constant-factor approximation of $\mathrm{OPT}_p(M_i)$ and therefore also of $\mathrm{OPT}_p(M)$, we obtain a p-signal schedule that is an $\mathcal{O}(\log \Gamma)$-approximation of $\mathrm{OPT}_p(M)$.

Theorem 2. *For every constant $p \geq 1$, there is an $\mathcal{O}(\log \Gamma)$-approximation algorithm for the problem of computing a shortest p-signal schedule for a given set of multicast requests, i.e., for the* M-SCHEDULING *problem.*

Since the partition of multicast requests into length classes and the greedy colouring of the unit disk graphs for each length class can be performed online, the same approach gives an $\mathcal{O}(\log \Gamma)$-competitive online algorithm for multicast scheduling. Furthermore, as pointed out by Halldórsson [10], approaches based on colouring of unit disk graphs are amenable to a distributed implementation.

3.1   Signal Strengthening

It is also interesting to relate the length of the optimal p-signal schedule to the optimal 1-signal schedule. The following result from [11] shows that in the unicast case, a larger SINR for all receivers can be achieved at a constant-factor loss in the schedule length.

Lemma 6. [11] *There is a polynomial-time algorithm that takes a p-signal schedule for a set of unicast links and refines it into a p'-signal schedule, for $p' > p$, increasing the number of slots by a factor of at most $\lceil 2p'/p \rceil^2$.*

Adapting this lemma to the multicast setting does not seem straightforward, but we are able to establish an analogous result at least for nearly equilength multicast links.

Lemma 7. *If there is a p-signal schedule for a set M of nearly equilength multicast groups that has length k, then there is a p'-signal schedule for M, for any constant $p' > p$, of length $\mathcal{O}(k)$. Moreover, such a schedule can be computed in polynomial time.*

Proof. Let $\mathcal{A}$ be a p-signal schedule for a set M of multicast groups. Let L_M be the set of unicast links obtained by taking the longest link ℓ_{v_1} from every multicast group m_v in M. It is clear that $\mathcal{A}$ can also be viewed as a p-signal schedule for L_M. As L_M is a set of unicast links, we can transform $\mathcal{A}$ into a p'-signal schedule $\mathcal{A}'$ for L_M by Lemma 6, such that the length of the schedule increases by only a constant factor. As the optimal p'-signal schedule for L_M cannot be longer than $\mathcal{A}'$, we have that the length of $\text{OPT}_{p'}(L_M)$, the optimal p'-signal schedule for L_M, is within a constant factor of the length of $\mathcal{A}$.

Consider the p'-signal schedule S_M computed for M by Algorithm 1 in polynomial time. By Lemma 5, the length of S_M is within a constant factor of $\text{OPT}_{p'}(L_M)$, and therefore also within a constant factor of the length of $\mathcal{A}$. Thus, S_M is a p-signal schedule for M that is within a constant factor of the length of $\mathcal{A}$.   □

Applying Lemma 7 to an optimal 1-signal schedule for M, we obtain the following corollary.

Corollary 2. *For any constant $p \geq 1$ and any set M of nearly equilength multicast groups, $\text{OPT}_p(M)$ is at most a constant factor longer than $\text{OPT}(M)$.*

This result shows that if we require strengthening of the SINR in a schedule, we will lose only a constant factor in the schedule length, at least for nearly equilength multicast requests.

4 Splittable versus Atomic Multicast

In this section we discuss the relationship between splittable and atomic multicast requests. For ease of presentation, we only consider 1-signal schedules in this section. For a given set M of multicast requests, denote by $\text{OPT}^s(M)$ the length of an optimal 1-signal schedule that is allowed to split a multicast request. As before, $\text{OPT}(M)$ denotes the length of an optimal 1-signal schedule with atomic multicasts.

Since every atomic schedule is also a splittable schedule, it is clear that $\text{OPT}^s(M) \leq \text{OPT}(M)$ for any set M of multicast requests. Furthermore, we have the following lemmas.

Lemma 8. *For any set M of nearly equilength multicast requests, $\mathrm{OPT}(M) = \mathcal{O}(\mathrm{OPT}^s(M))$.*

Proof. Let L_M be defined as in Section 3. We have $\mathrm{OPT}(L_M) \leq \mathrm{OPT}^s(M)$ since even a splittable schedule must schedule the longest link of each multicast group in some round. Furthermore, by Lemma 5 there is an atomic 1-signal schedule for M that is within a constant factor of $\mathrm{OPT}(L_M)$. □

Lemma 9. *For any set M of multicast requests, $\mathrm{OPT}(M) = \mathcal{O}(\log \Gamma) \cdot \mathrm{OPT}^s(M)$.*

Proof. Consider a partition of M into $\mathcal{O}(\log \Gamma)$ length classes M_i, such that each length class is nearly equilength. The maximum of $\mathrm{OPT}(L_{M_i})$ over all i is a lower bound on $\mathrm{OPT}^s(M)$. Furthermore, the algorithm of Section 3 computes an atomic schedule for M that is within a constant factor of the sum of the values $\mathrm{OPT}(L_{M_i})$ over all i. □

5   Throughput Maximisation

5.1   Algorithms

In this section, we discuss how the approach described in Section 3 can be adapted to the problem M-THROUGHPUT. We consider only atomic multicasts. For a given set M of nearly equilength multicast groups, one can construct the unit disk graph H as in Algorithm 1 and then compute a maximal independent set I in H, for example using a greedy algorithm. The set I forms a 1-signal set. It is known that in unit disk graphs, the size of any maximal independent set is within a factor of 5 of the maximum independent set [12].

Let $I^* \subseteq M$ be a 1-signal set of largest size. By Lemma 5, the unit disks in H corresponding to the multicast groups in I^* can be coloured with a constant number of colours. Hence, I^* contains a set of multicast groups that corresponds to an independent set in H of size $\Omega(|I^*|)$. The set I computed by the algorithm then also has size $\Omega(|I^*|)$ and therefore constitutes a constant-factor approximation of the largest 1-signal set.

For general sets of multicast requests, we can partition the multicast requests into $\mathcal{O}(\log \Gamma)$ length classes, compute a 1-signal set for each length class as described above, and output the largest of these 1-signal sets. This gives an $\mathcal{O}(\log \Gamma)$-approximation for M-THROUGHPUT. The same approach can be used to obtain a randomised $\mathcal{O}(\log \Gamma)$-competitive online algorithm. The randomisation is only needed to select one of the length classes at the beginning of the algorithm.

5.2   Online Lower Bound

In this section we present a lower bound showing that no deterministic online algorithm for the throughput problem can achieve competitive ratio better than $\Omega(\log \Gamma)$ even in the case of unicast requests. We make use of the following fact that was stated by Avin et al. [2].

Lemma 10. [2] *Two senders s_1 and s_2 cannot transmit successfully at the same time if their respective receiver is closer to the other sender i.e., if $\delta(s_1, r_1) > \delta(s_1, r_2)$ and $\delta(s_2, r_2) > \delta(s_2, r_1)$.*

Now utilising Lemma 10 we provide a construction bounding the performance of any arbitrary deterministic algorithm for the online variant of THROUGHPUT.

Theorem 3. *The competitive ratio of every deterministic online algorithm, even with arbitrary power assignments, is $\Omega(\log \Gamma)$ for* THROUGHPUT.

Proof. Consider the following construction. Let n be an arbitrary positive integer, and let $\Gamma = 2b^n$ for a sufficiently large constant $b > 1$. All senders and receivers are located on the x-axis, so we can identify a node with its x-coordinate.

Let A be an arbitrary deterministic online algorithm. The adversary first presents a request ℓ_0 with sender $s_0 = 2b^n$ and receiver $r_0 = 0$. The algorithm must accept ℓ_0 as otherwise its competitive ratio is unbounded if the request sequence stops here. Next, the adversary presents requests $\ell_1, \ldots, \ell_n$ where for each $1 \leq i \leq n$ the sender and receiver of ℓ_i are $s_i = -b^i$ and $r_i = b^i$, respectively.

By Lemma 10, the algorithm cannot accept any of the requests $\ell_1, \ldots, \ell_n$ as none of them can transmit at the same time as ℓ_0. It remains to show that an optimal solution can reject ℓ_0 and accept all other requests.

Let $\ell_1, \ldots, \ell_n$ transmit simultaneously using the square root power assignment, i.e., assign power $\sqrt{b^i}$ to s_i for all i.

The strength of the signal received at r_i from s_i is

$$\frac{\sqrt{b^i}}{(2b^i)^\alpha} = \frac{b^{(0.5-\alpha)i}}{2^\alpha}.$$

The total interference received at r_i is

$$\sum_{j<i} \frac{\sqrt{b^j}}{(b^j + b^i)^\alpha} + \sum_{j>i} \frac{\sqrt{b^j}}{(b^j + b^i)^\alpha}. \tag{3}$$

We can bound the first sum in (3) as follows:

$$\sum_{j<i} \frac{\sqrt{b^j}}{(b^j + b^i)^\alpha} \leq \sum_{j<i} \frac{\sqrt{b^j}}{(b^i)^\alpha} \leq \frac{\sqrt{b^i}}{(\sqrt{b} - 1) \cdot (b^i)^\alpha} = \frac{b^{(0.5-\alpha)i}}{\sqrt{b} - 1}$$

The second sum in (3) can be bounded as follows:

$$\sum_{j>i} \frac{\sqrt{b^j}}{(b^j + b^i)^\alpha} \leq \sum_{j>i} \frac{\sqrt{b^j}}{(b^j)^\alpha} = \sum_{j>i} b^{(0.5-\alpha)j} \leq 2 \cdot b^{(0.5-\alpha)(i+1)}$$

where the last inequality holds for sufficiently large b. The SINR at r_i is

$$\frac{b^{(0.5-\alpha)i}2^{-\alpha}}{b^{(0.5-\alpha)i}\left(\frac{1}{\sqrt{b}-1} + 2 \cdot b^{0.5-\alpha}\right)} = \frac{2^{-\alpha}}{\frac{1}{\sqrt{b}-1} + 2 \cdot b^{0.5-\alpha}}$$

For b a sufficiently large constant (chosen depending on α), the SINR is larger than 1 (or any other desired constant SINR threshold). $\square$

We remark that the lower bound of Theorem 3 applies even in the case where the algorithm is allowed to change the power assigned to previously accepted requests upon the acceptance of a new request.

6 Conclusion

In this paper we have studied wireless scheduling and throughput problems for multicast requests in the SINR model. We have presented $\mathcal{O}(\log \Gamma)$-competitive algorithms for both problems by exploiting and extending the relationship between SINR scheduling and unit disk graph colouring that has been established by Halldórsson for unicast links [10]. This shows that the approach of reducing SINR scheduling problems for nearly equilength links to unit disk graph colouring extends to multicast requests provided that the longest links in the multicast groups are nearly equilength. We have also given an $\Omega(\log \Gamma)$ lower bound on the competitive ratio of any deterministic online algorithm for throughput even in the case of unicast links and arbitrary power assignments, and discussed relationships between scheduling with atomic and splittable multicast requests.

Several questions are left open. First, it would be interesting to find out whether offline approximation algorithms with ratio better than $\mathcal{O}(\log \Gamma)$ exist for the multicast scheduling and throughput problems. Halldórsson's $\mathcal{O}(\log n \cdot \log \log \Gamma)$-approximation algorithm for unicast links seems difficult to extend to the multicast setting. Furthermore, it would also be useful to determine whether signal strengthening can be done for arbitrary multicast requests while losing only a constant factor. This is true for arbitrary unicast requests (Lemma 6), but our current proof of Lemma 7 works only for nearly equilength multicast requests. Finally, it would be interesting to know whether the factor $\mathcal{O}(\log \Gamma)$ bounding the difference in schedule length between atomic and splittable schedules in Lemma 9 can be reduced.

References

1. Andrews, M., Dinitz, M.: Maximizing capacity in arbitrary wireless networks in the SINR model: Complexity and game theory. In: INFOCOM, pp. 1332–1340 (April 2009)
2. Avin, C., Lotker, Z., Pignolet, Y.-A.: On the power of uniform power: Capacity of wireless networks with bounded resources. In: Fiat, A., Sanders, P. (eds.) ESA 2009. LNCS, vol. 5757, pp. 373–384. Springer, Heidelberg (2009)
3. Fanghänel, A., Geulen, S., Hoefer, M., Vöcking, B.: Online capacity maximization in wireless networks. In: Proceedings of the 22nd ACM Symposium on Parallelism in Algorithms and Architectures (SPAA), pp. 92–99. ACM, New York (2010)
4. Fanghänel, A., Kesselheim, T., Räcke, H., Vöcking, B.: Oblivious interference scheduling. In: Proceedings of the 28th ACM Symposium on Principles of Distributed Computing (PODC), pp. 220–229. ACM, New York (2009)
5. Fanghänel, A., Kesselheim, T., Vöcking, B.: Improved algorithms for latency minimization in wireless networks. In: Albers, S., Marchetti-Spaccamela, A., Matias, Y., Nikoletseas, S., Thomas, W. (eds.) ICALP 2009. LNCS, vol. 5556, pp. 447–458. Springer, Heidelberg (2009)

6. Goussevskaia, O., Halldórsson, M., Wattenhofer, R., Welzl, E.: Capacity of arbitrary wireless networks. In: INFOCOM, pp. 1872–1880 (April 2009)
7. Goussevskaia, O., Moscibroda, T., Wattenhofer, R.: Local Broadcasting in the Physical Interference Model. In: ACM SIGACT-SIGOPT International Workshop on Foundations of Mobile Computing (DialM-POMC), Toronto, Canada (August 2008)
8. Goussevskaia, O., Oswald, Y.A., Wattenhofer, R.: Complexity in geometric SINR. In: Proceedings of the 8th ACM International Symposium on Mobile Ad Hoc Networking and Computing (MobiHoc), pp. 100–109. ACM, New York (2007)
9. Gupta, P., Kumar, P.: The capacity of wireless networks. IEEE Transactions on Information Theory 46(2), 388–404 (2000)
10. Halldórsson, M.: Wireless Scheduling with Power Control. In: Fiat, A., Sanders, P. (eds.) ESA 2009. LNCS, vol. 5757, pp. 368–380. Springer, Heidelberg (2009), http://www.hr.is/faculty/mmh/papers/ESAfull.pdf
11. Halldórsson, M., Wattenhofer, R.: Wireless Communication is in APX. In: Proceedings of the 36th International Colloquium on Automata, Languages and Programming (ICALP). LNCS, vol. 5555, pp. 525–536. Springer, Heidelberg (2009)
12. Marathe, M.V., Breu, H., Hunt III, H.B., Ravi, S.S., Rosenkrantz, D.J.: Simple heuristics for unit disk graphs. Networks 25, 59–68 (1995)
13. Moscibroda, T.: The worst-case capacity of wireless sensor networks. In: Proceedings of the 6th International Conference on Information Processing in Sensor Networks (IPSN), pp. 1–10. ACM, New York (2007)
14. Moscibroda, T., Wattenhofer, R.: The complexity of connectivity in wireless networks. In: INFOCOM (2006)
15. Resta, G., Santi, P.: Latency and capacity optimal broadcasting in wireless multi-hop networks. In: ICC, pp. 1–6. IEEE, Los Alamitos (2009)

Deterministic Recurrent Communication and Synchronization in Restricted Sensor Networks*

Antonio Fernández Anta[1,2], Miguel A. Mosteiro[3,2], and Christopher Thraves[4]

[1] Institute IMDEA Networks, Leganés, Spain
[2] LADyR, GSyC, Universidad Rey Juan Carlos, Móstoles, Madrid, Spain
anto@gsyc.es
[3] Department of Computer Science, Rutgers University, Piscataway, NJ, USA
mosteiro@cs.rutgers.edu
[4] ASAP Project team, IRISA/INRIA Rennes, Campus Universitaire de Beaulieu,
35043 Rennes Cedex, France

Abstract. Monitoring physical phenomena in Sensor Networks requires guaranteeing permanent communication between nodes. Moreover, in an effective implementation of such infrastructure, the delay between any two consecutive communications should be minimized. The problem is challenging because, in a restricted Sensor Network, the communication is carried out through a single and shared radio channel without collision detection. Dealing with collisions is crucial to ensure effective communication between nodes. Additionally, minimizing them yields energy consumption minimization, given that sensing and computational costs in terms of energy are negligible with respect to radio communication. In this work, we present a deterministic recurrent-communication protocol for Sensor Networks. After an initial negotiation phase of the access pattern to the channel, each node running this protocol reaches a steady state, which is asymptotically optimal in terms of energy and time efficiency. As a by-product, a protocol for the synchronization of a Sensor Network is also proposed. Furthermore, the protocols are resilient to an arbitrary node power-up schedule and a general node failure model.

1 Introduction

A Sensor Network is an infrastructure deployed in a hostile or remote area for monitoring purposes. The basic entities of a Sensor Network are called *sensor nodes*, small devices provided with radio-communication, processing, and sensing capabilities. Upon being distributed at random in the area of interest, sensor nodes have to build a communication system from scratch. A strong shortcoming in Sensor Networks is the energy supply of sensor nodes. Consequently, one of

---

* This research was partially supported by Spanish MICINN grant no. TIN2008-06735-C02-01, Comunidad de Madrid grant no. S2009TIC-1692, EU Marie Curie International Reintegration Grant IRG 210021, NSF grant no. 0937829, and French ANR project Shaman.

C. Scheideler (Ed.): ALGOSENSORS 2010, LNCS 6451, pp. 62–73, 2010.

the main challenges is the efficient administration of such resource, extending the usability of the network. In sensor nodes, sensing and computational costs in terms of energy consumption are negligible with respect to radio communication. Thus, it is crucial to optimize the communication schedule. In a harshly restricted Sensor Network, the communication is carried out by means of a single and shared radio channel where nodes may broadcast messages to all neighboring nodes but no collision detection mechanism is available. Therefore, special mechanisms to effectively transmit or receive a message are required. Indeed, a node b receives a message transmitted from a neighboring node a only if neither b nor the other neighbors of b transmit at the same time. Otherwise, a collision occurs and the messages are garbled. Furthermore, b is not able to recognize the difference between this garbled message received and the background noise present in the channel if no transmission is produced.

The mechanism used by a node to decide to transmit or receive at any time is called the *transmission schedule*. Some transmission schedules use randomness to avoid collisions, but frequently involve a large number of redundant transmissions, consequently incurring in excessive energy consumption. On the other hand, deterministic transmission schedules, although efficient in terms of energy consumption, usually provide only large time guarantees for successful communication. Therefore, the problem addressed in this work, i.e., to find a deterministic transmission schedule with optimal time and energy guarantees of successful communication, is a fundamental question in Sensor Networks.

The rest of the document is organized as follow. In Sections 2, the model and problem definition are presented. In Section 3, our results are presented and contextualized with the previous results. Section 4 contains synchronization algorithms of independent interest. Finally, deterministic recurrent communication algorithms are introduced in Section 5.

2 Model and Problems Definition

Regarding network topology and connectivity, and node constraints, we use the restrictive model in [15,16,14] summarized here as follows.

NETWORK AND NODES: Let us denote with V the set of sensors. Each sensor node is assumed to have a unique identification number (ID) in $\{0, \ldots, n-1\}$. Sensors are expected to be deployed at random in the area of interest. Each sensor is provided with a radio system to communicate with the rest of the network, but each radio system has only a limited range for transmissions and receptions. It is assumed that the transmission range and the reception range are the same, and it is referred as the communication range. Consequently, each node is able to communicate with a restricted number of other sensors, the ones deployed within its communication range. In this work, we use an undirected graph $G = (V, E)$ to model the topology of the network. Each node in V represents a sensor node, and the link $(u, v) \in E$ represents that nodes u and v are in communication range[1]. Let us denote with $N(v)$ the set of neighbors of node v. Let $n = |V|$

---

[1] This models corresponds to a *Geometric Graph*. Generalizing the results to arbitrary graphs is left for future work.

denote the number of nodes in the network, and let $k = \max_{v \in V} |N(v)|$ be the maximum degree of a node in G (i.e., the network). Finally, we use D to denote the diameter of the network. Unless otherwise stated, we assume that n, k and D are known by all the nodes in the system. (We assume the precise values are known for clarity, but limiting that knowledge to asymptotically tight upper bounds yield the same results asymptotically.) Regarding computational resources of sensor nodes, node-memory size is restricted only to $O(k + \log n)$ bits. Were the deployment of nodes uniform (random geometric graph) as it is popularly assumed in the Sensor Networks literature [11,24], our protocols would work even if the node-memory size is restricted to just $O(\log n)$ bits.

LOCAL SYNCHRONY: Time is assumed to be slotted in equal-length *time slots* or *steps*. It is assumed that the length of a slot is sufficient to transmit one message, i.e., each transmission occurs in a given slot. Without loss of generality [23], it is assumed that the slots of all nodes are in phase, i.e., they all start and finish at the same time instants. For convenience, we assume a *global time* that takes non-negative integer values and advances one unit per step. Note that this is a fictional device and that the nodes do not have access to its value. For convenience we assume that the global time is the number of time steps since the first nodes in the system have been awakened. We assume the availability of a hardware clock mechanism at each node, denoted local-clock, such that, starting from 0 when the node is powered up, the clock is incremented by one automatically at the end of each time slot[2]. Then, for all $i \in V$ and $t \in \mathbb{Z}^+$, local-clock$_i(t)$ denotes the value of local-clock of node i at time step t before being incremented. In the first step t executed by a node i, local-clock$_i(t) = 0$.

NODE AWAKENING AND TYPES OF ADVERSARIES: Nodes are in two possible states, *sleeping* and *awake*. It is assumed that initially all nodes are sleeping. The nodes are assumed to be awakened by an adversary.[3] Without loss of generality, it is assumed that every node of the network is eventually awakened. In the rest of the paper x will be used to denote the first node awakened by the adversary, breaking ties arbitrarily. As x is always awake (see below), $\forall t \geq 0$: local-clock$_x(t) = t$.   Regarding node reliability, as customary in the Sensor Networks literature, we assume that nodes may fail. I.e., a node may crash and stop working. The adversary decides when to crash and recover (awake again) nodes. However, if crashes and recoveries occur arbitrarily, due to determinism, there exist topologies for which the adversary may stop a node from receiving any message, even if connectivity is required.[4] Thus, limitations to the crash/recovery schedule are in order. In this work, we consider node failures as long as: (i) the network stays connected (one connected component) at all times,

---

[2] Observe that, if not readily available, the described mechanism can be implemented as a software counter.

[3] In contrast with the wake-up problem studied in the literature, we do not assume that sleeping nodes may additionally be awaken by the transmission of a neighboring node.

[4] For any time slot t, if none or more than one neighbor transmit, do nothing. Otherwise, put the transmitter to sleep during t.

(ii) node x is always awake (in fact it would be enough if there is always some node that has the global time up and running), and (iii) each period when a node runs without failures lasts at least the length of the stabilization time (as defined in Section 2). In this work, we consider two types of adversaries.

Definition 1. *A τ-adversary is an adversary that awakens all the nodes of the network within a window time of size τ, i.e., no node is awakened at a time $t \geq \tau$. Additionally, a τ-adversary does not recover crashed nodes. The parameter τ is assumed known by the nodes.*

Definition 2. *An ∞-adversary is an adversary that has no restriction on when nodes are awakened.*

COMMUNICATION: Each radio system transmits and receives in a single and shared radio channel. Therefore, at each step, each node decides between transmission mode or reception mode. Moreover, node v *receives* from node u in a slot if and only if node u is the only neighbor of v transmitting in that slot, and v is in reception mode at that slot. In the case that two or more neighbors of node v transmit in the same slot a collision occurs at node v. A node v is not able to distinguish between silence (none of the nodes in $N(v)$ transmits) and collision. We denote the communication range as r. A customary assumption in Sensor Networks [11,24] is that nodes can adjust the power of transmission to a smaller level, introducing only a constant factor in the number of nodes that has to be deployed to maintain connectivity. Instead, for the sake of clarity, in this work we assume that nodes can duplicate their transmission range to $2r$. Likewise, such an assumption does not yield an extra asymptotic cost. Notice that, independently of this assumption, the maximum degree k and diameter D defined before correspond to the underlying graph G defined for range r.

Deterministic Recurrent Communication Problem. The problem solved in this paper is called *deterministic recurrent communication*. The goal in solving this problem is to provide a communication service that can be used by the components of a distributed application residing in different nodes to exchange *application messages*. Thus, the service must allow a component in a node to recurrently communicate with the components in neighboring nodes. For the sake of clarity, we assume that all nodes run application components that have an infinite supply of application messages to transmit.

Definition 3. *A distributed protocol solves the* deterministic recurrent communication *(DRC) problem if it guarantees that, for every step t and every pair $(u, v) \in E$, there is some step $t' \geq t$ such that, in step t', v receives an application message from u.*

The protocols proposed in this paper are adaptive, in the sense that when nodes are awakened, they run a *start-up phase*. During this phase, nodes use *control messages* to agree on a periodic transmission schedule. After the start-up phase, a *stable phase* starts in which they use the agreed transmission schedule to exchange application messages. For some of the protocols, control messages still have to be used in the stable phase. We use three goodness parameters to evaluate these protocols. The first one is the maximum number of steps of the start-up phase for any node, called the *stabilization time*. Then, we define the following metrics to evaluate energy and time efficiency *in the stable phase*. For any $(u, v) \in E$ and any $i > 1$, let $R_u^i(v)$ be the number of transmissions of u between the $(i-1)^{th}$ and the ith receptions of application messages from u at v, and $R_u(v) = \max_i R_u^i(v)^5$. In order to measure time we denote $\Delta R_u^i(v)$ the time (number of time slots) that are between the $(i-1)^{th}$ and the ith receptions of application messages from u at v, and $\Delta R_u(v) = \max_i \Delta R_u^i(v)^7$. We define the *message complexity* of a protocol for DRC as $\max_{(u,v) \in E} R_u(v)$. We define the *delay* of a protocol for DRC as $\max_{(u,v) \in E} \Delta R_u(v)$.

In this paper, the goal is to derive protocols that solve DRC with asymptotically optimal message complexity and delay, even if they incur in significant stabilization times. We design our protocols assuming the existence of an *oblivious deterministic recurrent communication protocol* that solves DRC with bounded delay and no start-up phase. In this protocol, whether a node u is in transmission or reception mode at step t is a function only of u's ID and local-clock$_u(t)$ (the number of steps u has been awake). Such oblivious deterministic protocols exist. An example is the Primed Selection communication protocol proposed in [15]. In the rest of the paper, the oblivious deterministic recurrent communication protocol will be modeled as a binary function ORC on $V \times \mathbb{Z}^+$. Then, for all $u \in V$ and all $j \in \mathbb{Z}^+$ we have $\text{ORC}(u, j) \in \{transmit, receive\}$. The delay of this protocol will be denoted by T. Since oblivious protocols have no start-up phase, this means that if nodes u and v, such that $(u, v) \in E$, are awake and run ORC, in every interval of T steps they will receive from each other.

The Synchronization Problem. As a by-product of the protocols proposed in this paper for DRC, we propose also deterministic protocols that solve the *synchronization problem* under both classes of adversaries defined. In the synchronization problem it is assumed that each node has a slot counter global-clock (incremented in every step) and a Boolean variable synced indicating whether it is synchronized or not. The slot counters of all synchronized nodes must have the same value. For each node $i \in V$ and time slot t, let global-clock$_i(t)$ and synced$_i(t)$ be, respectively, the slot counter and the Boolean variable of node i at the beginning of time slot t. We say that a network is *synchronized* at a time step $t \in \mathbb{Z}^+$ if, for all $i, j \in V$, such that synced$_i(t) = $ synced$_j(t) = true$, it holds that global-clock$_i(t) = $ global-clock$_j(t)$.

Definition 4. *We say that a protocol solves the* synchronization problem *if there exists a time t from which the protocol guarantees that the network is synchronized at all times after t, and every node that awakes eventually gets synchronized. The maximum time between a node awaking and getting synchronized is the* synchronization time *of the protocol.*

In the synchronization protocols proposed here each node initializes its counter global-clock to 0 and increments it by 1 every step. A node can also adopt a larger

---

⁵ If the maximum does not exist, this value is defined as ∞.

global-clock value from another node. Then, since x is the first node awake and it never fails, it will always have the largest global-clock counter, i.e., for each node $u \in V$ and each $t \geq 0$, if u is awake at time t then $\text{global-clock}_u(t) \leq \text{global-clock}_x(t)$. Moreover, $\forall t \geq 0 : \text{local-clock}_x(t) = \text{global-clock}_x(t) = t$.

3 Framing Our Results with Related Work

To the best of our knowledge, deterministic recurrent communication under a restricted Sensor Network model was only studied in [15] and later improved in [16]. It was shown in the latter an oblivious protocol with optimal message complexity and delay at most $k(n+k)(\ln(n+k)+\ln\ln(n+k))$, which was shown to be optimal delay-wise for a subclass of non-adaptive protocols for most values of k. For adaptive protocols, it was shown in that work a delay of $O(k^2 \log k)$ relaxing memory size constraints and an asymptotically optimal delay of $O(k)$ additionally limiting the adversarial node awakening schedule. In the present paper, a worst-case asymptotically optimal $O(k)$ delay bound is proven, even removing those restrictions.

The question of how to disseminate information in Radio Networks has led to different well-studied important problems such as *Broadcast* [2,21], *Selection* [20], and *Gossiping* [22,5]. These problems differ in the number of nodes that hold a possibly different message to disseminate to all nodes in the network. Although these are one-shot communication primitives, some of the results obtained could be used repeatedly to achieve recurrent communication.

Deterministic solutions [8,10] for Broadcast and Gossiping include assumptions such as simultaneous startup or the availability of a global clock, which are not feasible in Sensor Networks. The selection problem, on the other hand, was studied by Kowalski [20] in a model where the node awakening schedule is adversarial, proving the existence of a $O(k^2 \log n)$ algorithm and showing constructively how to obtain an algorithm that achieves $O(k^2 \text{ polylog } n)$. These results are obtained for a model where nodes turn off upon successful transmission. Thus, they do not apply to our setting.

In [1], Alon, Bar-Noy, Linial and Peleg gave a deterministic distributed protocol to simulate the message passing model in radio networks. Using this technique, each node receives a transmission of all its neighbors after $O(k^2 \log^2 n / \log(k \log n))$ steps. Again, simultaneous awakening of nodes is required, a feature that can not be assumed in restricted models of Sensor Networks. In the same paper, lower bounds for this problem are also proved by showing bipartite graphs that require $\Omega(k \log k)$ rounds. Bipartite graphs with maximum degree $\omega(1)$ are not embeddable in geometric graphs therefore these bounds do not apply to our setting.

Related lines of work from combinatorics include *selectors*, *selective-* and *strongly-selective families* [19,9,13,3]. The application of any of these combinatorial objects to recurrent communication in Radio Networks would require simultaneous awakening of the participating nodes. Within the scope of the *wake-up* problem, the existence of a combinatorial structure called *radio-synchronizer* was shown in [7], later explicited in [6]. The existence of an extension of radio-synchronizers, called *universal-synchronizers*, was also shown in the latter, and a constructive proof of universal-synchronizers was given in [4]. In Radio Networks terminology, a radio-synchronizer is an n-set of schedules of transmissions (one for each node) such that, for any node awakening schedule and for any subset of k nodes, there is a time step when exactly one of the k nodes transmits. Synchronizers (radio- or universal-) are of the utmost importance in Radio Networks because they tolerate arbitrary rotations of each schedule of transmissions. In other words, they can be used obliviously without assuming any specific node awakening schedule. Furthermore, due to the same reason, synchronizers could be used repeatedly to implement a recurrent communication primitive, as long as it is enough for each node to receive messages from *some* neighboring node infinitely many times. In the present paper, we study a recurrent communication primitive that requires each node to receive from *each* neighboring node infinitely many times. (See Definition 3.)

In order to compute a transmission schedule that solves DRC with asymptotically optimal delay bound, we include in the algorithms presented in this paper a synchronizing phase. Within the scope of Radio Networks, the problem of globally synchronizing the network has been recently studied in [12], but their model includes a single-hop network and many channels of communication.

The application of Radio Network wake-up protocols to global synchronization was studied in [7,6,4]. In their model, nodes may be awaken adversarially, but additionally they may be also awaken by the transmission of another node. The synchronization technique proposed takes advantage of the latter and works only after all nodes have been awaken. Thus, it can only be applied to our setting under a τ-adversary, adding an initial waiting phase to ensure that all nodes are awake before running that protocol. Extending the best running time obtained in [4] by the additional τ waiting steps gives $O(\tau + \min\{n, Dk\}k \text{ polylog } n)$. Whereas the synchronization algorithm of [18], suited here for a τ-adversary and using the ORC protocol of [15], yields a running time of $\tau + Dnk \log n$. Although which of these protocols is more efficient depends on the parameters instance, we propose the latter for clarity of the presentation towards the more general adversary. A more complete review of the related literature can be found in [17].

Our Results. In this work, we present an adaptive protocol that solves DRC asymptotically optimally for message complexity and delay efficiency measures. We model the arbitrary node awakening schedule, and node failures, with the two types of adversaries previously defined, τ-adversary and ∞-adversary. As a building block of our deterministic computation of an optimal transmission schedule, we include a synchronization algorithm for each of type of adversary. Once nodes are synchronized, we provide a $19(k + 1)$ coloring of the network, where k is the maximum degree[6]. Thus, the transmission schedule guarantees, in the case of the first adversary, that for every time interval of length $19(k + 1)$

---

[6] Recall that k is the maximum degree with communication range r. The proposed protocols use also a communication range of $2r$. The value $19(k + 1)$ is an upper bound on the maximum degree with this range.

slots, each node has at least one successful transmission to all its neighbors. In the case of the less restricted ∞-adversary, the transmission schedule has to be resilient to the awakening of new nodes. Thus, after synchronization, each time step is doubled extending the length of that interval to $38(k+1)$ slots. Due to the pigeonhole principle, these delays between reception of each neighboring node are asymptotically optimal.

Given that the efficient use of energy is crucial to extend the life-cycle of a sensor node, and that the radio-communication cost in terms of energy dominates other consumption factors, it is extremely important to minimize the number of transmissions produced that do not achieve effective application communication. The protocols presented in this paper are shown to have optimal message complexity of 0 for the restricted adversary, and a message complexity of $19(k+1)/n$ for the unrestricted adversary, which is asymptotically optimal if all nodes run application components that have an infinite supply of application messages to transmit.

4   Synchronization Protocols

In this section, we present the protocol that solves the synchronization problem under an ∞-adversary. For a τ-adversary, the synchronization protocol used is a re-creation of the algorithm presented in [18]. The interested reader may find the details in [17].

We present now the protocol CONTMAXSPREAD, designed to solve the synchronization problem against an ∞-adversary. Observe that, due to the nature of an ∞-adversary, any synchronization protocol has to keep sending synchronization messages during all its execution, even after the network has been synchronized. In this way, any new node awakened after the network is synchronized recognizes this fact, and joins the network adopting the common value of the global clock.

Hence, the synchronization protocol CONTMAXSPREAD has two phases, a *synchronization phase*, and an *application phase*. In the synchronization phase, the largest global-clock is spread through the network. However, as mentioned above, CONTMAXSPREAD keeps sending synchronization messages in the application phase. The protocol CONTMAXSPREAD sets up the synchronization flag synced to communicate the current synchronization state of the network (from a node's point of view). Roughly speaking, during the first $T_1 = 3n^2 + 2nT$ steps of the synchronization phase, a node listens for messages from the network. That listening part is devoted to provide the node with the current synchronization state of the network. If the network is synchronized, and some node has synced $= true$, when the node wakes up, it will know about it before the listening period is over and, without having to send any message will get synchronized. If that does not happen, during the next $T_2 = 2nT$ steps of the synchronization phase, the node transmits to its neighbors its value global-clock and its synchronization flag synced following ORC. As will be shown, at the end of this subphase the network (and hence the node) has to be synchronized. During the application phase, a node transmits its value global-clock and its synchronization flag synced (perhaps, piggybacked in an application message), but this time, the transmission is done in a round robin fashion, i.e., if the identifier of the node is equal to the value global-clock modulo n, then the node transmits. More details of the CONTMAXSPREAD protocol can be found in [17].

Lemma 1. *The global clock of a node u awakened before $T_1 + T_2$ satisfies that either* global-clock$_u(T_1 + T_2) \leq T_2$, *or* global-clock$_u(T_1 + T_2) =$ global-clock$_x(T_1 + T_2) = T_1 + T_2$.

Proof. Recall that the adversary is restricted so that the network is connected at all times and awake nodes are alive for at least the stabilization time. This means that, up to time $T_1 + T_2$, if node $u \in V$ is awake, there exists some *time ordered path* $x = v_0, v_1, \ldots, v_l = u$ (recall that x is the first node awake) in the network connecting x to u such that $l < n$ and, for all $0 < i \leq l$, local-clock$_{v_{i-1}}(t) \geq$ local-clock$_{v_i}(t)$. We call the *distance* from u to x as the smallest number of edges of any of these time ordered paths. Since all the time steps, and hence global clocks, considered in this proof are smaller than $T_1 + T_2$, then no node fails, and all awake nodes are in the synchronization phase of the algorithm, have a time ordered path to x, and have synced $= false$.

We show that a node u that at time $T_1 + T_2$ has a global clock different from x's must have global-clock$_u(T_1 + T_2) \leq T_2$. Let us consider a node u awakened before $T_1 + T_2$ and whose global clock at that time is global-clock$_u(T_1 + T_2) < T_1 + T_2$. A node that is awakened before T_1 and whose distance to x is d has the same global clock as x by time $T_1 + d \cdot T$. (Broadcast time in a network of awakened nodes, see [17] for details.) Thus, given that the distance is always less than n, a node awakened before T_1 has the the same global clock as x by time $T_1 + nT \leq T_1 + T_2$. Therefore, to complete the proof, it remains to consider the case where u was awakened at some time within the global-time interval $[T_1, T_1 + T_2)$. To prove the claim in that case, it is enough to prove that global-clock$_u(T_1 + T_2) =$ local-clock$_u(T_1 + T_2)$ because, given that u did not wake up before T_1, it holds that local-clock$_u(T_1 + T_2) \leq T_2$.

Let us assume, by way of contradiction, that u has global-clock$_u(T_1 + T_2) \neq$ local-clock$_u(T_1 + T_2)$. This means that u has received a message before time $T_1 + T_2$ with a field global-clock$'$ larger than its own global clock, and has adopted it. The value global-clock$'$ is received because some node v had global-clock$_v(t) =$ local-clock$_v(t) \geq T_1$ at some time $t < T_1 + T_2$, and transmitted this value (using schedule ORC). Let us denote the propagation path (not necessarily time ordered) of this value before reaching u as $v = q_0, q_1, \ldots, q_s = u$.

From $t < T_1 + T_2$, local-clock$_v(t) \geq T_1$, and $T_1 > T_2$, it is derived that v was awakened before T_1. Let d be the distance from v to x. Then, node v has the same global clock as x by time $T_1 + d \cdot T$. Then, by time $T_1 + d \cdot T$ v transmits, using the ORC schedule, the same global clock as x. Furthermore, it does this for at least $(2n - d)T$ steps.

Returning to the path $v = q_0, q_1, \ldots, q_s = u$, we have that q_1 must have received (and hence was awake) some message from $v = q_0$ (in particular, the global clock that was later propagated as global-clock$'$) before $T_1 + d \cdot T$. Furthermore, q_1 has received from v a message with the global clock of x by $T_1 + (d+1)T$. Applying the same argument, we conclude that q_2 received (and hence was awake) from q_1 before $T_1 + (d+1)T$ and has received the global clock of x by time $T_1 + (d+2)T$. Inductively, $q_s = u$ has received the global clock of x by time $T_1 + (d+s)T$. Since $d + s < 2n$, this mean that u has the same global clock as x by time $T_1 + T_2$, which is a contradiction.

Theorem 1. CONTMAXSPREAD *solves the synchronization problem under any* ∞-*adversary with synchronization time* $T_1 + T_2$, *where* $T_1 = 3n^2 + 2nT$ *and* $T_2 = 2nT$.

Proof (Proof sketch). To prove the theorem, it is enough to prove that, at any global time step $t \geq T_1 + T_2$, any node in the network is either synchronized with x, or it is still in the listening part of the synchronization phase. The proof of the following claim can be found in [17].

Claim. For any node $v \in V$ and any time step $t \geq T_1 + T_2$, it takes at most $3n^2$ time steps for v to have the global time (be synchronized), even under failures (as defined in Section 2), unless v goes back to sleep before.

Lemma 1 shows that at global time $T_1 + T_2$ a global-clock in the network is either synchronized with x's global clock, or its value is smaller than T_2, which is $3n^2$ time steps smaller than T_1. Consequently, at global time $T_1 + T_2$, every node who is transmitting messages does it with x's global clock. Then, any node with global clock smaller than T_2 receive x's global clock before its own global clock reaches the value T_1. Finally, due to the same reason, if a node is awakened at global time $t \geq T_1 + T_2$, before its local clock reaches the value $3n^2$, it receives a message with x's global clock. Then, that node is synchronized without transmitting itself in the synchronization phase.

5   Communication Scheme

In this section, we show how to solve DRC for τ- and ∞- adversaries. Both protocols are algorithmically similar and can be broadly described for each node $v \in V$ as follows. Upon waking up, v runs three phases: synchronization, coloring, and application. During the first phase, v synchronizes itself (as defined in Section 2) with the node x that woke up first in the network. During the second phase, v chooses a color that has not been chosen by any neighboring node. Finally, by mapping colors to time slots (thanks to the global synchronization achieved), the application phase of i corresponds to its stable phase. Given that the color chosen by v is unique within radius $2r$ of v, but the application messages are transmitted with radius r, all nodes within distance r of v receive v's application messages.

Moving to how do we implement each phase, synchronization is implemented using the protocols of Section 4 for the τ- and ∞- adversaries respectively. The coloring phase, on the other hand, is implemented by each node announcing the color chosen so that, by appropriate bookkeeping of the available colors at each node, nodes within distance $2r$ do not choose the same color (avoiding the hidden-terminal problem). To avoid collision of transmissions and simultaneous choice of the same color, taking advantage of the global synchronization achieved in the previous phase, each colored node chooses an available color and announces its choice in a time slot selected in Round-robin fashion according to ID. For the application phase, again thanks to the global synchronization achieved, each node transmits its application messages in Round-robin fashion, but now according to its color.

For the τ-adversary, thanks to the inclusion of a τ-long waiting period at the beginning of the synchronization phase, the above described phases are executed synchronously by all nodes in the network. In other words, all nodes in the network finish the synchronization (resp. coloring) phase and begin the coloring (resp. application) phase at the same time. For the ∞-adversary on the other hand, new nodes may be woken up while others are already in the coloring or application phases. Thus, control messages have to be sent always to handle these late arrivals. The transmissions corresponding to those control messages are produced in Round-robin fashion according to ID. The coexistence of both types of messages during the application phase is handled by devoting even slots (w.r.t. global time) to control messages and odd slots (w.r.t. global time) to application messages, at the cost of duplicating the time delay. The details of both algorithms can be found in [17].

Regarding the space complexity of these protocols, a node needs to store its own ID ($O(\log n)$ bits) and after the coloring phase one of $O(k)$ colors ($O(\log k)$ bits). Additionally, each node has to keep track of the colors still available ($O(k)$ bits), and maintains a counter that reach a maximum count in $O(kn)$ ($O(\log n)$ bits). Thus, the overall space complexity for each node is $O(k + \log n)$ bits. The stabilization time, delay, and message complexity of the protocols described can be proved applying the results of Section 4 and standard analysis of the Round-robin algorithms used. We establish those bounds in the following theorems. (The proofs can be found in [17].)

Theorem 2. *Given a Sensor Network of n nodes, the protocol presented in Section 5 solves the DRC problem under a τ-adversary with stabilization time at most $D \cdot T + \tau + n$, where T is the delay of the ORC protocol. The delay of this DRC protocol is $19(k+1)$ which is asymptotically optimal, and the message complexity is 0 which is optimal.*

Theorem 3. *Given a Sensor Network of n nodes, upon being woken up by a ∞-adversary, the protocol presented in Section 5 solves the DRC problem under an ∞-adversary with stabilization time at most $6n^2 + 4nT + 4n$, where T is the delay of the ORC protocol. The delay of this DRC protocol is $38(k+1)$ and the message complexity is $19(k+1)/n$, which are both asymptotically optimal.*

References

1. Alon, N., Bar-Noy, A., Linial, N., Peleg, D.: Single round simulation in radio networks. J. Algorithms 13, 188–210 (1992)
2. Bar-Yehuda, R., Goldreich, O., Itai, A.: On the time-complexity of broadcast in multi-hop radio networks: An exponential gap between determinism and randomization. JCSS 45, 104–126 (1992)

3. De Bonis, A., Gąsieniec, L., Vaccaro, U.: Generalized framework for selectors with applications in optimal group testing. In: Baeten, J.C.M., Lenstra, J.K., Parrow, J., Woeginger, G.J. (eds.) ICALP 2003. LNCS, vol. 2719, pp. 81–96. Springer, Heidelberg (2003)
4. Chlebus, B., Gąsieniec, L., Kowalski, D., Radzik, T.: On the wake-up problem in radio networks. In: Caires, L., Italiano, G.F., Monteiro, L., Palamidessi, C., Yung, M. (eds.) ICALP 2005. LNCS, vol. 3580, pp. 347–359. Springer, Heidelberg (2005)
5. Chlebus, B., Gąsieniec, L., Lingas, A., Pagourtzis, A.: Oblivious gossiping in ad-hoc radio networks. In: DIAL-M, pp. 44–51 (2001)
6. Chlebus, B., Kowalski, D.: A better wake-up in radio networks. In: PODC (2004)
7. Chrobak, M., Gąsieniec, L., Kowalski, D.: The wake-up problem in multi-hop radio networks. In: SODA (2004)
8. Chrobak, M., Gąsieniec, L., Rytter, W.: Fast broadcasting and gossiping in radio networks. In: FOCS (2000)
9. Clementi, A., Monti, A., Silvestri, R.: Selective families, superimposed codes, and broadcasting on unknown radio networks. In: SODA (2001)
10. Czumaj, A., Rytter, W.: Broadcasting algorithms in radio networks with unknown topology. In: FOCS (2003)
11. Doherty, L., Pister, K.S.J., El Ghaoui, L.: Convex optimization methods for sensor node position estimation. In: INFOCOM, pp. 1655–1663 (2001)
12. Dolev, S., Gilbert, S., Guerraoui, R., Kuhn, F., Newport, C.: The wireless synchronization problem. In: PODC (2009)
13. Dyachkov, A., Rykov, V.: A survey of superimposed code theory. Probl. Contr. Inform. Theor. 12(4) (1983)
14. Farach-Colton, M., Fernandes, R.J., Mosteiro, M.A.: Bootstrapping a hop-optimal network in the weak sensor model. ACM TALG 5(4), 1–30 (2009)
15. Fernández Anta, A., Mosteiro, M.A., Thraves, C.: Deterministic communication in the weak sensor model. In: Tovar, E., Tsigas, P., Fouchal, H. (eds.) OPODIS 2007. LNCS, vol. 4878, pp. 119–131. Springer, Heidelberg (2007)
16. Fernández Anta, A., Mosteiro, M.A., Thraves, C.: Deterministic recurrent communication in restricted sensor networks. INRIA RR 00486270 (2009)
17. Fernández Anta, A., Mosteiro, M.A., Thraves, C.: Deterministic recurrent communication and synchronization in restricted sensor networks. INRIA RR 00486277 (2010)
18. Gouda, M.G., Herman, T.: Stabilizing unison. IPL 35(4), 171–175 (1990)
19. Indyk, P.: Explicit constructions of selectors and related combinatorial structures, with applications. In: SODA (2002)
20. Kowalski, D.R.: On selection problem in radio networks. In: PODC, pp. 158–166 (2005)
21. Kushilevitz, E., Mansour, Y.: An $\Omega(D\log(N/D))$ lower bound for broadcast in radio networks. SICOMP 27(3), 702–712 (1998)
22. Liu, D., Prabhakaran, M.: On randomized broadcasting and gossiping in radio networks. In: Ibarra, O.H., Zhang, L. (eds.) COCOON 2002. LNCS, vol. 2387, pp. 340–349. Springer, Heidelberg (2002)
23. Roberts, L.G.: Aloha packet system with and without slots and capture. CCR 5(2), 28–42 (1975)
24. Song, W.-Z., Wang, Y., Li, X.-Y., Frieder, O.: Localized algorithms for energy efficient topology in wireless ad hoc networks. MONET 10(6), 911–923 (2005)

k^+ Decision Trees*
(Extended Abstract)

James Aspnes[1], Eric Blais[2], Murat Demirbas[3], Ryan O'Donnell[2], Atri Rudra[3],
and Steve Uurtamo[3]

[1] Department of Computer Science, Yale University
New Haven, CT 06520
aspnes@cs.yale.edu
[2] Department of Computer Science, Carnegie Mellon University
Pittsburgh, PA 15213
{eblais,odonnell}@cs.cmu.edu
[3] Department of Computer Science and Engineering, University at Buffalo
State University of New York, Buffalo, NY, 14260
{demirbas,atri,uurtamo}@buffalo.edu

Abstract. Consider a wireless sensor network in which each sensor has
a bit of information. Suppose all sensors with the bit 1 broadcast this
fact to a basestation. If zero or one sensors broadcast, the basestation
can detect this fact. If two or more sensors broadcast, the basestation
can only detect that there is a "collision." Although collisions may seem
to be a nuisance, they can in some cases help the basestation compute
an aggregate function of the sensors' data.

Motivated by this scenario, we study a new model of computation for
boolean functions: the 2^+ *decision tree*. This model is an augmentation
of the standard decision tree model: now each internal node queries an
arbitrary *set* of literals and branches on whether 0, 1, or at least 2 of the
literals are true. This model was suggested in a work of Ben-Asher and
Newman but does not seem to have been studied previously.

Our main result shows that 2^+ decision trees can "count" rather effectively. Specifically, we show that zero-error 2^+ decision trees can compute
the threshold-of-t symmetric function with $O(t)$ expected queries (and
that $\Omega(t)$ is a lower bound even for two-sided error 2^+ decision trees).
Interestingly, this feature is not shared by 1^+ decision trees. Our result
implies that the natural generalization to k^+ decision trees does not give
much more power than 2^+ decision trees. We also prove a lower bound of
$\tilde{\Omega}(t) \cdot \log(n/t)$ for the *deterministic* 2^+ complexity of the threshold-of-t
function, demonstrating that the randomized 2^+ complexity can in some
cases be unboundedly better than deterministic 2^+ complexity.

* James Aspnes is supported in part by NSF grant CCF-0916389. Murat Demirbas'
work was partially supported by NSF Career award #0747209. Ryan O'Donnell is
supported in part by NSF grants CCF-0747250 and CCF-0915893, a Sloan fellowship,
and an Okawa fellowship. Atri Rudra and Steve Uurtamo are supported in part by
NSF CAREER grant CCF-0844796.

C. Scheideler (Ed.): ALGOSENSORS 2010, LNCS 6451, pp. 74–88, 2010.

Finally, we generalize the above results to arbitrary symmetric functions, and we discuss the relationship between k^+ decision trees and other complexity notions such as decision tree rank and communication complexity.

1 Introduction

The motivation for our work comes from monitoring applications in wireless sensor networks. Consider the scenario where n sensors communicate directly with a basestation (i.e., a "single-hop" network). Each sensor contains one bit of information (e.g., "Is the temperature more than 70°F?") and the basestation wants to compute some aggregate function over this information (e.g., "Is the temperature more than 70°F for at least 10 of the sensors?"). How efficiently can the basestation compute the aggregate function? The naive way to compute the aggregate function is to query each sensor individually resulting in as many queries as the number of sensors n in the worst case.

We observe that a better solution is to use the broadcast primitive available in wireless networks. With a single broadcast message, the basestation may simultaneously ask a group of sensors if their bit is 1, and switches to the listening mode. There are three possible scenarios: either 0, 1, or at least 2 sensors reply. In the first two cases, the basestation can detect that exactly 0 or exactly 1 sensors in the group have replied. In the third case, there will be a collision in the sensors' replies. Conventional wisdom says that collisions are bad, and in fact protocols in wireless networks try to disambiguate collisions. In this scenario, however, collisions provide useful information: the basestation gets a quick feedback affirming that at least 2 sensors have replied in the queried group.

Such a quick in-network feedback collection primitive has many uses in wireless sensor network applications. For example for intrusion detection applications [2], a clusterhead can employ this primitive to quickly check if a threshold number of sensors have detected an intruder. The clusterhead may initiate the more costly actions to localize and classify the intruder, only if a threshold number of sensors detect the phenomena (i.e., after it is assured that this is not a false-positive due to wind, low-quality sensors, etc.).

The receiver side collision detection required for this primitive can easily be implemented in the existing sensor radios. Indeed, there has been recent work in using existing wireless sensor nodes to detect collisions and using this capability to design more efficient protocols [7,8,11].

Next, we present our theoretical framework for studying the problem above.

Decision trees. Decision trees provide an elegant framework for studying the complexity of boolean functions. The internal nodes of a decision tree are associated with *tests* on the input; the branches leaving a node correspond to the outcomes of the associated test; and, the leaves of the tree are labeled with output values. The main parameter of interest is the *depth* of the decision tree; i.e., the maximum number of tests made over all inputs. The decision tree complexity of a particular boolean function is defined to be the minimum of this parameter over all decision trees computing the function.

We can define different decision tree models by restricting the set of tests that can be performed at each internal node. In the *simple* decision tree model, each test queries the value of a single bit of the input. This standard model is extremely well-studied in theoretical computer science; see e.g. the survey of Buhrman and de Wolf [6]. Other models include *linear* decision trees, where the tests are signs of linear forms on the bits (see, e.g., [9]); *algebraic* decision trees, the generalization to signs of low-degree polynomials (see, e.g., [4]); k-AND decision trees [5], where the tests are ANDs of up to k literals; k-bounded decision trees [18], the generalization to arbitrary functions of up to k bits; and $\mathbb{F}_2$-linear decision trees [16], where the tests are parities of sets of input bits.

Closer to the interests of the present article are models where the tests are *threshold functions* of the input bits. When the tests can be ORs of input variables, the model is known as *combinatorial group testing* (see the book [10]). When the tests can count and branch on the number of inputs in any subset of variables, the model is connected to that of *combinatorial search* (see the book [1]). Finally, when the tests allowed are ORs of any subset of input *literals*, we have the decision tree model studied by Ben-Asher and Newman [3]. We call this last model the *1⁺ decision tree* model.

In this article, we initiate the study of the *2⁺ decision tree* model. If the algorithm at the basestation does not try to avoid collisions but instead uses them to determine when at least 2 sensors have replied, the complexity of computing the aggregate function is determined by the 2^+ decision tree complexity of the function. The tests in this model are on arbitrary subsets of the n input literals, and the branches correspond to the cases of either 0, 1, or at least 2 literals in the subset being true. (We will give a formal definition in Section 2.1.) We also introduce and examine the *k⁺ decision tree* model, a natural generalization of the 2^+ model in which the branches correspond to 0, 1, 2, ..., $k-1$, or at least k literals being true.

A similar motivation for 2^+ decision trees appears in the work of Ben-Asher and Newman [3]. They primarily studied the 1^+ model. The authors also mentioned that an Ethernet channel scenario — say, a single bus Ethernet network where the controller can detect any collisions in the network — yields a computational model equivalent to our 2^+ decision trees, but left the study of this model as an open problem. The 2^+ model has been considered before in the context of single-hop networks: see e.g., [15,13] and the references therein. These previous works considered some specific problems in the 2^+ model where as our results are more general.

Organization of the article. We defer the statement of our main results to Section 3, in order to first introduce formal definitions of our models. We prove our main results in Sections 4 and 5, and we present other results from the full version of this article in Section 6. Due to lack of space, the missing details including all the omitted proofs will appear in the full version of the paper.

2   Preliminaries

2.1   Definitions

In this article, we are concerned with boolean functions; i.e., functions of the form $f : \{0,1\}^n \to \{0,1\}$. We write a typical input as $x = (x_1, \ldots, x_n) \in \{0,1\}^n$, and write $|x|$ for its Hamming weight, namely $\sum_{i=1}^n x_i$. We also use the notation $[n] = \{1, \ldots, n\}$ and $\log(m) = \max\{\log_2(m), 1\}$.

A boolean function $f : \{0,1\}^n \to \{0,1\}$ is *monotone* if $f(x) \geq f(y)$ whenever $x \geq y$ coordinate-wise. A function f is *(totally) symmetric* if the value of $f(x)$ is determined by $|x|$. When f is symmetric, we write $f_0, f_1, \ldots, f_n \in \{0,1\}$ for the values of the function on inputs of Hamming weight $0, 1, \ldots n$, respectively. The functions which are both monotone and symmetric are the *threshold* functions. Given $0 \leq t \leq n + 1$, the *t-threshold* function $T_n^t : \{0,1\}^n \to \{0,1\}$ is defined by $T_n^t(x) = 1$ iff $|x| \geq t$.

For an arbitrary symmetric function f we recall the integer parameter $\Gamma(f)$, first introduced by Paturi [20], and related to the longest interval centered around $n/2$ on which f is constant:

$$\Gamma(f) = \min_{0 \leq \ell \leq \lceil n/2 \rceil} \{\ell : f_\ell = f_{\ell+1} = \cdots = f_{n-\ell}\}.$$

E.g., for the threshold functions we have $\Gamma(T_n^t) = \min\{t, n + 1 - t\}$.

k^+ **decision trees.** Let $1 \leq k \leq n$ be integers. A k^+ *decision tree* T over n-bit inputs is a tree in which every leaf has a label from $\{0,1\}$, every internal node is labeled with two disjoint subsets $Q_{\text{pos}}, Q_{\text{neg}} \subseteq [n]$, and the internal nodes have $k + 1$ outgoing edges labeled $0, 1, \ldots, k - 1$, and k^+. Every internal node is also called a *query*; the corresponding sets Q_{pos} and Q_{neg} are called the *positive query set* and *negative query set*. Given a boolean input $x = (x_1, \ldots, x_n) \in \{0,1\}^n$, the computation of T on x begins at the root of T. If that node is labeled by $(Q_{\text{pos}}, Q_{\text{neg}})$, computation proceeds along the edge labeled $0, 1, \ldots, k - 1$, or k^+ according to Hamming weight of the literal set $\{x_i : i \in Q_{\text{pos}}\} \cup \{\overline{x}_j : j \in Q_{\text{neg}}\}$; i.e., $\sum_{i \in Q_{\text{pos}}} x_i + \sum_{j \in Q_{\text{neg}}} \overline{x}_j$. The label k^+ has the interpretation "at least k." The computation of T on x then proceeds recursively at the resulting child node. When a leaf node is reached, the tree's output on x, denoted by $T(x)$, is the label of the leaf node. T is said to *compute* (or *decide*) a function $f : \{0,1\}^n \to \{0,1\}$ if and only if $T(x) = f(x)$ for all $x \in \{0,1\}^n$. The *cost* of T on x, denoted $\text{cost}(T, x)$, is the length of the path traced by the computation of T on x. The *depth* of the tree T is the maximum cost over all inputs. The *deterministic* k^+ *decision tree complexity* of a boolean function f, denoted $D^{(k^+)}(f)$, is the minimum depth of any k^+ decision tree that computes it.

As usual, we also introduce *randomized* k^+ decision trees. Formally, these are probability distributions $\mathcal{P}$ over deterministic k^+ decision trees. The *expected cost* of $\mathcal{P}$ on input x is $\mathbf{E}_{T \sim \mathcal{P}}[\text{cost}(T, x)]$. The expected cost of $\mathcal{P}$ itself is the maximum expected cost over all inputs x. Given a boolean function $f : \{0,1\}^n \to \{0,1\}$, the *error* of $\mathcal{P}$ on input x is $\mathbf{Pr}_{T \sim \mathcal{P}}[T(x) \neq f(x)]$. We say that $\mathcal{P}$ computes f

with *zero error* if this error is 0 for all inputs x (in particular, each deterministic T in the support of $\mathcal{P}$ must compute f). We say that $\mathcal{P}$ computes f with *two-sided error* if the error is at most $1/3$ for all inputs x. Note that both the expected cost measure and the error measure are worst-case over all inputs; we do not consider distributional complexity in this article. The *zero (respectively, two-sided) error randomized k^+ decision tree complexity* of a boolean function f, denoted $R_0^{(k^+)}(f)$ (respectively, $R_2^{(k^+)}(f)$), is the minimum expected cost over all distributions $\mathcal{P}$ which compute f with zero (respectively, two-sided) error. In this work, our randomized upper bounds will be for zero error k^+ computation and our randomized lower bounds for two-sided error.

We conclude by noting that the *simple* decision tree model is the 1^+ model with the extra restriction that the query sets Q_{pos} and Q_{neg} satisfy $|Q_{\text{pos}} \cup Q_{\text{neg}}| = 1$ at each node. We use the standard notation $D(f)$, $R_0(f)$, and $R_2(f)$ for the associated deterministic, 0-error, and 2-sided error complexities.

2.2   Related Work

Our main results concern the complexity of symmetric functions under the 2^+ decision tree model, as well as the relation between the deterministic, zero-error randomized, and two-sided error randomized complexities of functions under the k^+ decision tree model. In this section, we review some of the work done on similar problems in the simple and 1^+ decision tree models.

Simple decision trees. The computation of totally symmetric functions is not interesting in the simple decision tree model; it's easy to see that for nonconstant totally symmetric f we have $D(f) = n$ (and it's also known that even $R_2(f) \geq \Omega(n)$ [19]). But some of the most interesting open problems in the theory of simple decision trees concern functions that have a large "degree" of symmetry. Recall that a *graph property* for v-vertex graphs is a decision problem $f : \{0,1\}^{\binom{v}{2}} \to \{0,1\}$ which is invariant under all permutations of the vertices. Let f be a nonconstant *monotone* graph property. Two famous open problem in simple decision tree complexity are the evasiveness conjecture [21], that $D(f)$ equals $\binom{v}{2}$, and the Yao-Karp conjecture [22], that $R(f)$ must be $\Omega(v^2)$.

The relationship between deterministic and randomized complexity is another interesting aspect of simple decision trees. Perhaps surprisingly, it is known [19] that deterministic, zero-error randomized, and two-sided error randomized simple decision tree complexity are polynomially related for every boolean function; specifically, $D(f) \leq O(R_2(f)^3)$. On the other hand, it is not known whether $R_0(f) \leq O(R_2(f))$ holds for all f.

1^+ decision trees. In the 1^+ model, the complexity of symmetric functions becomes a natural question, and a non-trivial one. For example, we of course have $D^{(1^+)}(T_n^1) = 1$, but the value of even $D^{(1^+)}(T_n^2)$ is not immediately obvious. Ben-Asher and Newman point out that it is not hard to show that $D^{(1^+)}(T_n^t) \leq O(t \log(n/t))$, and they show that this bound is tight:

Ben-Asher–Newman Theorem [3]. *For $2 \leq t \leq n$, $D^{(1^+)}(T_n^t) = \Theta(t \log(n/t))$.*

Ben-Asher and Newman also consider randomized complexity. They sketch the proof of the fact that $R_0^{(1^+)}(T_n^2) \geq \Omega(\log n)$, and also observe that $R_2^{(1^+)}(T_n^2) = O(1)$. This leads to the interesting conclusion that unlike in the simple decision tree model, there is *no* polynomial relationship between $R_0^{(1^+)}$ and $R_2^{(1^+)}$ — indeed, $R_0^{(1^+)}(f)$ can be *unboundedly* larger than $R_2^{(1^+)}(f)$.

As we mentioned in the introduction, Ben-Asher and Newman leave the study of the 2^+ model as an open problem. In particular, they asked if their main theorem can be extended to $D^{(2^+)}(T_n^t) \geq \Omega(t \log(n/t))$, observing only a trivial $\Omega(t)$ lower bound.

3 Our Results

Our main results exactly characterize (up to constants) the zero and two-sided error randomized 2^+ complexities of all symmetric functions. We also nearly characterize the deterministic 2^+ complexity of symmetric functions; in particular, we answer the open question of Ben-Asher and Newman up to a $\log t$ factor.

Theorem 1. *For any symmetric boolean function $f : \{0,1\}^n \rightarrow \{0,1\}$, write $\Gamma = \Gamma(f)$. Then*

$$\Omega\big((\Gamma/\log \Gamma) \cdot \log(n/\Gamma)\big) \leq D^{(2^+)}(f) \leq O\big(\Gamma \cdot \log(n/\Gamma)\big),$$

$$R_0^{(2^+)}(f) = \Theta(\Gamma),$$

$$R_2^{(2^+)}(f) = \Theta(\Gamma).$$

In particular, the above bounds hold with $\Gamma = \min(t, n+1-t)$ for threshold functions $f = T_n^t$.

To get a feel for the theorem consider the threshold function $g = T_n^{100}$. Theorem 1 states that $R_0^{(2^+)}(g) = R_2^{(2^+)}(g) = O(1)$ while it can be shown that $R_0^{(2^+)}(g) \geq \Omega(\log n)$. On the other hand both $D^{(2^+)}(g) = D^{(1^+)}(g) = \Theta(\log n)$. The upper bounds and lower bounds of Theorem 1 are tackled in Sections 4 and 5 respectively.

An immediate corollary of Theorem 1 is that there is no polynomial relationship between deterministic and zero-error randomized 2^+ decision tree complexity; indeed, no bounded relationship at all. This is because for $t = O(1)$ we have $D^{(2^+)}(T_n^t) \geq \Omega(\log n)$, yet $R_0^{(2^+)}(T_n^t) = O(1)$. This latter result shows that the zero-error 2^+ decision tree model is quite powerful, being able to compute $T_n^{O(1)}$ with a number of queries *independent* of n.

Our upper bound $R_0^{(2^+)}(f) \leq O(\Gamma)$ relies essentially on the upper bound $R_0^{(2^+)}(T_n^t) \leq O(t)$, and to prove this we actually prove a stronger statement: any

"k^+ query" can be exactly simulated with an expected $O(k)$ many 2^+ queries. Consequently we deduce that the zero error randomized k^+ decision tree complexity of *any* boolean function is $O(k)$ times smaller than its 2^+ decision tree complexity.

Corollary 1. *For any function* $f : \{0,1\}^n \to \{0,1\}$, $R_0^{(k^+)}(f) \geq \Omega(R_0^{(2^+)}(f)/k)$.

The inequality in this corollary is best possible. Indeed, we show that for every symmetric function f it holds that $R_0^{(k^+)}(f) = \Theta(\Gamma(f)/k)$. A similar reduction can be made regarding deterministic k^+ complexity.

The full version of this article includes many other results regarding the k^+ decision tree complexity of general functions. We give a brief overview of some of these results in Section 6.

4   Upper Bounds

Appendix A reduces the computation of general symmetric functions to that of threshold functions. Thus in this section we only discuss computing threshold functions.

Our upper bound for the deterministic 2^+ complexity of thresholds follows immediately from the Ben-Asher–Newman Theorem (which in fact only needs 1^+ queries). We also have the following very straightforward extension:

Proposition 1. *Let* $1 \leq k \leq t \leq n$ *and* $0 \leq t \leq n+1$ *be integers. Then there exists a query algorithm that correctly decides whether* $|x|$ *is* $0, 1, \ldots, t - 1$, *or at least* t *in* $O(t/k \log(n/t))$ *queries. In particular,* $D^{(k^+)}(T_n^t) \leq \lceil \frac{t}{k} \rceil \cdot (2 \cdot \lceil \log \left(\frac{n}{t} \right) \rceil + 1)$.

Note that this Proposition bounds the 2^+ complexity of a k^+ query, which immediately implies for every f that $D^{(k^+)}(f)$ is never better than $D^{(2^+)}(f)$ by more than a $O(k \log(n/k))$ factor.

To complete the proof of the upper bounds in Theorem 1, it now suffices to analyze the zero-error randomized complexity of threshold functions, which we do in the following theorem:

Theorem 2. *Let* $2 \leq k \leq t \leq n$ *be integers. Then there is a randomized* k^+ *query algorithm which, given* $x \in \{0,1\}^n$, *correctly decides whether* $|x|$ *is* $0, 1, \ldots, t - 1$, *or at least* t, *using an expected* $O(t/k)$ *queries. In particular,* $R_0^{(k^+)}(T_n^t) \leq O(t/k)$. *Moreover, if* $t \leq k$ *then* $R_0^{(k^+)}(T_n^t) = 1$.

Corollary 1 follows directly from this theorem (using linearity of expectation), and as mentioned earlier Theorem 2 implies the upper bounds in Theorem 1.

The key to proving Theorem 2 is the following "COUNT" algorithm:

Theorem 3. *Let* $k \geq 2$. *There is an algorithm* COUNT *which on input* x, *outputs* $|x|$ *in an expected* $O(1 + |x|/k)$ *many* k^+ *queries.*

We will also need the following easier result:

Proposition 2. *For each $k \geq 1$ and each real t satisfying $k \leq t \leq n$, there is an $O(t/k)$-query zero-error randomized k^+ query algorithm which on input $x \in \{0,1\}^n$ has the following properties:*

(i) It makes (at most) $4t/k$ queries, with probability 1.
(ii) It outputs either "$|x| \geq t$" or "don't know."
(iii) If $|x| \geq 4t$, it outputs "$|x| \geq t$" with probability at least $1/4$.
(iv) If it ever outputs "$|x| \geq t$", then indeed $|x| \geq t$.

Proof. Let $m = \lfloor 4t/k \rfloor$. If $m \geq n$ we can solve the problem trivially by querying every bit. Otherwise, $1 \leq m \leq n$; we now partition the input coordinates randomly into m bins and perform a k^+ query on each. If at least t/k of the responses are "k^+" then we output "$|x| \geq t$" (which is certainly correct); otherwise we output "don't know."

Assume now that $|x| \geq 4t$; i.e., there are at least $4t$ "balls." The number of balls in a particular bin has distribution Binomial$(|x|, 1/m)$ and hence its mean $|x|/m$ is at least $4t/m \geq k$. It known that the median of a binomial random variable is at least the floor of its mean [14]; hence the probability that a bin has fewer than k balls is at most $1/2$. The expected fraction of bins with fewer than k balls is therefore at most $(1/2)m$; hence by Markov's inequality, the probability that there are more than $(2/3)m$ bins with fewer than k balls is at most $(1/2)/(2/3) = 3/4$. Thus with probability at least $1/4$ we see at least $(1/3)m$ bins with k^+ balls, and $(1/3)m = (1/3)\lfloor 4t/k \rfloor \geq t/k$. This completes the proof.

We remark that Proposition 2 works even if our k^+ queries only return the response "k^+" or "$< k$"; in particular, it holds even when $k = 1$. Theorem 3, however, needs the full power of k^+ queries.

Proof of Theorem 2. Consider the following algorithm:

1. Run COUNT till $4t/k$ queries are made or it halts. In the latter case return the output of COUNT and halt.
2. Run algorithm from Proposition 2.
   a. If the algorithm outputs "don't know" go to Step 1 else output "$|x| \geq t$" and halt.

The fact that this dovetailing algorithm's output is always correct follows from the correctness in Theorem 3 and Proposition 2. As for the expected number of queries used, if the input x satisfies $|x| \geq 4t$, then by the third property in Proposition 2, the dovetailing algorithm stops after at most an expected $32t/k$ queries. On the other hand, if $|x| < 4t$, by Theorem 3, the dovetailing algorithm stops after an expected $O(t/k)$ queries. Thus for any input the dovetailing algorithm makes at most an expected $O(t/k)$ many queries.

Proof Sketch of Theorem 3. Next, we sketch how to prove Theorem 3 using balls and bins analysis. The COUNT algorithm involves randomly partitioning the coordinates $[n]$ into some number of "bins." We think of the "balls" as being the indices for which the input x has a 1. With this framework set up, it is fairly easy to prove Proposition 2. We also prove Theorem 3 about the COUNT algorithm using the balls and bins framework. Suppose we toss the balls (1-coordinates) into bins and then make a k^+ query on each bin. Recall that this tells us whether the number of balls is 0, 1, 2, ..., $k - 1$, or $\geq k$. If a bin contains fewer than k balls, we say it *isolates* these balls. Whenever a bin isolates balls, we have made progress: we know exactly how many 1's are in x in the bin's coordinates. We can henceforth "throw away" these coordinates, remembering only the 1-count in them, and continue processing x on the substring corresponding to those coordinates in bins with at least k many 1's. Thus in terms of balls and bins, we can think of the task of counting $|x|$ as the task of isolating all of the balls. We note that the ability to isolate/count and throw away is the crucial tool that 2^+ queries gain us over 1^+ queries.

We now give a brief intuition behind the COUNT algorithm. Although the algorithm doesn't actually know $|x|$, the number of balls, if it could partition using $2|x|/k$ bins then that would likely isolate a constant fraction of the balls. If we could do this repeatedly while only using $O(\#\text{ balls remaining}/k)$ many queries, we will be able to construct the desired COUNT algorithm. Since we don't know the number of balls remaining, we can try using 2, 4, 8, etc., many bins. If we get up to around the "correct number" $2|x|/k$, we're likely to isolate a good fraction of balls; we can then reset back to 2 bins and repeat. Although we pay a query for each bin, we don't have to worry too much about doubling the number of bins too far; resetting becomes highly likely once the number of bins is at least the correct number. More worrisome is the possibility of resetting too early; we don't want to just keep isolating too few bins. However, we will show that if the number of bins is too small, we are very unlikely to get many isolating bins; hence we *won't* reset.

Statement of COUNT **algorithm.** We now present some more details on the COUNT algorithm. The COUNT algorithm is dovetailing of two other algorithms: A-COUNT (which in $O(A^2)$ queries can determine if $|x| \leq A$, where A is an absolute constant) and SHAVE (to be described soon). More precisely,

0. Set $X \leftarrow 0$.
1. Run A-COUNT till A^2 queries are made. If the algorithm halts with the answer w then halt and return $X + w$.
2. Run SHAVE till A^2 queries are made. Assume SHAVE has isolated the set of indices S (out of which w are 1s), update $X \leftarrow X + w$ and go to Step 1 with the input projected to indices outside of S.

The algorithm SHAVE is as follows:

Run PARTITION$^+(t)$ with t equal to 0; 0, 1; 0, 1, 2; 0, 1, 2, 3; ....
Halt as soon as one of the run halts.

The algorithm PARTITION$^+(t)$ runs another algorithm PARTITION(t) 50 times and halts the first time PARTITION(t) "accepts" and "rejects" if all the runs "reject." Finally, the PARTITION(t) algorithm is as follows:

1. Toss the indices into 2^t bins and do a k^+ query on each bin.
2. Call a bin "good" if the number of balls in it is in the range $[\frac{1}{4}k, \frac{3}{4}k]$.
3. If the fraction of good bins is at least $\frac{1}{20}$, declare "accept" and isolate the balls.
4. Otherwise declare "reject" and *do not* isolate any balls.[a]

---

[a] Not isolating any ball is just for the simplicity of analysis. In practice one should indeed isolate any ball that one can.

5   Lower Bounds

Deterministic lower bound

Lemma 1. *For any symmetric function* $f : \{0,1\}^n \rightarrow \{0,1\}$ *such that* $\Gamma = \Gamma(f) > 2$,

$$D^{(2^+)}(f) \geq \Omega\left((\Gamma/\log \Gamma) \cdot \log(n/\Gamma)\right).$$

(When $\Gamma \leq 2$, $D^{(2^+)}(f) \leq 1$.)

Proof. The statement about the $\Gamma \leq 2$ case is trivial. For $\Gamma > 2$, assume without loss of generality that $f_{\Gamma-1} \neq f_\Gamma$. (If the inequality does not hold, then $f_{n-\Gamma} \neq f_{n-\Gamma+1}$ and we exchange the roles of the 0 and 1 labels in the rest of the proof.) Assume also for now that $\Gamma/3$ and $3n/\Gamma$ are integers. We describe an adversary that constructs inputs of weight $\Gamma - 1$ or Γ while answering the 2^+ queries of the algorithm consistently.

The adversary maintains two pieces of information: a list of $m = \Gamma/3$ sets $U_1, \ldots, U_m$ of "undefined" variables and a set $I \subseteq [m]$ of the sets of undefined variables that are "active." Initially, $U_\ell = \{\frac{n}{m}(\ell - 1) + 1, \ldots, \frac{n}{m} \cdot \ell\}$ and $I = [m]$. For each query $(Q_{\text{pos}}, Q_{\text{neg}})$, the adversary proceeds as follows:

1. If there is an index $\ell \in I$ such that $|Q_{\text{pos}} \cap U_\ell| > |U_\ell|/m$, then the adversary answers "2^+", assigns the variables in $U_\ell \setminus Q_{\text{pos}}$ the value 0, and updates $U_\ell = U_\ell \cap Q_{\text{pos}}$. We refer to a query handled in this manner as an ℓ-query.
2. Otherwise, let $Q' \subseteq Q_{\text{neg}}$ be a set of size $|Q'| = \min\{2, |Q_{\text{neg}}|\}$. The adversary sets the variables in $U_\ell \cap (Q_{\text{pos}} \cup Q')$ to 0 and updates $U_\ell = U_\ell \setminus (Q_{\text{pos}} \cup Q')$ for each $\ell \in I$. It then returns the answer "0", "1", or "2^+", depending on the size of Q'. We refer to the query as a 0-query in this case.

After answering the query, each set U_ℓ of size $|U_\ell| < 3m$ is considered "defined." When the set U_ℓ is defined, the adversary updates $I = I \setminus \{\ell\}$. If I is still not empty, the adversary also sets 3 of the variables in U_ℓ to one. When the last set U_ℓ is defined, the adversary sets either 2 or 3 of its variables to one.

While not all the sets are defined, the answers of the adversary are consistent with inputs of weight $\Gamma - 1$ and Γ. Therefore, the algorithm must make enough queries to reduce the sizes of $U_1, \ldots, U_m$ to less than $3m$ each. Let $q = q_0 + q_1 + \cdots + q_m$ be the number of queries made by the algorithm, where q_0 represents the number of 0-queries and q_ℓ represents the number of ℓ queries, for $\ell = 1, \ldots, m$.

Consider now a fixed $\ell \in [m]$. Each ℓ-query removes at most a $1 - 1/m$ fraction of the elements in U_ℓ, and each 0-query removes at most $|U_\ell|/m + 2 \leq 2|U_\ell|/m$ elements. So $|U_\ell| < 3m$ holds only when

$$\left(\frac{n}{m}\right) \left(\frac{1}{m}\right)^{q_\ell} \left(1 - \frac{2}{m}\right)^{q_0} < 3m.$$

The inequality holds for each of $\ell = 1, \ldots, m$; taking the product of the m inequalities, we obtain $\left(\frac{n}{m}\right)^m \left(\frac{1}{m}\right)^{q_1 + \cdots + q_m} \left(1 - \frac{2}{m}\right)^{m \cdot q_0} < (3m)^m$, which implies (for $m \geq 4$)

$$\left(\frac{n}{3m^2}\right)^m < m^{q_1 + \cdots + q_m} \left(1 - \frac{2}{m}\right)^{-m \cdot q_0} \leq m^{q_1 + \cdots + q_m} 4^{2q_0} \leq m^{2(q_0 + q_1 + \cdots + q_m)}.$$

Taking the logarithm on both sides and dividing by $2 \log m$, we get $\frac{m}{2 \log m} \log \frac{n}{3m^2} < q_0 + q_1 + \cdots + q_m = q$. Recalling that $m = \Gamma/3$, we get the desired lower bound.

To complete the proof, we now consider the case where $\Gamma/3$ or n/m is not an integer. In this case, let Γ' be the largest multiple of 3 that is no greater than Γ, let $n' = n - (\Gamma - \Gamma')$, and let n'' be the largest multiple of m no greater than n'. Let the adversary fix the value of the last $n - n'$ variables to one and the previous $n' - n''$ variables to zero. We can now repeat the above argument with Γ' and n'' replacing Γ and n.

Randomized lower bound. We have the following result:

Lemma 2. *For any symmetric function $f : \{0,1\}^n \to \{0,1\}$ such that $\Gamma = \Gamma(f) > k$ and integer $k \geq \Gamma$,*

$$R_2^{(k^+)}(f) \geq \Omega\left(\Gamma/k\right).$$

When $\Gamma \leq k$, even $D^{(2^+)}f \leq 1$.

Proof. As in the proof of Lemma 1, assume w.l.o.g. that $f_{\Gamma-1} \neq f_\Gamma$. We prove the theorem using Yao's minimax principle. For $a \in \{\Gamma-1, \Gamma\}$, let $\mathcal{D}_a$ be the uniform distribution over all the inputs with exactly a of the first $2\Gamma - 1$ variables set to 1 and all other variables set to 0. Let $\mathcal{D}$ be the distribution on inputs obtained by randomly selecting $\mathcal{D}_\Gamma$ or $\mathcal{D}_{\Gamma-1}$ with equal probability and then drawing an input from the selected distribution. We will show that any deterministic k^+ decision tree algorithm $\mathcal{A}$ that tries to determine the value of an input drawn from $\mathcal{D}$ with $q < (2\Gamma - 1)/(72k)$ queries must err with probability greater than $1/3$.

Let $\mathcal{P}$ be a random process for answering queries from $\mathcal{A}$ while constructing an input from $\mathcal{D}$. The random process $\mathcal{P}$ starts by selecting an index α uniformly at random from the range $[2\Gamma-1]$, When the algorithm makes a query $(Q_{\text{pos}}, Q_{\text{neg}})$, the process $\mathcal{P}$ begins by randomly ordering the literals in $Q_{\text{pos}} \cup Q_{\text{neg}}$. It then processes the literals one by one – either using the value already assigned to the associated variable or randomly assigning a value to the variable if it is currently undefined – until either (a) k literals have been satisfied, or (b) all the literals in $Q_{\mathrm{pos}} \cup Q_{\mathrm{neg}}$ have been processed. In the first case, the answer "k^+" is returned; otherwise the answer returned corresponds to the number of satisfied literals.

After all the queries have been handled, the process $\mathcal{P}$ assigns random values to the variables in $[2\varGamma - 1] \setminus \{\alpha\}$ that are still undefined such that exactly $\varGamma - 1$ of them have the value 1. There are two possibilities: either x_α has been defined while answering one of the queries, or it is the last undefined variable. If the latter occurs, the process ends by flipping a fair coin to determine the value of x_α and the resulting Hamming weight of the input.

When x_α is the last undefined variable, its value is established by $\mathcal{P}$ *after* all the interaction with the algorithm is completed. Therefore, in this case the algorithm cannot predict the value of x_α – and, as a consequence, the value of the function on the input – with probability greater than $1/2$. So to complete the proof, it suffices to show that the probability that x_α is defined while answering the queries is less than $1/3$.

Let m be the total number of variables whose values are defined while answering the queries and ζ correspond to the event where α is defined while answering t he queries. Then

$$\Pr_{\mathcal{P}}[\zeta] = \sum_{t \geq 0} \Pr_{\mathcal{P}}[m = t] \cdot \Pr_{\mathcal{P}}[\zeta \mid m = t]$$

$$\leq \Pr_{\mathcal{P}}[m \geq (2\varGamma - 1)/6] + \Pr_{\mathcal{P}}[\zeta \mid m < (2\varGamma - 1)/6].$$

We now show that both terms and the right-hand side are less than $1/6$.

First, let's bound the probability that $m \geq (2\varGamma - 1)/6$. Let m_j be the number of variables that are assigned a value by the process while answering the jth query. Each variable assigned a random value satisfies its corresponding literal in the query with probability $\frac{1}{2}$, so $\mathbf{E}[m_j] \leq 2k$ for $j = 1, \ldots, q$. When $q < (2\varGamma - 1)/(72k)$,

$$\mathbf{E}[m] = \mathbf{E}\left[\sum_{j=1}^{q} m_j \right] \leq 2kq < \frac{1}{6} \cdot \left(\frac{2\varGamma - 1}{6} \right).$$

Therefore, by Markov's inequality, $\Pr[m \geq (2\varGamma - 1)/6] < 1/6$.

Finally, let us consider $\Pr_{\mathcal{P}}[\zeta \mid m < (2\varGamma - 1)/6]$. Note that α is chosen uniformly at random from $[2\varGamma - 1]$ by $\mathcal{P}$, so when $m < (2\varGamma - 1)/6$ variables have been defined while answering the queries, the probability that α is one of those variables is less than $1/6$.

6 Other Results

In the full version of this article, we prove a number of results about the deterministic k^+ complexity of non-symmetric functions. We state a number of these results in this section.

First, every boolean function has nontrivial deterministic k^+ complexity:

Theorem 4. *For all* $f : \{0,1\}^n \to \{0,1\}$, $D^{(k^+)}(f) \leq O(n/\log k)$.

The proof of this theorem uses a result from the combinatorial group testing literature [10]. The bound in Theorem 4 is sharp:

Theorem 5. *At least a* $1 - 2^{-2^{n-1}}$ *fraction of functions* $f : \{0,1\}^n \to \{0,1\}$ *satisfy the inequality* $D^{(k^+)}(f) \geq (n/\log(k+1))(1 - o_n(1))$.

We can furthermore exhibit simple explicit functions with this property:

Theorem 6. *Let* EQ $: \{0,1\}^n \times \{0,1\}^n \to \{0,1\}$ *be defined by* EQ$(x,y) = 1$ *iff* $x = y$. *Then* $D^{(k^+)}(\text{EQ}) \geq \Omega(n/\log k)$.

The proof of Theorem 6 is a direct corollary of a more general result linking deterministic k^+ complexity to communication complexity. Let CC(f) denote the deterministic 2-party communication complexity of f (for details, see [17]).

Theorem 7. *For any* $f : \{0,1\}^n \times \{0,1\}^n \to \{0,1\}$, $D^{(k^+)}(f) \geq \Omega(\text{CC}(f)/\log k)$.

Interestingly, the deterministic k^+ complexity of a function is also closely related to its simple decision tree *rank*. The notion of (simple) decision tree rank was first introduced by Ehrenfeucht and Haussler [12] in the context of learning theory, and has the following recursive definition. If T has a single (leaf) node we define RANK$(T) = 0$. Otherwise, supposing the two subtrees of T's root node are T_1 and T_2, we define RANK$(T) = \max\{\text{RANK}(T_1), \text{RANK}(T_2)\}$ if RANK$(T_1) \neq$ RANK(T_2), and RANK$(T) = \text{RANK}(T_1) + 1$ if RANK$(T_1) = \text{RANK}(T_2)$. For a boolean function f, we define RANK(f) to be the minimum rank among simple decision trees computing f.

Theorem 8. *For all* $f : \{0,1\}^n \to \{0,1\}$,

$$\text{RANK}(f)/k \leq D^{(k^+)}(f) \leq O\big(\text{RANK}(f)\log(n/\text{RANK}(f))\big).$$

Both bounds in this inequality may be tight. For the lower bound, it can be shown that for any symmetric function f we have RANK$(f) = \Theta(\Gamma(f))$. This implies that for $t = \Theta(n)$ we have RANK$(T_n^t) = \Theta(n)$; but for this t we also have $D^{(k^+)}(T_n^t) \leq O(n/k)$, by Proposition 1. This does not rule out a lower bound of the form $(\text{RANK}(f)/k) \cdot \log(n/\text{RANK}(f))$, but such a lower bound would be ruled out by the OR function, which has rank 1 but even 1^+ query complexity 1. The upper bound is tight in the case of the so-called ODD-MAX-BIT function, which has rank 1; it can be shown that $D^{(k^+)}(\text{ODD-MAX-BIT}) \geq \Omega(\log n)$, *independent* of k.

Finally, in contrast to the evasiveness conjecture (for simple decision trees), we show that the basic monotone graph property of *connectivity* has $o(v^2)$ deterministic 1^+ complexity:

Theorem 9. *For the connectivity graph property* CONN$_v : \{0,1\}^{\binom{v}{2}} \to \{0,1\}$ *it holds that* $D^{(1^+)}(\text{CONN}_v) \leq v(\lceil \log v \rceil + 1)$.

Acknowledgments

We thank Dana Angluin, Jiang Chen, Sarah C. Eisenstat, Onur Soysal and Yitong Yin for helpful discussions.

References

1. Aigner, M.: Combinatorial Search. Wiley-Teubner Series in Computer Science (1988)
2. Arora, A., Dutta, P., Bapat, S., Kulathumani, V., Zhang, H., Naik, V., Mittal, V., Cao, H., Demirbas, M., Gouda, M., Choi, Y.R., Herman, T., Kulkarni, S.S., Arumugam, U., Nesterenko, M., Vora, A., Miyashita, M.: A line in the sand: A wireless sensor network for target detection, classification, and tracking. Computer Networks (Elsevier) 46(5), 605–634 (2004)
3. Ben-Asher, Y., Newman, I.: Decision trees with boolean threshold queries. J. Comput. Syst. Sci. 51(3), 495–502 (1995)
4. Ben-Or, M.: Lower bounds for algebraic computation trees. In: STOC 1983, pp. 80–86 (1983)
5. Bshouty, N.H.: A subexponential exact learning algorithm for DNF using equivalence queries. Information Processing Letters" 59(3), 37–39 (1996)
6. Buhrman, H., de Wolf, R.: Complexity measures and decision tree complexity: A survey. Theoretical Computer Science 288(1), 21–43 (2002)
7. Chockler, G., Demirbas, M., Gilbert, S., Lynch, N.A., Newport, C.C., Nolte, T.: Consensus and collision detectors in radio networks. Distributed Computing 21(1), 55–84 (2008)
8. Demirbas, M., Soysal, O., Hussain, M.: Singlehop collaborative feedback primitives for wireless sensor networks. In: INFOCOM, pp. 2047–2055 (2008)
9. Dobkin, D., Lipton, R.J.: Multidimensional searching problems. SIAM Journal on Computing 5(2), 181–186 (1976)
10. Du, D.Z., Hwang, F.K.: Combinatorial Group Testing and its Applications. World Scientific, Singapore (2000)
11. Dutta, P., Musaloiu-e, R., Stoica, I., Terzis, A.: Wireless ack collisions not considered harmful. In: HotNets-VII: The Seventh Workshop on Hot Topics in Networks (2008)
12. Ehrenfeucht, A., Haussler, D.: Learning decision trees from random examples. Information and Computation 82(3), 231–246 (1989)
13. Goodrich, M.T., Hirschberg, D.S.: Efficient parallel algorithms for dead sensor diagnosis and multiple access channels. In: SPAA 2006: Proceedings of the eighteenth annual ACM symposium on Parallelism in algorithms and architectures, pp. 118–127. ACM, New York (2006)
14. Hamza, K.: The smallest uniform upper bound on the distance between the mean and the median of the binomial and Poisson distributions. Statistics and Probability Letters 23(1), 21–25 (1995)
15. Jurdzinski, T., Kutylowski, M., Zatopianski, J.: Energy-efficient size approximation of radio networks with no collision detection. In: Ibarra, O.H., Zhang, L. (eds.) COCOON 2002. LNCS, vol. 2387, pp. 279–289. Springer, Heidelberg (2002)
16. Kushilevitz, E., Mansour, Y.: Learning decision trees using the fourier spectrum. SIAM Journal on Computing 22(6), 1331–1348 (1993)

17. Kushilevitz, E., Nisan, N.: Communication Complexity. Cambridge University Press, Cambridge (1997)
18. Moran, S., Snir, M., Manber, U.: Applications of ramsey's theorem to decision tree complexity. J. ACM 32(4), 938–949 (1985)
19. Nisan, N.: CREW PRAMs and decision trees. SIAM Journal on Computing 20(6), 999–1007 (1991)
20. Paturi, R.: On the degree of polynomials that approximate symmetric boolean functions (preliminary version). In: STOC 1992, pp. 468–474 (1992)
21. Rosenberg, A.L.: On the time required to recognize properties of graphs: a problem. SIGACT News 5(4), 15–16 (1973)
22. Yao, A.C.C.: Monotone bipartite graph properties are evasive. SIAM Journal on Computing 17(3), 517–520 (1988)

A   From Threshold Functions to Symmetric Functions

The following simple observation shows that the k^+ decision tree complexity of any symmetric function is essentially determined by that of the threshold functions.

Lemma 3. *For any $2 \leq k \leq t \leq n$, assume that there are deterministic (or zero-sided error randomized) k^+ query algorithms that on input $x \in \{0,1\}^n$ can determine whether $|x|$ is $0, 1, \ldots, t-1$ or at least t with $Q_1^{(k)}(t, n)$ queries (in expectation resp.) and if $|x|$ is $n, n-1, \ldots, n-t+1$ or at most $n-t$ with $Q_0^{(k)}(t, n)$ queries (in expectation resp.). Then for any symmetric function f, there is a deterministic (zero-sided error randomized resp.) $k+$ query algorithm that decides f with $Q_1^{(k)}(\Gamma(f), n) + Q_0^{(k)}(\Gamma(f), n)$ k^+ queries (in expectation resp.).*

Proof. The algorithm for f is a simple one: first run the given algorithm and decide if $|x|$ is $0, 1, \ldots, \Gamma(f) - 1$ or at least $\Gamma(f)$. Note that if $|x| < \Gamma(f)$, then since we know $|x|$, we can determine $f(x)$. Similarly, using the other algorithm we can determine $|x|$ if $|x| > n - \Gamma(f)$ in which case we again know $f(x)$ exactly. Thus, the only case left is $\Gamma(f) \leq |x| \leq n - \Gamma(f)$. However, in this case by definition of $\Gamma(\cdot)$, the value of f is constant (and hence, we can determine $f(x)$).

It is easy to check that the query complexity of the algorithm above is at most $Q_1^{(k)}(\Gamma(f), n) + Q_0^{(k)}(\Gamma(f), n)$.

Brief Announcement: Regional Consecutive Leader Election in Mobile Ad-Hoc Networks

Hyun Chul Chung[1],[*], Peter Robinson[2],[**], and Jennifer L. Welch[1],[*]

[1] Texas A&M University, Department of Computer Science & Engineering,
College Station TX 77843, USA
{h0c8412,welch}@cse.tamu.edu

[2] Technische Universität Wien, Embedded Computing Systems Group (E182/2)
Treitlstrasse 1-3, A-1040 Vienna, Austria
robinson@ecs.tuwien.ac.at

Abstract. In this paper we introduce the regional consecutive leader election (RCLE) problem, which extends the classic leader election problem to the continuously-changing environment of mobile ad-hoc networks. We assume that mobile nodes can fail by crashing, and might enter or exit the region of interest at any time. We require the existence of certain paths which ensures a bound on the time for propagation of information within the region. We present and prove correct an algorithm that solves RCLE for a fixed region in 2 or 3-dimensional space. Our algorithm does not rely on the knowledge of the total number of nodes in the system nor on a common startup time. Additionally, we introduce a condition on mobility that is sufficient to ensure the existence of the paths required by our RCLE algorithm.

Problem Description. We consider leader election among mobile nodes that reside within a fixed geographic region R. The nodes communicate via wireless broadcasts and are subject to crash failures. We assume the locations of the nodes ensure a bounded communication diameter D, meaning that if a node in R initiates the propagation of a message at some time t, then the message will be relayed through at most D hops to any node that stays in the region sufficiently long after time t. We also assume that the execution of mobile nodes is carried out in synchronous rounds and each node knows its exact location and time information, which can be provided by a GPS device, for example. We define the problem of electing a leader among mobile nodes within an arbitrary fixed region as the *Regional Consecutive Leader Election* (RCLE) problem. Roughly speaking, an algorithm solves the RCLE problem if the following properties hold:

(*Agreement*) All nodes in the region that elect a leader elect the same leader.

(*Termination*) If a live (i.e. not yet crashed) node p remains in the region for a sufficiently long period of time, then p must elect a leader within bounded time.

---

[*] The work of Hyun Chul Chung and Jennifer L. Welch was supported in part by Texas Higher Education Coordinating Board NHARP grant 000512-0130-2007.
[**] Peter Robinson has been supported by the Austrian Science Foundation (FWF) project P20529.

C. Scheideler (Ed.): ALGOSENSORS 2010, LNCS 6451, pp. 89–91, 2010.

(*Validity*) If some live node p in the region elects a leader, then that leader node must have been in the region in the near past.

(*Stability*) If some live node p in the region stops considering some other node q as the leader, then q has either crashed or left the region in the near past.

Algorithm. In the full paper [1,2], we present and prove correct an algorithm for the RCLE problem. The proposed algorithm guarantees that the node that has been in the region R the longest has priority for becoming the leader. An informal description of the algorithm follows.

Once a leader is elected, it generates a "leader" message every D rounds, which is propagated throughout R. The propagation is ensured by the "relaying" message communication pattern employed, in which every node sends the contents of its message buffer at every round. There are two situations in which a node p must elect (or re-elect) a leader. One situation is when p has already chosen a leader but p fails to receive a message from the leader in a timely fashion; this situation occurs if the leader crashes or leaves the region. The other situation is when p enters the region.

In order to elect (or re-elect) a leader, p generates an "instance" message containing p's id, the current round number, and the round number when p first entered R. If, during the next $2D$ rounds, p does not receive a leader message and does not receive an instance message that was generated by a node that entered R earlier than p did, then p elects itself as leader. On the other hand, if p receives a leader message before $2D$ rounds elapse, then p adopts the generator of that message as its leader. Finally, if, during those $2D$ rounds, p does not receive a leader message but does receive one or more instance messages that were generated by nodes that entered R earlier than p did, then, among the generators of those received instance messages, p sets the generator that entered R the earliest as its "candidate leader" and waits for a specific number of rounds which depends on the round when the candidate leader generated the instance message. If p receives a leader message from its candidate leader during this waiting period, then it elects that node as leader, otherwise it initiates a new instance message.

The Condition on Mobility. We also discuss what assumptions are necessary to guarantee a bounded communication diameter D for nodes within the region. For this end, we introduce a condition on mobility that ensures that information propagates towards its destination in every round.

We first define some basic properties for our mobility condition. Let R be a 2-dimensional rectangular region.[1] Fix a constant δ such that $\delta > 0$. Given two positions ϕ_1 and ϕ_2, let $dist(\phi_1, \phi_2)$ be the Euclidean distance between ϕ_1 and ϕ_2.

To specify which broadcasts are received by a process in a round, we use the notion of two processes p and q being *connected in the round*: this means that throughout the round, the Euclidean distance between p and q is at most C, the (common) wireless communication radius.

---

[1] Our results can easily be extended to 3 dimensions by considering R to be a rectalgular cuboid instead of a rectangle.

Definition 1 (Well-directed Propagation Sequence). *Let $p_0, p_1, \ldots, p_{n-1}$ be a sequence of nodes such that p_i is at position $\phi_i = (x_i, y_i)$ at the beginning of round $r + i$, $0 \le i \le n - 1$, and let $\phi_n = (x_n, y_n)$ be any position in R. Without loss of generality, assume that $x_0 \le x_n$ and $y_0 \le y_n$.*[2]

The sequence of positions $\phi_0, \phi_1, \ldots, \phi_n$ is called a well-directed propagation sequence from p_0 to ϕ_n starting at round r, *denoted as $S^r_{\phi_0 \leadsto \phi_n}$, if it holds that*
(a) ϕ_0 and ϕ_n are both in R,
(b) p_i broadcasts in round $r + i$,
(c) p_i and p_{i+1} are live and connected in round $r + i$, $0 \le i \le n - 2$, and throughout round $r + n - 1$, p_{n-1} is live and within distance C of ϕ_n,
(d) (Progress) $\delta \le dist(\phi_i, \phi_{i+1})$, $0 \le i \le n - 1$, and
(e) (Well-directed) $x_i \le x_{i+1}$ and $y_i \le y_{i+1}$, $0 \le i \le n - 1$.

Intuitively speaking, the (well-directed) requirement of Definition 1 says that as information propagates to its destination, it should lie within a certain geographic sector and the (progress) requirement of Definition 1 says that information gets closer to its destination in each round. The (well-directed) requirement in conjunction with the (progress) requirement, as we discuss below, allows us to calculate an upper bound on the length of the sequence.

Suppose nodes move in such a way that the following condition is satisfied:

Mobility Assumption: *For every node p that is live throughout round r and broadcasts a message at the beginning of round r at position ϕ_p in R, and for all positions ϕ_q in R, there exists a well-directed propagation sequence $S^r_{\phi_p \leadsto \phi_q}$ starting at round r.*

Then, we obtain the bounded communication diameter $D = \lceil \frac{L_x + L_y}{\delta} \rceil$ where L_x and L_y are the width and height of region R, respectively.

References

1. Chung, H.C., Robinson, P., Welch, J.L.: Regional consecutive leader election in mobile ad-hoc networks. Technical Report 12/2010, Vienna University of Technology, Embedded Computing Systems Group (E182/2), Treitlstr. 1-3, 1040 Vienna, Austria (2010)
2. Chung, H.C., Robinson, P., Welch, J.L.: Regional consecutive leader election in mobile ad-hoc networks. In: Proc. 6th International Workshop on Foundations of Mobile Computing (DIALM-POMC 2010) (to appear in September 2010)

---

[2] One can easily adjust the coordinate system to obtain this property.

From Key Predistribution to Key Redistribution*

Jacek Cichoń, Zbigniew Gołębiewski, and Mirosław Kutyłowski**

Institute of Mathematics and Computer Science, Wrocław University of Technology
{firstname.familyname}@pwr.wroc.pl

Abstract. One of crucial disadvantages of key predistribution schemes for ad hoc networks is that if devices A and B use a shared key K to determine their session keys, then any adversarial device that holds K can impersonate A against B (or vice versa). Also, the adversary can eavesdrop communication between A and B for the lifetime of the system.

We develop a dynamic scheme where a system provider periodically broadcasts random temporal keys (e.g. via a GSM network) encrypted with keys from the main predistribution pool. Shared temporal keys (and not the keys from the main pool) are used to establish session keys. The trick is that the scheme broadcast is organized in such a way that with a high probability two devices share much more temporal keys than the keys from the main pool of keys. It is a kind of paradox, but this makes it possible not only to protect communication against an adversary that has collected a large fraction of keys from the main pool, but also makes the system well suited for authentication purposes.

Keywords: key predistribution, wireless ad hoc network, eavesdropping, attack detection, dynamic key management.

1 Introduction

One of the key security challenges for ad hoc wireless networks of tiny artefacts is to protect node to node wireless communication. It concerns confidentiality, message integrity as well as authentication of the nodes. While these problems have satisfactory solutions for standard networks, there are many reasons for which these techniques are inadequate or infeasible in case networks of tiny artefacts. Unfortunately, lack of really good solutions in this area is a source of many risks and severely reduces market chances of these networks.

So far usage of asymmetric cryptographic techniques for tiny devices is regarded as limited, even if there is a significant progress in adjusting asymmetric techniques to limitations of tiny devices. On the other hand, symmetric techniques are generally accepted as implementable on most devices (even if there is a struggle to adjust them to the requirements of ultra lightweight devices).

One of the fundamental techniques in the area of symmetric solutions is random key predistribution [1]. For this approach, a system provider generates a large pool of keys $\mathcal{K}$. Before a device gets deployed in the network, it gets a *random* subset of keys from

---

* Partially supported by EU within the 7th Framework Programme, contract 215270 (FRONTS).
** Contact author: Miroslaw.Kutylowski@pwr.wroc.pl

C. Scheideler (Ed.): ALGOSENSORS 2010, LNCS 6451, pp. 92–104, 2010.

$\mathcal{K}$ of cardinality k. The parameter k is chosen as a function of the size n of $\mathcal{K}$. The main idea is that due to the birthday paradox already for k of order $\sqrt{n}$, two random k-element subsets of $\mathcal{K}$ have a common key with a fairly large probability. In this scenario, if two devices want to establish a secure link, they derive a session key from the shared key(s).

Advantages and Disadvantages of Key Predistribution Schemes. Key predistribution has many notable advantages. First, there are no major scalability problems. For a reasonable size of the key pool there is practically unlimited number of different k-element subsets of the pool of keys. Choosing the keys at random for a given device requires no bookkeeping of already used subsets.

However, there are substantial disadvantages as well. It is impossible to guarantee that a pair of devices really shares a key – due to random character of key assignment it may happen that no key is shared even if their expected number is one or more. Irregularities in the number of shared keys can be avoided by a careful choice of the subsets of keys (see e.g. combinatorial designs [2]). One can also increase the number of keys per device [3] so that multiple keys are shared by communicating devices with a fair probability. However, in order to get k shared keys the size of the random subsets has to be at least of the order $n^{(k-1)/k}$, where n is the size of the key pool. Another approach is to use indirect links: if a device A and B have no shared key, but there is a different device C in their range so that A shares a key with C and B shares another key with C, then A and B can communicate securely via C in order to establish a session key [4,3].

Eavesdropping and Impersonation. The main problem of random key predistribution and its variants is lack of resilience against collecting the keys. by an adversary. Namely, the adversary can get some of the devices and retrieve the keys from them (the devices are to be cheap and so they are not necessarily tamper resistant). Moreover, the adversary might be an internal one - a user or users holding some number of devices and using them in a malicious way. Namely, assume that a device A establishes a link with a device B. The session key depends on a key K (or keys) shared by A and B. However, due to the key predistribution mechanism, K is kept by many other devices, the adversary having any of them can eavesdrop the messages exchanged by devices A and B. Moreover, since implicit authentication of B is based on knowledge of K, the adversary can impersonate B.

There are some efforts to deter such attacks. One of them is to use q-composite schemes [3]: in order to establish a link at least q shared keys are necessary. Since the adversary has to hold all shared keys used by communicating parties, this seems to improve significantly resilience to the attack. However, in order to guarantee q shared keys, each device must hold a much larger fraction of keys from the key pool. This in turn makes collecting the keys by the adversary much faster. It turn out that using q-composite schemes improves the situation for adversaries holding relatively few devices. and has the opposite effect if the adversary holds relatively many devices.

Ideally, each pair of devices should get a unique shared key. However, this is hardly possible in practice, since in a system consisting of N devices each of them would have to hold $N-1$ keys and the set of devices would have to be fixed in advance. This can be improved by Blom [5] by an algebraic construction: a separate key can be computed for every pair of devices and this key remains inaccessible for the adversary as long as he holds key material from less than λ devices. There are some other designs of this kind (e.g. [6]) reducing the number of keys per device. Still, there is a problem of adversaries collecting devices. In case of [6] it suffices to collect $2 \log N$ devices to break the system of N devices completely.

Let us remark that the situation is much easier, if the devices are not mobile and their so leaking a key to the adversary has a limited impact (see e.g. [7]).

Some progress against the adversary collecting the keys has been achieved in [8] – adversary's costs are increased by a (small) constant factor. With a few *levels* of the same key the chances of the adversary are decreased by a constant factor.

Design Goals. Our goal is to strengthen the key predistribution scheme so that it better protects the system against collecting key material by an adversary aiming to impersonate devices or to eavesdrop encrypted communication.

As devices communicate between themselves in a wireless way, it can also be assumed that they could also be controlled by a broadcast infrastructure run by the system provider. For instance, a GSM network or an overlay broadcasting system can be used for this purpose. On the other hand, cooperation with the infrastructure should be limited in bandwidth and frequency. Preferably, there should be no uploading data from devices to the system, as it may cause high energy usage of battery operated devices.

Our Contribution. We propose schemes with temporal keys broadcasted by the system provider. They have the following properties:

- if devices A and C communicate, but C impersonates itself as B, then after broadcasting new temporal keys A discovers fraud with a fair probability (this holds even if C collects some number of keys from other devices),
- an adversary that collects a (not too large) fraction of keys from the pool is cannot decrypt all traffic between a pairs of devices. With a high probability there will be some time intervals, when he cannot decrypt the messages.

In Sect. 4 we also show a mechanism related to the main construction for revoking the keys from predistribution.

2 Dynamic Key Redistribution

2.1 Model

Our system consists of the following components:

Devices: they are sensor devices, or mobile devices etc. which need to establish protected communication links between themselves, each device is capable of holding a limited number of keys and can use symmetric encryption, a hash function and a pseudo-random number generator.

Broadcasting system: it is a broadcasting wireless system that covers the area of operation of the devices - each device is in its range and can receive the messages sent by this system. The messages sent by the system do not depend on the receivers' locations. The broadcasting system is run by the system provider.

At each moment of system operation there is one or more key pools. If $\mathcal{K} = \{K_1, \ldots, K_n\}$ is such a pool, then each device holds a limited number of keys from $\mathcal{K}$. Each device holds an ID; the identifiers of the keys accessible to the device must be easy to derive from the ID of the device. For instance, node v_S holds the set of keys $\mathcal{K}_S = \{K_{s_1}, \ldots, K_{s_k}\} \subset \mathcal{K}$, where $(s_1, \ldots, s_k, \ldots) = R(S, t)$, t is a current public parameter, and R is a pseudo-random number generator yielding numbers in the range $[1, n]$.

Like in the standard key predistribution scheme we assume that if devices v_c, v_d meet and wish to establish a secured link, they first exchange their ID's. Then each device determines the ID's of the keys shared by v_c, v_d, say $K_{u_1}, \ldots, K_{u_b}$ with $u_1 < u_2 < \ldots < u_b$. Then the session key is computed from

$$H|(K_{u_1}, \ldots, K_{u_b}, c, d, t),$$

where t is some current parameter (like date and time), H is a hash function and $H|(-)$ denotes the output of H truncated to the number of bits of the session key.

2.2 Scheme Description

The system provider periodically exchanges the keys used by the devices. The new keys are broadcasted in an encrypted form. Since the devices are not physically available, the exchange need to be performed by broadcasting the new keys. Of course, the new keys must be accessible to the entitled devices only. Since the only secret material stored in the devices are the old keys from the pool, the broadcaster uses them to encrypt the new keys.

Assume that $\mathcal{K} = \{K_1, \ldots, K_n\}$ is the current pool of keys used by the devices and the system provider decides to provide a new pool of keys $\widetilde{\mathcal{K}} = \{\widetilde{K}_1, \ldots, \widetilde{K}_n\}$.

A naïve solution is to transmit the following sequence of ciphertexts:

$$E_{K_1}(\widetilde{K}_1), E_{K_2}(\widetilde{K}_2), \ldots, E_{K_n}(\widetilde{K}_n)$$

However, the only advantage of such a scheme is limiting the number of ciphertexts encrypted with the same key that can be recorded from the network. It does not help against impersonation or similar misuse of keys, as if an adversary uses K_i for the attack, then he will use $\widetilde{K}_i$ in the same way.

The main idea of our scheme is that after the key update the indexes of the keys shared by two devices change. Our goal is the following property:

Proposition 1. *If at some moment devices A and B establish session key using the keys $K_{u_1}, \ldots, K_{u_b}$ that they share, then after performing key update they share keys with different indexes, say $\widetilde{K}_{u'_1}, \ldots, \widetilde{K}_{u'_{b'}}$ where $\{u_1, \ldots, u_b\} \neq \{u'_1, \ldots, u'_{b'}\}$ with high probability. Moreover, knowledge of shared keys before the update does not suffice to learn the shared keys after the update.*

In our architecture there two pools of keys. One of them is the main pool $\mathcal{K}$, which is unchanged except for rebuilding the system. Unlike for the classical key predistribution scheme, $\mathcal{K}$ is not used for establishing connections between the devices. Its purpose is to encrypt the current values of the keys from the second pool $\widetilde{\mathcal{K}}$, which are updated as frequently as needed. The keys from pool $\widetilde{\mathcal{K}}$ are used for establishing pairwise session keys.

The pool $\widetilde{\mathcal{K}}$ contains exactly n/m keys generated at random. Parameter m will be carefully chosen, generally $m \geq 2$ is a small constant. During a key update each key $\widetilde{K}_i$ is broadcasted m times, encrypted by m different keys from pool $\mathcal{K}$, namely by ciphertexts

$$E_{K_{\pi(i,1)}}(\widetilde{K}_i), \ldots, E_{K_{\pi(i,m)}}(\widetilde{K}_i)$$

where π is a bijection between $\{1, \ldots, n/m\} \times \{1, \ldots, m\}$ and $\{1, \ldots, n\}$ chosen in a pseudo-random way. The ciphertexts are transmitted according to the order of the keys used for encryption, that is as

$$E_{K_1}(\ldots), E_{K_2}(\ldots), \ldots, E_{K_n}(\ldots) \,.$$

Proposition 2. *Devices A and B may share a key $\widetilde{K}_i$ for two reasons:*

Case 1: *A and B share a key $K_j \in \mathcal{K}$, and this key has been used to encrypt $\widetilde{K}_i$,*

Case 2: *one device holds K_j, the other one holds $K_{j'}$, and $\pi(i,u) = j$, $\pi(i,v) = j'$, for $u \neq v$ so that both A and B get $\widetilde{K}_i$, but they neither share K_j nor $K_{j'}$.*

The shared keys from $\widetilde{K}$ from Case 2 are called accidental.

2.3 Communication Complexity

Key update requires transmitting n ciphertexts. For the example values $n = 2^{16}$ and key length 128, the volume of the ciphertexts to be sent is 2^{23} bits long, that is, 32KB, which is acceptable for a GSM transmission. Each device has to listen to a small fraction of transmission, namely of the size $\sqrt{n} \cdot 128 = 2^{15}$ bits, that is, 128B. If we use a larger number of keys such as $n = 2^{20}$ (a pool with over one million keys), we typically store 2^{10} keys in a device, so 512B, which is quite a lot. Still, the transmission volume is 2^{27}b=128MB. For transmission speed 2Mb/sec, it takes roughly one minute to send the keys.

3   Properties of Dynamic Key Redistribution

First we consider the number of keys from pool $\widetilde{\mathcal{K}}$ shared by two devices after a key redistribution. Our goal is to show that there are quite many such keys (much more than in case of the keys from $\mathcal{K}$). Later we shall see that it leads to quite reliable authentication of devices and message confidentiality, when the keys of $\widetilde{\mathcal{K}}$ are renewed.

Theorem 1. *Assume that the key pool $\widetilde{\mathcal{K}}$ contains n/m keys, each encrypted with m different keys from $\mathcal{K}$ ($|\mathcal{K}| = n$) during the key update. Assume that each device holds exactly k keys each from the pool $\mathcal{K}$. Then :*

1. *the expected number of keys from $\mathcal{K}$ shared by devices A and B chosen at random equals*

$$k^2/n \, ,$$

2. *the expected number of keys from $\widetilde{\mathcal{K}}$ shared by A and B equals*

$$\frac{n\left(\binom{n}{k} - \binom{n-m}{k}\right)^2}{m\binom{n}{k}^2} \, .$$

Remark 1. By Theorem 1 we can easily compute the expected number of accidental keys shared by two devices as the difference of the expressions from points 2 and 1. As the expression from point 2 is hard to interpret, we later provide some estimations and "thumb rules". Nevertheless, the expressions from Theorem 1 can be used for numerical calculations.

Proof. In the proof we heavily use tools from the analytic combinatorics, which turn out to be extremely useful here. For more information concerning these techniques we refer the reader to [9,10]. From now on we assume that the reader is familiar with basic methods from this field.

Computing the Number of Shared Keys from $\mathcal{K}$. [1] Devices A and B pick at random k different keys each from pool $\mathcal{K}$. Below we calculate the expected number of keys that they share. Let $\mathcal{Z}$ denote a combinatorial class that describes one key from pool $\mathcal{K}$. Then $\mathcal{Z} = (\{\epsilon, a, b\}, |.|)$ where $|\epsilon| = 1, |a| = z$ and $|b| = u$. One can read this as follows: if device A holds the key K_i, then it is marked by a. Analogously, if the device B holds the key K_i, then it is marked by b. If neither A nor B holds the key K_i, then it is marked by a neutral element ϵ. Obviously, the key can be held simultaneously by A and B, then it is marked by a and b. The generating function of the class $\mathcal{Z}$ is

$$Z(z, u) = 1 + z + u + zu \, .$$

Since we are interested in the number of keys shared by A and B, we introduce parameter χ. It associates the number of keys shared by A and B to the distribution of keys in the devices A and B. Since zu describes a key shared by A and B, we multiply it by a formal variable w that marks χ. Therefore, we obtain the multivariate generating function

$$Z'(z, u, w) = 1 + z + u + wzu \, .$$

Let $\mathcal{U}$ denote the class describing the key pool $\mathcal{K}$. Since the size of $\mathcal{K}$ equals n, the generating function that describes the pool $\mathcal{K}$ is

$$U(z, u, w) = (Z'(z, u, w))^n \, .$$

---

[1] For this case it is relatively easy to compute the expected value with elementary methods. However, we use this part to warm up before the next subsection.

By [9], the expected value of the parameter χ is given by the formula

$$E[\chi] = \frac{[z^k][u^k]\frac{\partial U(z,u,w)}{\partial w}\Big|_{w=1}}{[z^k][u]U(z,u,1)} , \tag{1}$$

where $[z^k]f(z)$ denotes the coefficient of z^k in $f(z)$. By straightforward calculations we get

$$\frac{\partial U(z,u,w)}{\partial w}\Big|_{w=1} = nuz(1+z)^{n-1}(1+u)^{n-1} ,$$

and

$$U(z,u,1) = (1+u)^n(1+z)^n .$$

Now we can apply these values for (1):

$$E[\chi] = \frac{[z^k][u^k]nuz(1+z)^{n-1}(1+u)^{n-1}}{[z^k][u^k](1+u)^n(1+z)^n} =$$

$$\frac{n([z^{k-1}](1+z)^{n-1})([u^{k-1}](1+u)^{n-1})}{([z^k](1+z)^n)([u^k](1+u)^n)} =$$

$$\frac{n\binom{n-1}{k-1}\binom{n-1}{k-1}}{\binom{n}{k}\binom{n}{k}} = \frac{k^2}{n} .$$

This concludes the proof of the first part of Theorem 1.

Computing the Number of Shared Keys from $\widetilde{\mathcal{K}}$. Let $\mathcal{P}$ be the combinatorial class that describes a key $\widetilde{K} \in \widetilde{\mathcal{K}}$. Each key from the pool $\widetilde{\mathcal{K}}$ is encrypted by exactly m keys from the pool $\mathcal{K}$. Thus, the generating function of $\mathcal{P}$ equals

$$P(z,u) = Z(z,u) = (1 + z + u + zu)^m$$

$$= \sum_{j_1+j_2+j_3+j_4=m} \binom{m}{j_1, j_2, j_3, j_4} 1^{j_1} z^{j_2} u^{j_3} (zu)^{j_4} .$$

Since we are interested in the number of keys from the pool $\widetilde{\mathcal{K}}$ shared by A and B, we introduce parameter $\widetilde{\chi}$. It associates the number of keys from the pool $\widetilde{\mathcal{K}}$ shared by A and B to the distribution of keys from the pool $\mathcal{K}$ in the devices A and B.

A key $\widetilde{K} \in \widetilde{\mathcal{K}}$ is shared by A and B, if it is encrypted by at least one of the keys of the device A from the pool $\mathcal{K}$ and one of the keys of the device B from the pool $\mathcal{K}$. Therefore, we multiply the sum:

$$\sum_T \binom{m}{j_1, j_2, j_3, j_4} 1^{j_1} z^{j_2} u^{j_3} (zu)^{j_4} ,$$

where T is a set of quadruples (j_1, j_2, j_3, j_4) satisfying the conditions

$$(j_1 + j_2 + j_3 + j_4 = m) \wedge \neg(j_1 + j_2 = m \vee j_1 + j_3 = m)$$

by a formal variable w that marks $\widetilde{\chi}$. Thus, $P'(z, u, w)$ equals

$$1 + \sum_{x=1}^{m} \binom{m}{x} z^x + \sum_{x=1}^{m} \binom{m}{x} u^x + w \cdot \sum_{(j_1, j_2, j_3, j_4) \in T} \binom{m}{j_1, j_2, j_3, j_4} 1^{j_1} z^{j_2} u^{j_3} (zu)^{j_4}$$

$$= 1 + ((1+z)^m - 1) + ((1+u)^m - 1) +$$
$$w\left((1 + z + u + zu)^m - 1 - ((1+z)^m - 1) - ((1+u)^m - 1)\right)$$
$$= w((1+u)(1+z))^m - (w-1)((1+u)^m + (1+z)^m - 1) .$$

Since the pool $\widetilde{\mathcal{K}}$ contains $\frac{n}{m}$ keys, the generating function describing the whole pool $\widetilde{\mathcal{K}}$ is given by $R(z, u, w) = (P'(z, u, w))^{\frac{n}{m}}$.

By Equation 1 we calculate the expected number of keys from $\widetilde{\mathcal{K}}$ shared by the devices A and B:

$$\partial_w R(z, u, w)\big|_{w=1} =$$
$$\frac{n}{m} \left(((1+u)(1+z))^{n-m}(1 - (1+u)^m - (1+z)^m + ((1+u)(1+z))^m)\right) =$$
$$\frac{n}{m}((1+z)(1+u))^{n-m}\left(((1+z)(1+u))^m + 1 - (1+z)^m - (1+u)^m\right) =$$
$$\frac{n}{m}\left((1+z)^n(1+u)^n + (1+z)^{n-m}(1+u)^{n-m} - \right.$$
$$\left. (1+z)^n(1+u)^{n-m} - (1+z)^{n-m}(1+u)^n\right) .$$

Since $[z^k][u^k](1+z)^x(1+u)^y = [z^k](1+z)^x[u^k](1+u)^y$, we have

$$[z^k][u^k]\partial_w R(z, u, w)\big|_{w=1} =$$
$$\frac{n}{m}\left([z^k](1+z)^n[u^k](1+u)^n + [z^k](1+z)^{n-m}[u^k](1+u)^{n-m} - \right.$$
$$\left. [z^k](1+z)^n[u^k](1+u)^{n-m} - [z^k](1+z)^{n-m}[u^k](1+u)^n\right) =$$
$$\frac{n}{m}\left(\binom{n}{k}^2 + \binom{n-m}{k}^2 - 2\binom{n}{k}\binom{n-m}{k}\right) = \frac{n}{m}\left(\binom{n}{k} - \binom{n-m}{k}\right)^2 .$$

The denominator of Equation 1 is given by

$$[z^k][u^k]R(z, u, 1) = [z^k][u^k](1 + z + u + zu)^n = [z^k](1+z)^n[u^k](1+u)^n = \binom{n}{k}^2.$$

Hence,

$$E[\widetilde{\chi}] = \frac{[z^k][u^k]\partial_w R(z, u, w)\big|_{w=1}}{[z^k][u^k]R(z, u, 1)} = \frac{n\left(\binom{n}{k} - \binom{n-m}{k}\right)^2}{m\binom{n}{k}^2} . \qquad \square$$

Diagram 1 shows the values of expected values from Theorem 1 for different values of k and m. Below we give also some approximations.

Corollary 1. *Let m be fixed and $k = \Theta(\sqrt{n})$. Then*

$$E[\widetilde{\chi}] = \frac{m}{n}k^2 + O\left(\frac{1}{\sqrt{n}}\right) .$$

Proof. Notice that using Exp-Log transform and expansion $\ln\frac{1}{1-x} = \sum_{j\geq 1}\frac{x^j}{j}$ we have

$$\frac{\binom{n-m}{k}}{\binom{n}{k}} = \frac{(n-m)^{\underline{k}}}{n^{\underline{k}}} = \prod_{a=0}^{k-1}\left(1-\frac{m}{n-a}\right) = \exp\left(-\sum_{a=0}^{k-1}\ln\frac{1}{1-\frac{m}{n-a}}\right) =$$

$$\exp\left(-\sum_{a=0}^{k-1}\sum_{j\geq 1}\frac{\left(\frac{m}{n-a}\right)^j}{j}\right) = \exp\left(-\sum_{a=0}^{k-1}\frac{m}{n-a}-\sum_{a=0}^{k-1}\sum_{j\geq 2}\frac{\left(\frac{m}{n-a}\right)^j}{j}\right) =$$

$$\exp\left(-\sum_{a=0}^{k-1}\frac{m}{n-a}\right)\exp\left(-\sum_{a=0}^{k-1}\sum_{j\geq 2}\frac{\left(\frac{m}{n-a}\right)^j}{j}\right).$$

Since m is fixed, $k = \Theta(\sqrt{n})$ and $\frac{m}{n-a} \leq \frac{m}{n-k}$ for $0 \leq a \leq k-1$, we have

$$\sum_{a=0}^{k-1}\sum_{j\geq 2}\frac{\left(\frac{m}{n-a}\right)^j}{j} = \sum_{a=0}^{k-1}O\left(\left(\frac{1}{n-a}\right)^2\right) = O\left(k\left(\frac{1}{n-k}\right)^2\right) = O\left(\frac{1}{n}\right).$$

Moreover,

$$\sum_{a=0}^{k-1}\frac{m}{n-a} = m(H_n - H_{n-k}) = m\left(\ln(n)-\ln(n-k)+O\left(\frac{1}{n}\right)\right),$$

so

$$\frac{\binom{n-m}{k}}{\binom{n}{k}} = \exp\left(m\left(\ln\left(\frac{n-k}{n}\right)+O\left(\frac{1}{n}\right)\right)\right)\exp\left(O\left(\frac{1}{n}\right)\right) =$$

$$\left(1-\frac{k}{n}\right)^m\exp\left(O\left(\frac{1}{n}\right)\right) = \left(1-\frac{k}{n}\right)^m + O\left(\frac{1}{n}\right).$$

Therefore

$$E[\tilde{\chi}] = \frac{n}{m}\left(1-(1-\frac{k}{n})^m+O(\frac{1}{n})\right)^2 =$$

$$\frac{n}{m}\left(\frac{km}{n}+O(\frac{k}{n})^2+O(\frac{1}{n})\right)^2 = \frac{n}{m}\left(\frac{km}{n}+O(\frac{1}{n})\right)^2 =$$

$$\frac{n}{m}\left((\frac{km}{n})^2+O(\frac{km}{n^2})+O(\frac{1}{n^2})\right) = \frac{n}{m}\left((\frac{km}{n})^2+O(\frac{1}{n^{\frac{3}{2}}})\right) = \frac{k^2m}{n}+O(\frac{1}{\sqrt{n}}).$$

$\square$

As we have seen, if we apply dynamic key redistribution with parameter m, then the number of keys shared is approximately m for standard values of k and n (instead of just 1 shared key in case of random key predistribution). So taking a small value like $m = 16$ leads to quite many shared keys for a pair of devices. Now we check what are the consequences of this fact for an adversary trying to hold a broken link between devices A and B using keys stored in device C (recall that for the standard random key predistribution if this link is broken, then it lasts forever!).

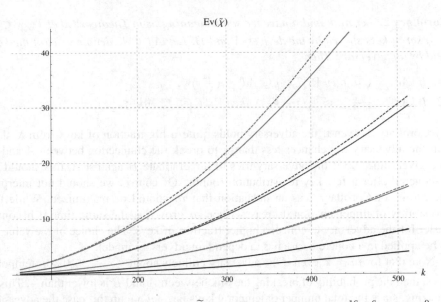

Fig. 1. The expected number of keys from $\widetilde{\mathcal{K}}$ shared by A and B for $n = 2^{16}$, $2^6 \leq k \leq 2^9$ and $m = 1$ (black plot), $m = 2$ (blue plot), $m = 4$ (dark pink plot), $m = 8$ (dark red plot), $m = 16$ (green plot) (dashed plots present approximations from Corollary 1)

Theorem 2. *Let m, k and n have the same meaning as in Theorem 1. Let $k \leq \frac{n}{m}$. Assume that the number of keys from $\widetilde{\mathcal{K}}$ shared by devices A and B is m. Then the probability that a random device C holds all temporal keys shared by A and B is at most*

$$\left(\frac{km}{n}\right)^m.$$

Proof. Assume that after redistribution of the keys from pool $\widetilde{\mathcal{K}}$ $\left(|\widetilde{\mathcal{K}}| = \frac{n}{m}\right)$, the devices A and B share a set $T_{A,B} \subset \widetilde{\mathcal{K}}$ temporal keys ($|T_{A,B}| = m$) and the device C holds a set $T_C \subset \widetilde{\mathcal{K}}$ temporal keys ($|T_c| \leq k$). We shall estimate probability that $T_{A,B} \subseteq T_C$.

Let Q be a random subset of the temporal keys $\widetilde{\mathcal{K}}$ of cardinality k. An easy domination argument shows that $\Pr[T_{A,B} \subseteq T_C] \leq \Pr[T_{A,B} \subseteq Q]$. Next, we have

$$\Pr[T_{A,B} \subseteq Q] = \frac{\binom{\frac{n}{m}-m}{k-m}}{\binom{\frac{n}{m}}{k}} = \frac{\binom{\frac{n}{m}-m}{k-m}}{\left(\frac{n}{m}\right)^m \binom{\frac{n}{m}-m}{k-m}} = \frac{k^{\underline{m}}}{\left(\frac{n}{m}\right)^{\underline{m}}}.$$

If $m < \frac{n}{m} - 1$ and $k < \frac{n}{m}$, then $(k - (a+1))/(\frac{n}{m} - (a+1)) < (k-a)/(\frac{n}{m} - a)$. Therefore

$$\Pr[T_{A,B} \subseteq Q] \leq \left(\frac{k}{\frac{n}{m}}\right)^m = \left(\frac{km}{n}\right)^m. \qquad \square$$

Corollary 2. *Let* m, k *and* n *have the same meaning as in Theorem 1. Let* $T_{A,B} \subset \widetilde{\mathcal{K}}$ *be a set of keys shared by the devices* A *and* B. *Let* $Ad \subset \widetilde{\mathcal{K}}$ *denote a set of the keys held by an adversary. Then*

1. *If* $|Ad| = \sqrt{n}$, *then* $\Pr[T_{A,B} \subseteq Ad] \leq (\frac{m}{\sqrt{n}})^m$.
2. *If* $|Ad| < \frac{n}{m2^{1/m}} \approx \frac{n}{m}(1 - \frac{\ln 2}{m})$, *then* $\Pr[T_{A,B} \subseteq Ad] < \frac{1}{2}$.

By Corollary 2, even if the adversary holds quite a big fraction of keys from $\widetilde{\mathcal{K}}$ then still the adversary has chances less than $\frac{1}{2}$ to break the connection between A and B at a given time. So if the adversary tries to impersonate B against A, this should be discovered after a few key redistribution rounds. Of course, we should not interpret the results of Corollary 2 as an indication that m should be maximized. While the probability of impersonation decreases when m grows, at the same time it becomes easier for the adversary to collect a higher fraction of keys. The choice of the value m to be applied in a concrete case has to depend on adversary model.

Note that for $m = 2$, even if the adversary collects about $\frac{n}{2} \cdot \frac{1}{\sqrt{2}} \approx 0.35n$ temporal keys, then the probability of breaking the link between A and B is lower than $\frac{1}{2}$. This is amazing, since the total number of temporal keys is $\frac{1}{2} \cdot n$, i.e. in this case the adversary holds about 70% of the temporal keys! If the number of keys held by the adversary is lower, then the probability of breaking the link drops quite fast due to the exponent m in the expression $(\frac{km}{n})^m$. Note also that this decrease is very rapid for higher values of m. A down side of this approach is that the total number of temporal keys is lower and it is easier to collect most keys.

4 Revocation Mechanism

Now we sketch a mechanism of device revocation. For random key predistribution device revocation is hardly possible. One solution would be to revoke all keys from compromised devices. However, this may lead to a substantial reduction of the number of keys in the system. For instance, if each device holds $\sqrt{n}$ out of n keys in the pool, then after revoking $\sqrt{n}$ devices the expected number of revoked keys is close to $(1 - e^{-1})n \approx 0.63n$. In this case, the probability of finding a shared key by two devices is reduced to about $e^{-e^2} \approx 0.0006$. Below we propose a mechanism that alleviates this problem.

Full Key Update Mechanism. The new keys are generated at random by the system provider. In order to encrypt them always a pair of keys from the old pool is used. Say, if K_i and K_j have been chosen for encrypting $\widetilde{K}_l$, then the ciphertext is takes the form

$$E_{h(K_i, K_j, t)}(\widetilde{K}_l) \tag{2}$$

where h is some cryptographic hash function and t is some current parameter (e.g. time). The key point is that for retrieving $\widetilde{K}_l$ one needs both K_i and K_j.

Now imagine an $n \times n$ matrix, where rows and columns are indexed by the keys from $\mathcal{K}$ (the old pool of keys). We use only the part of the matrix below the main diagonal; let us call it $\mathcal{B}$. An entry of $\mathcal{B}$ is either empty, or contains a ciphertext of the form described in (2). Namely, if the broadcasted set of encrypted keys contains the ciphertext $E_{h(K_i,K_j,t)}(\widetilde{K}_l)$, then we put it into the entry indexed by row label K_i and column label K_j. If no ciphertext encrypted with $h(K_i, K_j, t)$ is sent, then we leave this entry empty.

The key feature of the algorithm is that:

- each key from $\widetilde{\mathcal{K}}$ is contained in several ciphertexts,
- only a limited number of pairs (K_i, K_j) is used.

It is an important point that we do not transmit n^2 ciphertexts (which would be impractical), but only such a number that, in average, each device gets about k keys (parameter k is chosen according to key predistribution policy). Note that a device holding k keys can decrypt entries from a submatrix of size $k \times k$, with $k(k-1)/2$ locations in $\mathcal{B}$. Hence, in order to get probability of getting a given key from $\widetilde{\mathcal{K}}$ equal to approximately k/n, we have to insert the ciphertext of the key in randomly chosen locations w times, where:

$$(1 - \tfrac{0.5k(k-1)}{0.5n(n-1)})^w \approx 1 - \tfrac{k}{n}.$$

For

$$w = \tfrac{n}{k} + \tfrac{1}{2} - \tfrac{1}{6}\tfrac{k}{n} + O((\tfrac{k}{n})^2)$$

both expressions become equal. If we choose a standard value for parameter k, i.e. $k \approx \sqrt{n}$, then $w \approx \sqrt{n}$. So one has to determine:

- $n \cdot w$ random locations in $\mathcal{B}$ for nonempty entries,
- an assignment of these locations to the keys from $\widetilde{\mathcal{K}}$, so that each of them gets w locations.

These data are determined from the output of a pseudo-random number generator with a seed z chosen by the system provider for a given change of the key pool. The transmission starts with the seed z, followed by the non-empty entries of $\mathcal{B}$, listed in the row-major order. After receiving the seed z, each device can reconstruct the mapping of keys to the transmission times and determine which ciphertexts it can decrypt with the keys from $\mathcal{K}$ that it knows. The seed z is retained in order to determine which keys are received by which device.

Revocation Mechanism. So far, we have not explained how to revoke certain devices (not really the keys!). If a device A has to be revoked, then no key pair (K_i, K_j) known to A should correspond to a nonempty entry in $\mathcal{B}$. In fact, we do not have to change the algorithm described above considerably: it suffices to put void keys in all entries of $\mathcal{B}$, where according to the above procedure a new key would be transmitted.

Let us observe that the mechanism described does not change considerably the number of keys obtained by non-revoked devices. Indeed, consider revoking $\sqrt{n}$ devices. They correspond to $\sqrt{n}$ submatrices of size $\sqrt{n} \times \sqrt{n}$. So the total space occupied by these submatrices is at most $n^{1.5}$, that is, the fraction $1/\sqrt{n}$ of $\mathcal{B}$. As each device is to get about $\sqrt{n}$ keys, in average only a few of them would be void.

Side Effects. There are some heavy side effects of the full key update mechanism, if we perform it many times. Namely, it may happen during a step of evolution that a device gets more than k keys from the new pool, or conversely, less than k keys. In the last case, during the next update step this device is further disadvantaged, since it can decode ciphertexts from less positions of B. So, "the rich become richer and the poor become more poor". This finally leads to degradation of the system. For further details see a forthcoming extended version of this paper.

References

1. Eschenauer, L., Gligor, V.D.: A key-management scheme for distributed sensor networks. In: Atluri, V. (ed.) ACM Conference on Computer and Communications Security, pp. 41–47. ACM, New York (2002)
2. Çamtepe, S.A., Yener, B.: Combinatorial design of key distribution mechanisms for wireless sensor networks. In: Samarati, P., Ryan, P.Y.A., Gollmann, D., Molva, R. (eds.) ESORICS 2004. LNCS, vol. 3193, pp. 293–308. Springer, Heidelberg (2004)
3. Chan, H., Perrig, A., Song, D.X.: Random key predistribution schemes for sensor networks. In: IEEE Symposium on Security and Privacy, p. 197. IEEE Computer Society, Los Alamitos (2003)
4. Anderson, R., Chan, H., Perrig, A.: Key infection: smart trust for smart dust. In: Proceedings of the 12th IEEE International Conference on Network Protocols, ICNP 2004, pp. 206–215 (2004)
5. Blom, R.: An optimal class of symmetric key generation systems. In: Beth, T., Cot, N., Ingemarsson, I. (eds.) EUROCRYPT 1984. LNCS, vol. 209, pp. 335–338. Springer, Heidelberg (1984)
6. Kulkarni, S., Bezawada, B., Gouda, M.G.: Optimal key distibution for secure communication. University of Texas atAustin MSU-CSE-07-189 (2007),
   http://www.cse.msu.edu/publications/tech/TR/MSU-CSE-07-189.ps
7. Liu, D., Ning, P., Du, W.: Group-based key pre-distribution in wireless sensor networks. In: WiSe 2005: Proceedings of the 4th ACM Workshop on Wireless Security, pp. 11–20. ACM, New York (2005)
8. Cichoń, J., Grząślewicz, J., Kutyłowski, M.: Key levels and securing key predistribution against node captures. In: Dolev, S. (ed.) ALGOSENSORS 2009. LNCS, vol. 5804, pp. 64–75. Springer, Heidelberg (2009)
9. Flajolet, P., Sedgewick, R.: Analytic Combinatorics, 1st edn. Cambridge University Press, Cambridge (2008)
10. Hofri, M.: Analysis of algorithms: computational methods and mathematical tools. Oxford University Press, Oxford (1995)

In-network Coding for Resilient Sensor Data Storage and Efficient Data Mule Collection

Michele Albano[1] and Jie Gao[2]

[1] Instituto de Telecomunicações (IT), Aveiro, Portugal
michele@av.it.pt
[2] Department of Computer Science, Stony Brook University, USA
jgao@cs.sunysb.edu

Abstract. In a sensor network of n nodes in which k of them have sensed interesting data, we perform in-network erasure coding such that each node stores a linear combination of all the network data with random coefficients. This scheme greatly improves data resilience to node failures: as long as there are k nodes that survive an attack, all the data produced in the sensor network can be recovered with high probability. The in-network coding storage scheme also improves data collection rate by mobile mules and allows for easy scheduling of data mules.

We show that using spatial gossip we can compute the erasure codes for the entire network with a total of near linear message transmissions, thus improving substantially the communication cost in previous scheme [5]. We also extend the scheme to allow for online data reconstruction, by interleaving spatial gossip steps with mule collection. We present simulation results to demonstrate the performance improvement using erasure codes.

Keywords: Sensor Networks, Erasure Coding, Resilient Storage, Data Mule.

1   Introduction

Data representation is a central problem in sensor network design. How to represent sensor data and where to store it greatly influence the design of other operation modules. In the most straightforward scheme, the sensor readings are simply kept in the sensor's local flash drives. However, this scheme is vulnerable to node failures: when a node stops being functional (by natural disasters, human/animal intrusion, or due to energy depletion), the data stored on the broken nodes is lost as well.

The issue of data storage and representation is also closely related to the data collection mechanism that gathers the sensor data to a base station. Earlier schemes have mostly adopted data collection trees and used multi-hop routing, e.g., in TinyDB [19]. This scheme presents the problem that nodes near the base station relay more traffic than an average node, and thus would use up their energy sooner. This will create a network hole around the base station that isolates the base station from the rest of functioning sensor network. For this reason, data collection by a mobile base station, called *data mule*, becomes attractive [8, 16, 23, 10, 26].

A data mule tours around in the network and retrieves data through direct communication with a sensor in close proximity. The mule can be either a vehicle/robot specifically employed for this task, or existing mobile entities (e.g., wild animals) that collect

C. Scheideler (Ed.): ALGOSENSORS 2010, LNCS 6451, pp. 105–117, 2010.

data in an opportunistic manner. For dedicated mules, the problem of motion planning and coordination is not trivial. A natural metric to plan routes is to minimize the total travel distance (proportional to delay or energy consumption) of the data mules. This becomes the multiple traveling salesman problem (mTSP), which is NP-complete and does not have any efficient approximation algorithms [4]. Existing solutions for mule planning are all heuristic schemes [8, 16, 23, 10, 26]. Alternatively, a practically appealing solution is to let data mules follow random movement, which requires minimum coordination. The downside is that we encounter the coupon collector problem. Specifically, if the data mule visits a random node each time, initially it picks up new data with high probability from each visited node. After the data mule has collected a substantial fraction of all the data from the network, it is highly likely that the next random node encountered has been visited before. Thus it takes the mule a long time to aimlessly walk in the network and hope to find the last few pieces. Theoretically for a random walk to cover a grid-like network, the number of steps is quadratic in the size of the network [17].

In many applications the sensor network is to detect target presence or other discrete events. Only a subset of sensors may have interesting data to report (we will denote these sensors as *data nodes* and the other ones as *storage nodes*) and the locations of these sensors are uncertain before hand (see [6]). Before the data mule visits the data nodes they have no idea where they are. Thus any pre-defined motion planning is inefficient as the mules may visit many nodes without anything to report. One can alleviate this problem by data replication (s.t. some storage nodes hold data copies). But one data mule may collect data that has been collected before; and multiple mules may collect the same piece of data due to lack of coordination.

In-network Coding. Consider the following simplified setting with k sensors with data and altogether n nodes that can possibly store it. Typically k is a fraction of n. We apply *erasure coding*, which transforms k data blocks into n codewords such that the original data can be recovered from any k codewords. Thus, as long as data mules collectively gather k codewords, the original data can be successfully reconstructed at the base station.

Using erasure codes for data storage brings two benefits for data mule collection: (1) sensor data is preprocessed in the network. Nodes with interesting data will initiate the encoding procedure and will preload useful information into other nodes in the network. Should only a small set of unknown sensors hold data to report, the data mule would not need to acquire the location of these sensors and can pick up data from any sensor; (2) Using erasure codes solves the coupon collector problem. The mules only needs to pick up a sufficient number of codewords, and it takes only linear time for random walk to achieve that [3]. The challenge of using erasure codes for sensor data storage is to develop distributed encoding algorithm with low communication cost.

Our Contribution. In this work, we construct the erasure codes with *near linear* message cost. In particular, we use spatial gossip in which each node p chooses another node q with probability proportional to $1/|pq|^3$, where $|pq|$ is the Euclidean distance between p and q. The gossip proceeds in synchronous rounds. In each round, every node with data (either its own data or data received in previous rounds) multiplies its data by a random coefficient and sends it to another node chosen with the above spatial distribution. A node may receive messages from multiple other nodes, in this case it will store the summation of the received data and its current data. After $O(\text{polylog}n)$ rounds, each node in the network stores a random linear combination of the original data. Once a node i receives data from node j, either directly or indirectly, some linear combination with the data of node i will be delivered to all other nodes that j communicates with in the following rounds. Thus data will be disseminated in an exponential rate. Using spatial gossip to build the in-network codes limits the total number of transmissions needed to build the erasure codes to $O(n\,\text{polylog}n)$, that is substantially smaller than the cost $O(n\sqrt{n})$ of the state of the art [5].

In addition to the basic mule collection, we also consider time critical applications for which we would like to reconstruct data as soon as the data mule acquires new information. For this, we keep all the computed coded values in the sensors, instead of replacing them with the newly computed codeword. If we denote the number of original data pieces in a linear combination as the *degree* of the codeword, this strategy considers increasing the degree of the codewords "slowly". In the first rounds, the sensors exchange the original data, so that initially the mule will pick up data in the original form. Gradually when the mule has collected a sufficiently large subset of data, it becomes harder to encounter new original data. Now we use gossip algorithm to exchange codewords of degree 2, and 3, and so on. For each piece of coded data collected, the mule will use its available data to reconstruct the original data. This is motivated by the idea of growth code developed by Kamra et al [9].

1.1 Related Work

In-network Coding. In the past, random linear codes have been proposed for improving sensor data resilience [5]. In that scheme each node that produced some data sends its data to $O(\log k)$ randomly chosen storage nodes. A storage node that receives multiple data from different data nodes saves a linear combination of them with random coefficients. The paper showed that a random set of k storage nodes can recover the original data with high probability. But the total message cost is $\widetilde{O}(n\sqrt{n})$ for uniformly randomly distributed sensors.

Fountain codes and other erasure codes have been used for in-network coding [14, 13, 2, 1] as well. These papers use random walk with the Metropolis algorithm to disseminate packets from data nodes. More variations have also been introduced such that small node failures can be recovered locally [15], or more important data is recovered with higher probability. For all these schemes, the message cost is super linear.

Data Collection by Mules. Most prior work on using mobile mules for data collection has focused on the system issues [8, 16, 23, 10, 26]. The scheduling problem is more challenging if both latency and energy consumption are under consideration. A lot of interesting work has been done on mule scheduling [24, 25]. We will not survey them here, since our objective is to prepare the data in the network in a nice format such that data collection is easy even for a mule performing a random walk.

Gossip Algorithms. Gossip algorithms have been extensively studied. See the survey [7] and the book [22] for references. There have been lots of variations depending on which node is selected to gossip to, and what information is exchanged between two gossip partners. Of particular relevance to our work is spatial gossip proposed by Kempe et al [12]. Our analysis uses a theorem proved in [12] to prove an upper bound on its convergence rate. The application of gossip algorithm in computing codewords in sensor network with near linear message cost, to our knowledge, has not been done before.

2   In-network Coding by Spatial Gossip

We assume that n sensors are in the network but only k of them have data to report at any moment. These nodes are called *data nodes* and the rest are denoted as *storage nodes*. We assume that the storage quota at each node is limited. For simplicity we assume that the data at a storage node almost hit the quota, so we can not put more data than one data symbol into a storage node.

Distributed Erasure Codes. *Erasure coding* transforms a message of m blocks into a longer message with M blocks, $M > m$, such that the original message can be recovered from a subset of the M blocks. In our case we use random linear codes over a finite Galois field $GF(q)$, $q = 2^b$. An original data piece is a vector of $GF(q)$ and is called a *symbol*. There are k symbols $\{s_1, s_2, \cdots, s_k\}$ distributed in the network. A *codeword* is a linear combination of the k symbols, denoted as $w = \sum_{i=1}^{k} \lambda_i s_i$, where λ_i's are coefficients. The calculation above is under the arithmetic of the Galois Field. The size of a codeword w is the same as the size of the symbols (b-bits long). The *degree* of a codeword w is the number of non-zero coefficients. Now suppose we have n codewords $w_1, w_2, \cdots, w_n$, with $w_j = \sum_{i=1}^{k} \lambda_{ij} s_i$. This coding scheme can be represented by the k by n generator matrix $G = \{\lambda_{ij}\}$. Take $w = (w_1, w_2, \cdots, w_n)$, $s = (s_1, s_2, \cdots, s_k)$. Thus $w = sG$.

The property required for decoding the symbols by using any k codewords is that any k columns from G form a full rank matrix G'. The decoding procedure is essentially solving a linear system $w' = sG'$ in $GF(q)$ and recover s, e.g., by Gaussian elimination.

The coefficients are taken as elements of $GF(q)$ as well and have b bits. The coefficients are delivered and stored along with the codeword. This causes storage/transmission overhead. However, we can make the overhead arbitrarily small by amortization over time by coding a long stream of data with the same set of coefficients.

Erasure Code Constructed by Spatial Gossip. We use spatial gossip to construct an erasure code in a distributed manner. At the beginning some subset of k nodes in the network has interesting data — the symbols s_i. We take t as the indicator of the number of rounds that have been executed. The current codeword at node j is denoted as $w_j^t = \sum_{i=1}^{k} \lambda_{ij}^t s_i$.

At round t, sensor x takes a random coefficient λ_x^t and updates its own codeword as $w_x \leftarrow \lambda_x^t \cdot w_x$. Suppose at this point w_x is $\sum_{i=1}^{k} \beta_i s_i$. The node x will choose a geographical location y^* and sends its current codeword w_x, as well as the current coefficients of the codeword $\{\beta_i\}$, to the node y closest to y^* (for example, by using geographical routing [11, 21]). In particular, y^* is selected with probability $p(x, y^*) = 1/(2\pi r^3)$, where

$r = |xy^*| \geq 1$. Since the sensors are distributed nearly uniformly, the probability that a node y is chosen is also proportional to $1/|xy|^3$. The proof is given in [21] and is not repeated here.

A node at round t may receive multiple messages from different nodes. It simply stores the summation of the incoming data and its own codeword as its current codeword. The coefficients of w_j^t are updated by the summation of the according coefficients. Notice that the degree of the codeword at any node is monotonically non-decreasing. The following theorem has been proved in [12] regarding spatial gossip:

Theorem 1. *The symbol from a data node x is propagated to a node y with probability $1 - O(1/d)$ after $O(\log^{3.4} d)$ rounds, where $d = |xy|$.*

We run the spatial gossip algorithm for $m = O(\log^{3.4} n)$ rounds so that for each data node x and any storage node y, y's codeword contains the symbol from x with high probability $1 - O(1/n)$. Recall that at round t, the node x takes a random number λ_x^t and multiplies it with the current codeword. The coefficient for symbol i in the final erasure code at node j is the multiplication of m random numbers corresponding to the nodes on the path of propagation from i to j, and is null with a very small probability $O(1/n)$.

3 Data Recovery and Mule Collection

Data Recovery Upon Node Failures. The goal of the spatial gossip is to construct erasure codes on the sensors. The codewords from any k nodes can be used to recover the original symbols. That is, take the matrix G' such that the j-th column is the vector of the coefficients of the j-th node. We would like G' to have full rank. From the discussion in the previous section, each element of G' is 0 with very small probability $O(1/n)$ and is otherwise the multiplication of m random numbers. We show in the following theorem that the probability of G' having full rank is very high. The proof of the following theorem is similar to the one in [5].

Theorem 2. *Take the codewords from any k nodes in the network and the corresponding k by k generator matrix G', G' has full rank with high probability $(1 - k/q)c(k)$, where $c(k) \to 1$ when $k \to \infty$.*

Proof. G' is a matrix with each element as some random variable determined by the gossip process. We just need to show that the determinant of G' is not zero. There are two possibilities for $\det(G')$ to be zero. In the first case, $\det(G')$ is identically zero regardless of the random coefficients selected in the gossip algorithm – for example, the entries of one column are all zero. To analyze the chance for this to happen, we take a bipartite graph β on vertex set X and Y, where X represents the data nodes and Y represents the storage nodes taken to recover the original data. $|X| = |Y| = k$. There is an edge between vertex x_i and y_j if there is a non-zero element at position (i, j) of G'. Edmonds' Theorem [20] says that if there is a perfect matching in β then $\det(G')$ is not identically zero. By our gossip algorithm, each edge ij is present with probability $1 - O(1/n)$. By the same analysis as in [5] we can see that the graph β has a perfect matching with high probability. Thus $\det(G')$ is not identically zero w.h.p.

In the second case, the determinant of G' happens to be zero for the specific random coefficients that we choose. This is a rare event and the probability that this happens can be bounded with Schwartz-Zippel Theorem [20]. The degree of $\det(G')$ is k. All the random coefficients are chosen from the field $GF(q)$. Thus $\text{prob}\{\det(G') = 0\} \leq k/q$.

In-network Coding Facilitating Mule Collection. When the data in the network is stored in terms of erasure codes, data collection by data mules is much easier. This scheme works very well with opportunistic data mules, whose movements are not under our control. As long as the opportunistic data mules visit k different nodes somehow, they can reconstruct the data from the entire network.

Moreover, with network coding a dedicated data mule does not need to know in advance which nodes have data and thus must be visited (in fact, it is impossible to know this in advance unless these data nodes report to the base station, in which case they can just report the data instead). It is also not necessary to plan very carefully what routes to follow so as to visit all the nodes in the network.

Online Mule Collection and Data Reconstruction. In the basic mule collection we first perform the in-network coding before mule collection. When events are time-critical, we would like to reconstruct data as soon as the mule collects something new. Initially we prefer data stored in its original form. At later data collection rounds it is difficult to discover a new data and higher degree symbols will become useful. We put a cap on the degree of the codewords in the gossip rounds. The cap grows with the number of gossip rounds.

What is the optimal mechanism to increase the cap of the degree of the codewords with the number of rounds remains an open question and our future work. For centralized LT codes, it has been proved that *Soliton* distribution [18] achieves the optimal rate and in practice the *robust Soliton* distribution has a more stable performance. We are not able to directly apply these results in our case due to the complex nature of nodes gossiping (codewords are moved around, instead of original data symbols). We learned through the simulations presented in next section that a practical scheme is to initially set the cap as a constant (in fact 1) to allow the data mule to collect enough original data, then let the cap grow as a linear function, so that the data mule can reconstruct data from almost each new data symbol.

4 Simulations

All the simulations were performed on sensor networks featuring 700 nodes including 100 data nodes, all uniformly randomly distributed inside a 50 by 50 square. The communication graph is modeled as a unit disk graph with communication range 3. For each data collection trial, a full reconstruction of data means that the base station received from the data mules enough codewords to be able to decode all the produced data.

In each set of simulations, $10 \sim 20$ sensor networks were randomly created. For each of them 100 different sets of data nodes were simulated. For each data production scenario $45 \sim 50$ data dissemination rounds were completed. After each round of data dissemination, 100 data collection experiments were performed, each one featuring a single data mule collecting codewords.

We evaluate different data collection strategies: *Random polling:* the data mule collects data from nodes selected uniformly at random in the network, this is implemented by the data mule doing random walk and picking up codewords during the motion; *Random straight line walk:* the data mule walks along a random line in the sensor network and collects data from the nodes that are closest to the line; *Clustered collection:* the data mule chooses a random location in the sensor network and collects data from near the location until k codewords are collected.

Communication Cost and Data Recovery Rate. We tested four different schemes, depending on what format of the data is exchanged and which node to send. A node with data may send either a single original data symbol or a codeword to a recipient. We denote the corresponding scheme by *non-coded gossip* or *coded gossip* method. In both cases, a storage node keeps a codeword (using random linear codes) of the incoming data packets. A node may send its data to a recipient chosen uniformly at random over all the nodes, or with some spatial distribution. We call the corresponding scheme *uniform gossip* or *spatial gossip*. Combining the choices, four different strategies are evaluated in our simulations. Specifically the non-coded uniform gossip method is the one in [5]. Our scheme is spatial coded gossip. The data collection scheme uses *clustered collection* in this set of experiments.

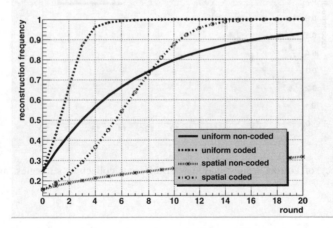

Fig. 1. Frequency of correct reconstruction with different data dissemination strategies, against round number

Figure 1 shows data recovery rate. The uniform non-coded gossip strategy initially performs better, similarly to the uniform coded gossip strategy. Then the spatial coded gossip strategy outperforms the uniform non-coded gossip strategy and behaves similar to the uniform coded gossip strategy. The number of rounds that were necessary to perform data dissemination for uniform non-coded gossip is 230 (not shown in the

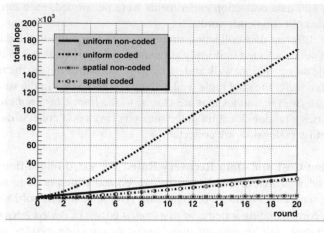

Fig. 2. Total number of communication hops for different data dissemination strategies, against round number

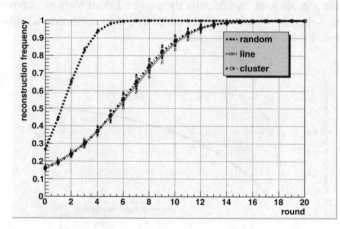

Fig. 3. Frequency of correct reconstruction with different collection strategies, against round number

figure). 20 rounds are enough to reconstruct data most of the times for spatial coded and non-coded gossip strategies. Figure 2 shows the total communication cost to move data around, against the round number. The uniform coded gossip strategy, with the best data recovery performance, is extremely expensive, as almost everyone sends data to random others. In summary, our scheme has the best combined performance than the other strategies in terms of lower message cost and higher data recovery rate.

Data Collection Strategies. We tested the three different data collection strategies introduced at beginning of this section. Figure 3 shows the frequency that the mules were able to correctly reconstruct all the data, against the number of rounds that were performed. The random polling method is the most expensive one for the data mule. It also has the highest reconstruction rate with a smaller standard deviation when the number of gossip rounds is small. Nevertheless, when we execute about 18 gossip rounds, all three data collection movement schemes can fully reconstruct the network data for all the trials we tested. This shows the erasure codes constructed with spatial gossip allow for flexible choice of data mule movement patterns.

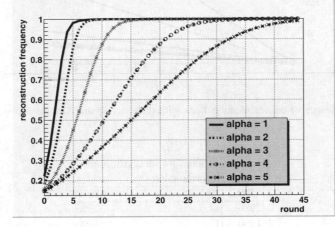

Fig. 4. Frequency of correct reconstruction with different Spatial Gossip exponents, against round number

Varying the Exponent for Spatial Gossip. We vary the exponent of the spatial distribution: in each round each node p selects one receiver node q, with probability proportional to $1/(d_{i,j})^{\alpha}$, and the analyzed αs were $1, 2, 3, 4, 5$. The simulations aim at finding out which exponent performs better in terms of reconstruction frequency and communication cost.

Figure 4 shows the frequency that the mules were able to correctly reconstruct all the data, against the round number. Figure 5 shows the total communication cost to move data around, against the round number. With a smaller α, the data storage scheme has higher communication cost and higher reconstruction probability. The communication cost that the network incurs to ensure correct data reconstruction is presented in the table in Figure 6. With the same reconstruction performance, the total message cost is the smallest when $\alpha = 3$, which corroborates our theoretical analysis.

Online Reconstruction. We introduce a network wide parameter called the "maximum codeword degree" to restrict the degree of the codeword at each round. The parameter can be changed after every round. Figure 7 shows this parameter as a function of the gossip round used in the simulation. The parameter is 1 for the first 40 rounds, then it increases in a sublinear manner up to round 80, after which it becomes a linear function of the round number.

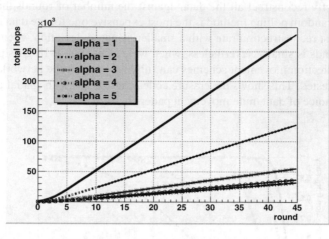

Fig. 5. Total number of communication hops with different Spatial Gossip exponents, against round number

α	cost per round	# rounds for successful reconstruction	total cost
1	6500	10	65000
2	2980	11	32780
3	1300	19	24700
4	867	39	33813
5	758	50	37900

Fig. 6. Total communication cost for correct data reconstruction with different Spatial Gossip exponents

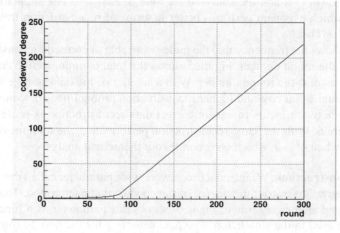

Fig. 7. Maximum codeword degree as function of the current gossiping round

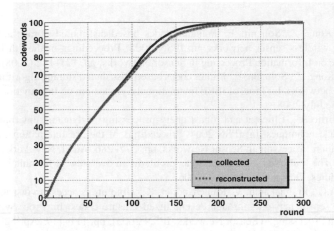

Fig. 8. Number of data reconstructed vs collected against the round number

From the point of view of the sensors, the algorithm is the same for each node. A node has a "current codeword", and a storage list. Initially, the "current codeword" is initialized to a produced data if the sensor is a data node, else it is initialized to null. The storage list is initialized with the "current codeword". In each gossip round, each sensor selects a recipient with spatial distribution, then it sends to it its "current codeword". Each sensor puts all the received codewords into its storage list, then it creates its next "current codeword" combining elements of the storage list. Elements chosen at random from the storage list are combined to create a new "current codeword" that has a degree equal or less to the "maximum codeword degree". After each gossip and random walk round, the data mule downloads from a sensor all the codewords it has into its storage list, then the data mule reconstructs all the original data symbols it can.

Figure 8 compares the number of reconstructed data against the number of independent codewords collected by the data mule, for each round. Simulations show that this strategy is able to collect a large number of data as soon as codewords are downloaded. On the other hand, the data mule is less efficient in reconstructing all the data than in the previous scenario, since it needs to collect more than 100 codewords to complete its job. We put a cap on the current codeword's degree, and this leads to a slowdown in information dispersal with respect to a scenario where the codeword degree is as high as it can get. The maximum degree of codewords initially stays 1, to help with the online reconstruction, since a data mule can extract automatically original data from codewords of degree 1. Later the maximum codeword degree increases quickly, thus the mule can cope with high degree codewords leveraging on all the original data it has already reconstructed.

Future Work. In our future work, we would like to explore two directions. First, what is the optimal strategy for the cap of the codeword degree for online data reconstruction? Second, if the network data has spatial correlation, how do we exploit it in the network coding scheme?

References

1. Aly, S.A., Kong, Z., Soljanin, E.: Fountain codes based distributed storage algorithms for large-scale wireless sensor networks. In: IPSN 2008: Proceedings of the 7th International Conference on Information Processing in Sensor Networks, pp. 171–182 (2008)
2. Aly, S.A., Kong, Z., Soljanin, E.: Raptor codes based distributed storage algorithms for wireless sensor networks. In: Proc. of IEEE International Symposium on Information Theory, pp. 2051–2055 (July 2008)
3. Avin, C., Brito, C.: Efficient and robust query processing in dynamic environments using random walk techniques. In: IPSN 2004: Proceedings of the 3rd International Symposium on Information Processing in Sensor Networks, pp. 277–286. ACM, New York (2004)
4. Bektas, T.: The multiple traveling salesman problem: an overview of formulations and solution procedures. Omega 34, 209–219 (2006)
5. Dimakis, A.G., Prabhakaran, V., Ramchandran, K.: Ubiquitous access to distributed data in large-scale sensor networks through decentralized erasure codes. In: Proc. Symposium on Information Processing in Sensor Networks (IPSN 2005), pp. 111–117 (April 2005)
6. Gao, J., Guibas, L.J., Hershberger, J., Milosavljević, N.: Sparse data aggregation in sensor networks. In: Proc. of the International Conference on Information Processing in Sensor Networks (IPSN 2007), pp. 430–439 (April 2007)
7. Hedetniemi, S.M., Hedetniemi, S.T., Liestman, A.: A survey of gossiping and broadcasting in communication networks. Networks 18(4), 319–349 (1988)
8. Jea, D., Somasundara, A.A., Srivastava, M.B.: Multiple controlled mobile elements (data mules) for data collection in sensor networks. In: Prasanna, V.K., Iyengar, S.S., Spirakis, P.G., Welsh, M. (eds.) DCOSS 2005. LNCS, vol. 3560, pp. 244–257. Springer, Heidelberg (2005)
9. Kamra, A., Misra, V., Feldman, J., Rubenstein, D.: Growth codes: maximizing sensor network data persistence. In: SIGCOMM 2006: Proceedings of the 2006 Conference on Applications, Technologies, Architectures, and Protocols for Computer Communications, pp. 255–266. ACM, New York (2006)
10. Kansal, A., Rahimi, M., Kaiser, W.J., Srivastava, M.B., Pottie, G.J., Estrin, D.: Controlled mobility for sustainable wireless networks. In: IEEE Sensor and Ad Hoc Communications and Networks (SECON 2004) (2004)
11. Karp, B., Kung, H.: GPSR: Greedy perimeter stateless routing for wireless networks. In: Proc. of the ACM/IEEE International Conference on Mobile Computing and Networking (MobiCom), pp. 243–254 (2000)
12. Kempe, D., Kleinberg, J., Demers, A.: Spatial gossip and resource location protocols. In: STOC 2001: Proceedings of the Thirty-Third Annual ACM Symposium on Theory of Computing, pp. 163–172. ACM Press, New York (2001)
13. Lin, Y., Li, B., Liang, B.: Differentiated data persistence with priority random linear codes. In: ICDCS 2007: Proceedings of the 27th International Conference on Distributed Computing Systems, Washington, DC, USA, p. 47. IEEE Computer Society, Los Alamitos (2007)
14. Lin, Y., Liang, B., Li, B.: Data persistence in large-scale sensor networks with decentralized fountain codes. In: Proc. of the 26th IEEE INFOCOM 2007 (May 2007)
15. Lin, Y., Liang, B., Li, B.: Geometric random linear codes in sensor networks. In: Proc. IEEE International Conference on Communications ICC 2008, May 19-23, pp. 2298–2303 (2008)
16. Lindner, W., Madden, S.: Data management issues in periodically disconnected sensor networks. In: Proceedings of Workshop on Sensor Networks at Informatik (2004)
17. Lovasz, L.: Random walks on graphs: A survey. Bolyai Soc. Math. Stud. 2, 353–397 (1996)
18. Luby, M.: Lt codes. In: FOCS 2002: Proceedings of the 43rd Symposium on Foundations of Computer Science, Washington, DC, USA, p. 271. IEEE Computer Society, Los Alamitos (2002)

19. Madden, S., Franklin, M.J., Hellerstein, J.M., Hong, W.: TAG: a tiny aggregation service for ad-hoc sensor networks. SIGOPS Oper. Syst. Rev. 36(SI), 131–146 (2002)
20. Motwani, R., Raghavan, P.: Randomized Algorithms. Cambridge University Press, Cambridge (1995)
21. Sarkar, R., Zhu, X., Gao, J.: Hierarchical spatial gossip for multi-resolution representations in sensor networks. In: Proc. of the International Conference on Information Processing in Sensor Networks (IPSN 2007), pp. 420–429 (April 2007)
22. Shah, D.: Gossip Algorithms. In: Foundations and Trends in Networking, Now Publishers Inc. (2008)
23. Shah, R., Roy, S., Jain, S., Brunette, W.: Data MULEs: Modeling a three-tier architecture for sparse sensor networks. In: IEEE SNPA Workshop (May 2003)
24. Sugihara, R., Gupta, R.K.: Improving the data delivery latency in sensor networks with controlled mobility. In: Nikoletseas, S.E., Chlebus, B.S., Johnson, D.B., Krishnamachari, B. (eds.) DCOSS 2008. LNCS, vol. 5067, pp. 386–399. Springer, Heidelberg (2008)
25. Sugihara, R., Gupta, R.K.: Optimizing energy-latency trade-off in sensor networks with controlled mobility. In: INFOCOM 2009 (2009)
26. Vincze, Z., Vida, R.: Multi-hop wireless sensor networks with mobile sink. In: CoNEXT 2005: Proceedings of the 2005 ACM conference on Emerging network experiment and technology, pp. 302–303. ACM Press, New York (2005)

Monitoring Churn in Wireless Networks

Stephan Holzer[1], Yvonne Anne Pignolet[2],
Jasmin Smula[1], and Roger Wattenhofer[1]

[1] Computer Engineering and Networks Laboratory (TIK), ETH Zurich, Switzerland
[2] IBM Research, Zurich Research Laboratory, Switzerland

Abstract. Wireless networks often experience a significant amount of churn, the arrival and departure of nodes. In this paper we propose a distributed algorithm for single-hop networks that detects churn and is resilient to a worst-case adversary. The nodes of the network are notified about changes quickly, in asymptotically optimal time up to an additive logarithmic overhead. We establish a trade-off between saving energy and minimizing the delay until notification for single- and multi-channel networks.

1 Introduction

In traditional (wired) distributed systems the *group membership problem* has been studied thoroughly (we refer to [6] for a survey). The basic premise of group membership is to know which other nodes are there, for instance to share the load of some task. Nowadays Wireless LAN or Bluetooth often replace large parts of wired networks since one does not have to build an expensive communication infrastructure first, but can communicate in "ad hoc" mode immediately. This motivates a revisit of the *group membership problem* in a wireless context: Imagine for example a bunch of wireless sensors, distributed in an area to observe that area. From time to time some of the nodes will fail, maybe because they run out of energy, maybe because they are maliciously destroyed. On the other hand, from time to time some more sensors are added. Despite this *churn* (nodes joining and leaving), all nodes should be aware of all present nodes, with small delay only. To account for the self-organizing flavor and the wireless context we decided to change the name from group membership to *self-monitoring* in this paper. We present an efficient algorithm for the self-monitoring problem in an adversarial setting.

Reducing the frequency of checking for changes, and thus the number of messages exchanged per time period, prolongs the time interval until every node is informed about changes. Since energy as well as communication channels are scarce resources for wireless devices, we evaluate a trade-off between energy and delay / runtime for single- and multi-channel networks. For single-channel networks, our algorithm can be applied to multi-hop networks using [2], which shows that algorithms designed for single-hop networks can be efficiently emulated on multi-hop networks.

C. Scheideler (Ed.): ALGOSENSORS 2010, LNCS 6451, pp. 118–133, 2010.

2   Model

The network consists of a set of wireless nodes, each with a built-in unique ID. All nodes are within communication range of each other, i.e., every node can communicate with every other node directly (single-hop). New nodes may join the network at any time, and nodes can leave or crash without notice. This fluctuation of nodes in the network is called churn. We exclude Byzantine behavior and assume that as soon as a node crashes, it does not send any messages anymore. Due to the churn, the number of nodes in the network varies over time. To simplify the presentation of the algorithms and their analysis, we assume time to be divided into synchronized time slots. Messages are of bounded size, each message can only contain the equivalent of a constant number of IDs. We first assume that the number of properly divided communication channels is rather large, a requirement we drop later. In each time slot a node v is in one of three operating states: transmit (v broadcasts on channel k), receive (v monitors channel k) or sleep (v does not send or receive anything). A transmission is successful, if exactly one node is transmitting on channel k at a time, and all nodes monitoring this channel receive the message sent. If more than one node transmits on channel k at the same time, listening nodes can neither receive any message due to interference (called a *collision*) nor do they recognize any communication on the channel (this is known as *no collision detection*). The energy dissipation of v is defined to be the sum of the energy for transmission and reception. Because in current embedded systems transmitting and receiving consumes several orders of magnitude more energy than sleeping or local computations, we set the energy consumption for being in state transmit or receive to unity and neglect the energy used in state sleep or for local computations. The nodes have sufficient memory and computational power to store an *ID table* containing all IDs of currently participating nodes and execute the provided algorithms. n_t denotes the number of entries in the ID table at time t.

At any time, an adversary may select arbitrary nodes to crash, or it may let new nodes join the network. However, the adversary may not modify or destroy messages. Since messages have bounded size, nodes can learn at most a constant number of identifiers per message. As each node can only receive at most one message per time slot, any algorithm needs at least c_{min} time units on average (for some constant c_{min}) to learn about *one* crash or join. In other words, if *on average* more than rate $r_{max} := c_{min}^{-1}$ nodes crash (or join) per time unit, no algorithm can handle the information (cf. [5] for the maximum tolerable average message rate in a dynamic broadcast setting). In the following, we will define an adversary and monitoring algorithm accordingly. Denote by b the number of crashes/joins that happen in a maximal burst and by $\tilde{b}$ the maximal burst-size that an algorithm tolerates.

Definition 1 (c-Adversary, $(c, \tilde{b})$-Adversary). *We call an adversary a c-adversary if it lets nodes join and crash arbitrarily as long as: First, there remains at least one node knowing the ID table in the network at any time. Second, on average the number of adversarial joins/crashes is at most one node in c time* *slots. The adversary has full knowledge of the algorithm and can coordinate crash and join events with the aim of making the algorithm fail. A $(c, \tilde{b})$-adversary is a c-adversary whose churn is bounded by a constant $\tilde{b}$ during every period of $c \cdot \tilde{b}$ time slots.*

3   Monitoring Algorithm

The algorithm we propose is asymptotically optimal in the sense that it can survive in a setting where on average one crash or join occurs in c time units, for a constant $c > c_{\min}$. We can tolerate bursty churn (a large number of nodes joining or leaving during a small time interval). Similarly to an optimal algorithm, we need time to recover from bursts since the number of newly joining (or crashed) nodes is bounded according to the message size. The algorithm can also tolerate churn while trying to recover from previous bursts; again the only limit is the learning rate of $r_{\max}$ IDs per time unit. Indeed, the adversary may crash all but one node at the same instant (killing all nodes is a special case, leading to an initialization problem, which we do not address here). Clearly, learning churn takes time, depending on the bursts. If there is a burst of β joins or crashes, an optimal algorithm needs at least $\beta \cdot c_{\min}$ time until the corresponding information at all nodes is up-to-date. Similarly, our algorithm needs time $\beta \cdot c$. If bursts happen while recovering from previous bursts, delays will take longer due to the constant learning rate. Up to a logarithmic additive term, the learning delay of the algorithm is asymptotically optimal: the algorithm handles the maximum average rate of churn any algorithm can tolerate in this communication model.

Our algorithm is partially randomized. However, randomness is only required for detecting new nodes since this part cannot be done in a deterministic fashion. All other parts of the algorithm are deterministic, which might be of interest in a setting where only updates on crashed nodes are needed and no nodes join the network.

Main Theorem 1. *We construct a* monitoring algorithm *that tolerates c-adversaries with maximum burst size b with logarithmic additive overhead: $O(b + \log n_t)$ time slots after an event all nodes have updated the corresponding entries in their ID tables.*

Proof. From a family of FBMAS $\{A_{\tilde{b}}\}_{\tilde{b} \in \mathbb{N}}$ that tolerate $(c/4, \tilde{b})$-adversaries we construct a monitoring algorithm B. Each $A_{\tilde{b}}$ might fail if the churn is too large – since we do not know b beforehand, we derive an algorithm B that adapts to the bursts by searching for a good value for $\tilde{b}$ with a binary doubling search procedure. It executes algorithms $A_{\tilde{b}_i}$ from the above family with estimated values $\tilde{b}_i$ for b, starting with $\tilde{b}_1 := \log n_t$ (we do not start with $\tilde{b}_1 = 1$ because the running time of A always exceeds $\log n_t$ due to the dissemination step). If algorithm A detects its failure, we know that an algorithm A tolerating $(\frac{c}{4}, \tilde{b}_i)$-adversaries is not sufficient and B doubles the estimated value of b to $\tilde{b}_{i+1} := 2\tilde{b}_i = 2^i \log n_t$.

Let the adversary's maximal burst be b. After at most $\log(b/\log n_t) + 1$ repetitions, the algorithm A succeeds and so does B. The total time needed by B is at most

$$\sum_{i=1}^{\log\left(\frac{b}{\log n_t}\right)+1} \frac{c}{4} \cdot (\tilde{b}_i + \log n_t) \quad < \quad \sum_{i=0}^{\log\left(\frac{b}{\log n_t}\right)} 2^{i-1} c \log n_t \quad \leq \quad \frac{cb}{\log n_t} \log n_t \quad = \quad c \cdot b.$$

Remark 1 (Adaptivity). After a maximal burst of size b happened, the above procedure always needs as much time as it needed for the big burst for all later bursts. The algorithm can be modified to update a network the quicker the smaller the current burst is by setting the estimate $\tilde{b}$ to $\tilde{b}_1$ after every successful update (proofs would need to be adjusted slightly in a few spots).

From now on, we will use the term "FBMA" as an abbreviation for "fixed burst monitoring algorithm". Let us now consider the FBMA $A_{\tilde{b}}$, ALGORITHM 1. In order to work correctly if the bursts are smaller than anticipated and to detect its failure it requires the following invariant.

Invariant 2. *All nodes that have been in the network for $\Theta(n_t)$ time slots have the same view of the network, i.e., their ID table always contains the same entries. Nodes that joined more recently know their position in the ID table.*

To ensure that this invariant holds when starting the algorithm, we may assume that at time 0 there is only a single designated node active, and all other nodes still need to join. This leads to the same sorted *ID table* at all nodes.

Algorithm 1. $A_{\tilde{b}}$ for a fixed $\tilde{b} \in \mathbb{N}$

---

loop forever // nodes have same ID table (INVARIANT 2)
1: partition nodes into sets of size $O(\min(\tilde{b}, n_t))$;
2: detect crashed nodes in each set on separate channels in parallel;
3: detect joined nodes;
4: disseminate information on crashed and joined nodes to all nodes;
5: stop if burst too large;
6: all nodes update their *ID table*;

Theorem 3. *If INVARIANT 2 holds at the start, then for all $\tilde{b} \in \mathbb{N}$, FBMA $A_{\tilde{b}}$ (ALGORITHM 1) tolerates $(c, \tilde{b})$-adversaries for a constant c. Furthermore each node detects if the algorithm failed $c \cdot (\tilde{b} + \log n_t)$ time slots after a stronger adversary caused a burst larger than $2\tilde{b}$. The energy consumption and the time for detection is asymptotically optimal.*

Proof. In brief, ALGORITHM 1 repeats a loop consisting of six steps to maintain up-to-date information in the *ID tables* of the nodes. Each step is fully distributed and does not need a central entity to control its execution. Subsequently, we call one execution of the loop of the FBMA $A_{\tilde{b}}$ a *round*.

Step 1 – partition nodes into sets: Nodes are divided into $N \in O(1 + n_t/\tilde{b})$ sets $V := \{S_1, \ldots, S_N\}$. Based on the information in their *ID table*, the nodes can determine which set they belong to by following a deterministic procedure. Each set appoints nodes as representatives of the set and designates their replacements in case they crash. Time $O(1)$.

Step 2 – detect crashed nodes in each set on separate channels: Each set $S_I \in V$ executes an algorithm to detect its crashed nodes. No communication between sets takes place. To avoid collisions each set carries out its intra-set communication on a separate channel. To find out if any of the set members in S_I have crashed, each node sends a "hello" message in a designated time slot. All other nodes of the set detect who did not send a message and generate the information to disseminate: a list of so-called update items U_I (details in SECTION 3.2). Time $O(\min(\tilde{b}, n_t))$.

Step 3 – detect joined nodes: New nodes listen to learn the tolerated burst size $\tilde{b}$ and when to try joining. They send requests to join to S_1 with probability $1/\tilde{b}$. In expectation at least one node can join in a constant number of rounds if the estimate $\tilde{b}$ is in $\Omega(b)$. Detected joiners are added to U_1 together with a note that they joined. After $O(\tilde{b} + \log n_t)$ time slots S_1 decides whether the estimate $\tilde{b}$ needs to be doubled due to too many joiners. Its decision is correct with high probability (whp), that is with probability greater than $1 - n_t^{-\gamma}$ for any but fixed constant γ (details in SECTION 3.3). Time $O(\tilde{b} + \log n_t)$.

Step 4 – disseminate information on crashed and joined nodes to all nodes: Now every set S_I has a list U_I of update items containing the IDs of crashed and joined nodes in the set. To distribute this information, each set becomes a vertex of a balanced binary tree and the representative nodes communicate with the representatives of neighboring vertices in the tree according to a pre-computed schedule. If a representative crashes, there are $\tilde{b}$ replacements to take over its job. No collisions occur due to the schedule (details in SECTION 3.4). Time $O(\tilde{b} + \log n_t)$.

Step 5 – stop if burst too large: If the adversary is too strong, information on some of the sets is missing, or more than $\tilde{b}$ nodes crashed or tried to join. In this case, all nodes are notified and the execution of the algorithm stops (details in SECTION 3.5). Time $O(\tilde{b} + \log n_t)$.

Step 6 – all nodes update their *ID table*: If the algorithm did not stop, every node now has the same list $U = \bigcup_{I=1}^{N} U_I$ and can update its *ID table*. INVARIANT 2 holds. Time $O(1)$.

Newly arrived nodes do not know the *ID table* yet and have to learn the IDs of all present nodes in asymptotically optimal time, described in SECTION 3.5. However, even with incomplete *ID tables* they can participate in the algorithm, see SECTION 3.6.

While steps 1 and 6 are executed locally and hence the time complexity is constant, steps 2–5 require communication between nodes. The following sections describe the steps in more detail and examine their time complexity as well as prove that the INVARIANT 2 at the beginning of the loop holds (as long as b is bounded by $\tilde{b}$ – else the algorithm will detect that it failed). We focus on $n_t \geq 2\tilde{b} + 2$, as in the case $n_t < 2\tilde{b} + 2$ the statements hold due to simple facts like "there will always remain at least one node in the network".

3.1   Partition Nodes into Sets (Step 1)

Compute sets: If $\tilde{b} \geq n_t/6 - 6$, the network forms one large set. If $\tilde{b} < n_t/6 - 6$, let $s := 2\tilde{b} + 2$ and partition the n_t nodes into $N := \lceil \frac{n_t}{s} \rceil - 1$ sets $S_1, \ldots, S_N$. Each set is of size s, except S_N which contains between s and $2s - 1$ nodes. The nodes are assigned to the sets in a canonical way, based on their ID's position in the sorted *ID table* $\{id_1 < id_2 < \cdots < id_N\}$. Set S_I is the set $S_I := \{id_{(I-1)\cdot s+1}, \ldots, id_{I \cdot s}\}$ for $1 \leq I \leq N - 1$ and $S_N = \{id_{(N-1)\cdot s+1}, \ldots, id_{N \cdot s}, \ldots, id_{n_t}\}$. We denote the index of S_I by a capital I and call it the ID of the set. Let us denote the set of all sets $\{S_1, \ldots, S_N\}$ by V (since the sets will be the vertices of a communication graph in the dissemination step 4). Note that there is no ambiguity in the mapping of nodes to sets.

Compute representatives: In the subsequent steps, the sets will communicate with each other. To this end, representative senders and receivers are chosen to act on behalf of the set. Moreover, for each representative, the set appoints $\tilde{b}$ replacement nodes to monitor the representative and take over if it crashes. Each set S_I designates two sets of nodes $R^{sender} := \{id_{(I-1)\cdot s}, \ldots, id_{(I-1)\cdot s+\tilde{b}}\}$ and $R^{receiver} := \{id_{(I-1)\cdot s+\tilde{b}+1}, \ldots, id_{I \cdot (i-1)+|S_I|-1}\}$, each consisting of $\tilde{b} + 1$ nodes. In each set we appoint the node with smallest ID to be the representative sender/receiver of S_I, denoted by r_I^{sender}, $r_I^{receiver}$. Its replacements are the other $\tilde{b}$ nodes in $R^{receiver}$ and R^{sender}. The ith replacement node of a representative (which is the node with i^{th}-smallest ID of the corresponding set) will take over the role of the representative in case the representative as well as the replacement nodes 1 to $i - 1$ crashed. After computing S_{I_v} each v can check easily if it is its set's representative sender/receiver or the ith replacement by looking at its position in the sorted ID table. The replacement nodes listen in all time slots whether their representative is sending or receiving messages in order to detect its failure and have the same knowledge as the representative. Thus they are able to take over the representative's role immediately. To keep things simple we often write that "S_I sends an update item to S_J" instead of "the representative sender r_I^{sender} of S_I sends information on some crashed or new node to the representative receiver $r_J^{receiver}$ of S_J". In some cases the introduced notation of representatives is used to clarify what exactly the algorithm does. As no communication is necessary for this step, the time complexity is $O(1)$.

3.2   Detect Crashed Nodes in Each Set in Parallel (Step 2)

Let the time slot in which the current round of the algorithm starts be t_0. All nodes that crash in time slot $t_0 + 1$ or later might not necessarily be detected during this execution of the loop but in the next one, i.e. at most $O(\tilde{b} + \log n_t)$ time slots later. Each set S_I detects separately, which of its members crashed. Set S_I uses the channel I for communication among its set members to avoid collisions with other sets.

Each node v is assigned a unique time slot to inform the other set members of its state (ALGORITHM 2, lines 4–5). In all other time slots, v listens to the other set members to determine crashed nodes, i.e., when v does not receive a message in the time slot corresponding to a certain ID (line 6) it assumes that the node with this ID has crashed and adds it to U_I (line 7).

Theorem 4. *When repeating* ALGORITHM 2 *continuously, crashed nodes are detected at most two rounds ($O(\tilde{b})$ time slots) if $b < \tilde{b}$.*

Proof. There are $O(\tilde{b})$ nodes in each set, thus each set can complete the crash detection in $O(\tilde{b})$ time slots. If there are N channels available, all sets can execute this algorithm simultaneously. If a node crashes after sending its "I'm here!" message, its failure is detected the next time ALGORITHM 2 is executed.

Corollary 1. *The monitoring algorithm detects crashes in $O(b+\log n_t)$ if $b < \tilde{b}$.*

3.3   Detect Joined Nodes (Step 3)

Apart from detecting nodes that have disappeared, the network needs to be able to integrate new nodes. ALGORITHM 4 describes the behavior of nodes of the network and AL-GORITHM 3 the behavior of nodes eager to join the network. Let $j \le \tilde{b}$ be the number of such joiners. They listen on channel 1 for the representative of the corresponding set S_1 to

---

Algorithm 2. Crash Detection

1: compute index i_v of v's ID and I_v of v's set S_{I_v};
2: $U_{I_v} := \emptyset$
3: **for** $k := 0, \dots, |S_{I_v}| - 1$ **do**
4:    **if** $i_v == I_v \cdot |S_{I_v}| + k$ **then**
5:      send "Im here!" on channel I_v;
6:    **else if** no message received on channel I_v **then**
7:      $U_{I_v} := U_{I_v} \cup \{id_{I_v \cdot |S_{I_v}|+k}\}$;

---

announce the current number of nodes n_t and the estimated $\tilde{b}$. When they have received such a message, they wait for a time slot and then try to join by sending a message with their ID with probability $p := 1/\tilde{b}$ on channel 1. If there has not been a collision, the representative sender of the set S_1 replies to the successful joiner with a welcome message. Otherwise each unsuccessful joiner repeats sending messages with this probability followed by listening for a reply or a stop message in the next time slot. The representative sender transmits a stop message after $d \cdot \max(\log n_t, \tilde{b})$ time slots for some constant d. The probability that a joiner is successful is constant if $j < \tilde{b}$ and hence the joiners attach to the network in a constant number of rounds in expectation.

Lemma 1. *In expectation a node attaches to the network within 4 rounds if $j < \tilde{b}$.*

Proof. Since $j < \tilde{b}$ the probability that a joiner is successful in a certain time slot is at least $1/\tilde{b}(1 - 1/\tilde{b})^{j-1} \ge \frac{1}{e\tilde{b}}$. Thus the probability that a joiner is the only sender at least once during $\tilde{b}$ time slots is greater than $1 - (1 - \frac{1}{e\tilde{b}})^{\tilde{b}} > 1 - e^{-e^{-1}} > 0.3$. Hence the expected number of rounds until a node has joined is less than 4.

The set S_1 is able to detect if the current estimate for $\tilde{b}$ is in the correct order of magnitude by letting the representative sender transmit messages every second time slot reserved for the joiners until it tried $d' \log n_t$ times for some constant d' to be defined later. Hence, every second opportunity for new nodes to join is blocked $d' \log n_t$ times. The other nodes in S_1 count the number of times the representative sender of S_1 transmits successfully. If this number is less than a threshold $\tau = 2d' \log n_t \cdot e^{-2} \cdot (1 - 2/\tilde{b})$, the set decides that $\tilde{b}$ is too small for the current number of joiners and lets the other sets know about this in the next step. To this end, all nodes in S_1 insert an additional update item to U_1 which has highest priority to be forwarded to all other nodes.

Using Chernoff bounds we can show that this decision is correct w.h.p. (see the technical report of this paper [8] for a proof). This procedure

---

Algorithm 3. Join Algorithm

For new nodes that want to join

1: **while** *attached* == *false* **do**
2:   **repeat**
3:     listen on channel 1;
4:   **until** received message "$\tilde{b}$ bursts"
5:   $p := 1/\tilde{b}$;
6:   **loop**
7:     send message "hello, id" on channel 1;
8:     listen on same channel;
9:     **if** received welcome message **then**
10:       *attached* := *true*;
11:     **else if** received "stop joining" **then**
12:       break;

Algorithm 4. Join Detection

For nodes in the network

1: $count := 0$;
2: **for** $k := 0, \ldots, d \cdot \max(\log n_t, \tilde{b})$ **do**
3:   **if** ($I_v == 1$ and k mod $4 == 0$ and
    $k < d' \log n_t$ and $i_v == r_v^{sender}$) **then**
4:     send message "$\tilde{b}$ bursts";
5:   **else if** received message from r_v^{sender} **then**
6:     $count := count + 1$;
7:   **else if** message from joiner id_j received **then**
8:     **if** $i_v == r_v^{sender}$ **then**
9:       send message "welcome";
10:     $U_{I_v} := U_{I_v} \cup \{id_j\}$;
11: **if** $count \geq \frac{d' \log n_t}{2e}(\frac{1}{2} + \frac{1}{e})$ **then**
12:   $U_{I_v} := U_{I_v} \cup \{$"$\tilde{b}$ too small"$\}$;
13: **if** $i_v == r_v^{sender}$ **then**
14:   send message "stop joining";

---

only prolongs the period until nodes are detected by a constant factor.

Remark 2. As discussed in Section 5, there exist energy-efficient size approximation algorithms. However, letting an unknown number of nodes join cannot be solved with the help of these algorithms, since they do not handle node failures and they do not give high probability results for a small number of joining nodes.

After joining, the new nodes listen on channel 1 until the end of the current loop. In addition, they (and the old nodes in the network) have to execute the algorithm described in Section 3.6 to get to know all the nodes that are currently in the network.

Remark 3. We could use more sets than S_1 to listen to joining nodes. As we only need to make sure that new nodes can join in a constant number of rounds and that the error probability is low, we use only the set S_1 for simplicity's sake.

3.4   Disseminate Crash/Join-Information to All Nodes (Step 4)

In the previous sections we discussed how each set S_I detects crashed nodes and accepts new nodes that want to join the network. This information is stored in a (possibly empty) list U_I of *update items*, where each update item consists of the ID of the node it refers to and whether the node has crashed or joined the network. This list U_I needs to be distributed to all other sets. To this end, the representatives of each set communicate with representatives of other sets to compute the set $U = \bigcup_{I=1}^{N} U_I$ of all changes in the network.

Theorem 5. *If $b \leq \tilde{b}$ (otherwise the algorithm stops in STEP 5), the update items are disseminated within time $O(\tilde{b} + \log n_t)$ with ALGORITHM 5.*

Idea: First, the sets are mapped to vertices of a communication graph G (in our case this will be a tree[1]). This can be done deterministically within each node and no messages need to be exchanged. Second, neighboring sets exchange information repeatedly until the information reaches all sets. See ALGORITHM 5 for a description in pseudo-code.

Definition 2 (Family of communication graphs). *Let $\mathcal{C}$ be an infinite family of communication graphs $C_N = (V_N, E_N)$ over N vertices which have the property, that the in-degree and the out-degree of each vertex are bounded by d_N, each. Furthermore we require that each C_N can be computed deterministically only from knowledge of N, as well as a schedule s_N of length l_N, where*
$$s_N : V_N \times \{1, \ldots, l_N\} \longrightarrow \{1, \ldots, N\} \times \{1, \ldots, N\}, (v, t) \longmapsto (\kappa_{send}, \kappa_{receive})$$
that tells each vertex $v \in V$ that it should send in time slot $t \in \{1, \ldots, l_N\}$ on channel $\kappa_{send} \in \{1, \ldots, N\}$ and receive on channel $\kappa_{receive} \in \{1, \ldots, N\}$ respectively – in such a way that within l_N time slots all neighbors of G are able to exchange exactly one message containing one update item without collisions.

Definition 3 (Trees). *Let $\mathcal{C} := \{C_N \mid N \in \mathbb{N}\}$ be the family of balanced binary trees over N nodes. In $C_N := (V_N, E_N)$ we have the vertices $V_N := \{1, \ldots, N\}$ and for each vertex $v \in V_N \setminus \{1\}$ there are directed edges $(v, \lfloor v/2 \rfloor)$ and $(\lfloor v/2 \rfloor, v)$ connecting v to its parent $\lfloor v/2 \rfloor$.*

Lemma 2. *A schedule s_N of length 4 can be computed deterministically for any member C_N of the above tree family.*

Proof. Each node v in odd levels of the tree (that is $\lfloor log_2(v) \rfloor$ is odd) will exchange one message (both ways) with child $2v$ in the first time slot and with child $2v + 1$ in the second time slot – observe that children are in even levels. Then each node v in even levels of the tree will exchange one message (both ways) with child $2v$ in the third time slot and with child $2v + 1$ in the fourth time slot. Every node u will send only on its own channel u to avoid collisions – receivers will tune to this channel. The complete schedule is given by

---

[1] We decided to present the algorithm in this slightly more general way such that it will be easy to replace the family of communication graphs. This is useful to handle unreliable communication where information being transported from a leaf to the root is very unlikely. Using expander graphs might help in this case, since they also have logarithmic diameter and constant degree but are more robust: after a short time (say $f(n)$) the information will be copied to $2^{f(n)/O(1)}$ nodes with not too small a probability. Compared to the tree, it is more likely that at least one of the many copies of the information will reach the destination.

$$s_N(v,1) = \begin{cases} (v, 2v) & : \lfloor \log_2(v) \rfloor \text{ is odd} \\ (v, \lfloor v/2 \rfloor) & : \lfloor \log_2(v) \rfloor \text{ is even} \end{cases} \quad s_N(v,2) = \begin{cases} (v, 2v+1) & : \lfloor \log_2(v) \rfloor \text{ is odd} \\ (v, \lfloor v/2 \rfloor) & : \lfloor \log_2(v) \rfloor \text{ is even} \end{cases}$$

$$s_N(v,3) = \begin{cases} (v, 2v) & : \lfloor \log_2(v) \rfloor \text{ is even} \\ (v, \lfloor v/2 \rfloor) & : \lfloor \log_2(v) \rfloor \text{ is odd} \end{cases} \quad s_N(v,4) = \begin{cases} (v, 2v+1) & : \lfloor \log_2(v) \rfloor \text{ is even} \\ (v, \lfloor v/2 \rfloor) & : \lfloor \log_2(v) \rfloor \text{ is odd} \end{cases}$$

If a channel (vertex) on (to) which a node v should send or listen is not in the range of $\{1, \ldots, N\}$, then v can be sure that the corresponding node does not exist and just sleeps in this slot – this will happen for the root and the leaves.

Corollary 2. *The family of trees* $\mathcal{C} := \{C_N \mid N \in \mathbb{N}\}$ *from* DEFINITION 3 *combined with the schedules* s_N *from* LEMMA 2 *is a family of communication graphs, where the diameter of* C_N *is* $2 \cdot \lceil \log n_t \rceil$, *the in-degree as well as the out-degree of each node are bounded by* $d_N = 3$ *and the length of any schedule* s_N *is* 4.

In the first part of the algorithm, all nodes start with the same *ID table*, what we can assume according to INVARIANT 2. From the information n_t stored in the ID table, each set v of the N sets computes deterministically without communication (line 1) the communication graph $G := C_N$ as well as the schedule S_N of length l_N.

In the second part of the algorithm, $O(diameter(G) + \tilde{b})$ phases, each of $l_N + d_N$ time slots, are executing. During each phase each vertex is able to send one update item to each of its (at most) d_N out-neighbors and receive one update item from each of its (at most) d_N in-neighbors. This communication takes place by adhering to the previously computed schedule s_N of length l_N. Thus in each phase each vertex exchanges messages with its

---

Algorithm 5. Deterministic Dissemination

Sender:
1: compute schedule s_N for
   $G := C_N := (\underbrace{\{S_1, \ldots, S_N\}}_{\text{vertices } V_N}, \underbrace{E_N}_{\text{edges}});$
2: $U' := \emptyset$;
3: **for** $t = 1, \ldots, diameter(G) + \tilde{b}$ **do**
4:    **for** $j = 1, \ldots, l_N$ **do**
5:       $item_{send} := \min_{item \in U \setminus U'}\{D\}$
          or "no news" if U empty;
6:       send $item_{send}$ on channel $s_N(I_v, j)_1$;
7:       $U' := U' \cup \{item_{send}\}$;
8:    **for** $j = l_N + 1, \ldots, l_N + d_N$ **do**
9:       receive item $item_{receive}$ on channel I_v;
10:      $U := U \cup \{item_{receive}\}$;
11: send U on channel I_v;

Receiver
1: compute schedule s_N for
   $G := C_N := (\underbrace{\{S_1, \ldots, S_N\}}_{\text{vertices } V_N}, \underbrace{E_N}_{\text{edges}});$
2: **for** $t = 1, \ldots, diameter(G) + \tilde{b}$ **do**
3:    **for** $j = 1, \ldots, l_N$ **do**
4:       receive $item_j$ on channel $s_N(I_v, j)_2$;
5:    **for** $j = l_N + 1, \ldots, l_N + d_N$ **do**
6:       send $item_j$ on channel I_v
          unless it is "no news";
7:       $U := U \cup \{item_j\}$;

---

neighbors. The vertices maintain two lists of update items. In the first list U are the items the set knows of, while the second list U' contains the items it has forwarded already. In the first of all phases, the first list is set to $U := U_I$, the list of the IDs determined in the detection step, and the second list $U' := \emptyset$ is empty (line 3). After the completion of the second part, U equals U' and contains all items. In each phase, set S_I sends the information of the lowest ID in $U \setminus U'$ to its (at most) d_N out-neighbors and receives (at most) d_N update items from its d_N in-neighbors. Depending on the outcome of each phase, the lists U and U' are updated.

First we show that exchanging messages with neighboring vertices is possible for two representatives in each set within time $l_N + d_N$ if none of them crashes (LEMMA 3). We argue later in LEMMA 5 that we can tolerate $\tilde{b}$ crashes during the execution and in SECTION 4 we establish a time/energy/channel trade-off for fewer channels.

Lemma 3. *All sets transmitting update items to their (at most) d_N out-neighbors and receiving (at most) d_N update items from their (at most) d_N in-neighbors takes time $l_N + d_N$ when the number of channels N is equal to the number of sets and no node crashes.*

Proof. We adhere to the schedule s_N. As we noted before, all nodes computed the same graph G and schedule s_N such that all global communication activities are consistent with the local computation of v. This takes l_N time. Afterwards the receiver $r_I^{receiver}$ reports the newly received update items (there are at most d_N, one from each neighbor) to r_I^{sender} on the set's channel I during time slots $l_N + 1, \ldots, l_N + d_N$ of this phase (lines 5–6 of the receiver's part). r_I^{sender} receives this information and adjusts U and U' accordingly (lines 8–10 of the sender's part). All these computations happen in a deterministic way based on the same information (stored in each node) and yield the same schedule for the whole graph in each node.

Observe that no set (vertex) crashes completely as the adversary is bounded to let at most $\tilde{b}$ nodes crash during the execution of the algorithm. Hence there are $\tilde{b}$ nodes ready to replace the representatives. In LEMMA 5 we prove that repeating the procedure from LEMMA 3 $O(diameter(G) + \tilde{b})$ times will lead to full knowledge of U. First we prove a weak version of this lemma (LEMMA 4). We extend this lemma to hold despite crashes during execution (LEMMA 5).

Lemma 4. *All vertices can learn the set U that contains all update items after $O(diameter(G) + \tilde{b}) \cdot (l_N + d_N))$ time slots if no nodes crash during the execution of this algorithm.*

Proof. W.l.o.g., let $U := \{item_1, \ldots, item_{\tilde{b}}\}$ be a sorted list of update items. By induction on i we prove that $item_i$ is known to all vertices S_I in G after $O((diameter(G) + i) \cdot (l_N + d_N))$ time slots of executing ALGORITHM 5 if no nodes crash during the execution.

Base case $i = 1$: Any representative v that receives $item_1$, will always immediately communicate $item_1$ to its neighbors in the next phase since $item_1$ is the first item in v's sorted list $U \setminus U'$. Thus item $item_1$ will have been broadcast to all nodes after $diameter(G) + 1$ phases if no nodes crash during this computation.

Inductive step $i \to i + 1$: Let us assume the induction hypothesis for i. Item $item_{i+1}$ can only be delayed (in line 5 of the sender's part) by items with smaller indices. Let $item_j$ be the item with the largest index that delays $item_{i+1}$ on any of the shortest paths to any of the vertices in G. Then $item_{i+1}$ is known by all vertices in G one phase after $item_j$. By the induction hypothesis, this is after $diameter(G) + j + 1$ phases. We remember $j \leq i$ to obtain the induction hypothesis for $i + 1$.

Lemma 5. LEMMA 4 *holds for up to $\tilde{b}$ nodes crashing during the execution.*

Proof. If a representative crashes during the dissemination step (either a sender or a receiver), a replacement node realizes the crash of its representative at most one phase later since the replacement is listening to all actions of the representatives and thus detects whether it sent all messages it was supposed to send. If it did not send a message during a phase it must have crashed and the next replacement node steps up to be the new representative (in case no information needs to be sent by a representative in a time slot it does not matter whether it crashed). This is possible since the replacement nodes have exactly the same information as the representative and know when the representative should send what message. For the same reason they are able to know how many replacements happened before and thus when it is their turn to jump in to retransmit the necessary message in the next phase after the crash. Since at most $\tilde{b}$ nodes can crash, there will never be more than $\tilde{b}$ retransmissions necessary. This can lead to a delay of at most $\tilde{b}$ phases and the statement follows.

Proof (Proof of THEOREM 5*).* We combine LEMMA 4 and LEMMA 5 as well as use the fact that in the communication graphs provided by the tree family from COROLLARY 2, for all values of $N \in \mathbb{N}$ we have $diameter(C_N) = O(\log n_t), d_N = 3$ and that the schedule-length of s_N is $l_N = 4$.

As a consequence, all representatives and replacements of S_I know all the update items available after $O(\log n_t + \tilde{b})$ time slots. Thus all nodes in any set S_I are aware of all crashed and new nodes at the time when the algorithm started (and also of some crashes/joins that happened during the algorithm's execution, but not necessarily all of those). This proves LEMMA 3.

3.5 Stop If Burst Too Large (Step 5)

In this step, the sets determine whether the algorithm failed due to too large a burst – that is more than $\tilde{b}$ nodes joined or crashed (within time $c\tilde{b}$). To distinguish sets that do not have any information to forward from sets of which all members crashed, we let each set S_I send "I'm here!" in its scheduled time slots without new information to be sent.

Theorem 6. *If $b > \tilde{b}$ then $O(\log n_t + \tilde{b})$ time slots after the dissemination step all nodes have the same information: Either they have noticed that the burst is too large and stopped the execution or all have the same information on network changes.*

Proof. Set S_1 knows with high probability if too many nodes tried to join and forwarded this information in the dissemination step. Thus all nodes are aware of this event at the end of step 4 of the FBMA $A_{\tilde{b}}$ if it occurs: if the decision of S_1 is wrong, the algorithm still works properly, it just takes longer until all nodes which to join the network are included, however, all nodes receive the same information.

If one or more sets S_I completely crash before or during step 4, its neighbors immediately know that more than $\tilde{b}$ nodes crashed and the algorithm might fail (e.g. the communication graph might be disconnected and not all nodes will have been delivered the same information). The neighbors of S_I then broadcast this information through the communication graph with highest priority. Even if further sets crash completely and the failure message originated by the neighbors of S_I does not reach all sets, the neighbors of the other crashed sets will start propagating such a message through the network as well. After $O(\log n_t + \tilde{b})$ phases all representatives are informed if one or more sets did not receive all the information: If no set crashed then after $\log n_t + \tilde{b}$ phases all sets have all the update items. If a set crashes before all sets have this information, then $\log n_t + \tilde{b}$ phases later all sets are informed of a failure, no matter how many sets crash now. If a set crashes afterwards, the update information has reached all sets already and thus all surviving sets can continue with this information.

The last possibility of an adversary to disturb the self-monitoring process consists in letting more than $\tilde{b}$ nodes crash even though all sets survive. By extending the dissemination phase by a constant number of time slots, we can ensure that all sets notice if more than $\tilde{b}$ update items have been disseminated and conclude that the adversary exceeds the bound of $\tilde{b}$. Therefore, also in this case a potential failure of the algorithm is known to all nodes after the dissemination step. Thus, the algorithm guarantees that all sets have the same set of update items at the end of a successful round if it did not stop the execution.

3.6 Participating without Complete *ID Table*

Note that the joiners can already participate in the information-dissemination algorithm without knowing the complete ID table: When a new node v is detected by the network, the node that is the oldest in the network according to the timestamp (ties are broken by ID) tells v the smallest ID of a node w in the network that is larger than v's ID. This is possible since the oldest node is guaranteed to have a complete ID table. Joiner v now assumes to have this position in the ID table. After the dissemination step has finished, node v determines the number $c^<$ of crashed nodes with IDs smaller than v and subtracts $c^<$ from its assumed position. Then v counts $j^<$, the number of nodes that joined the network with an ID smaller than itself and adds $j^<$ to its assumed position. Thus there is only one node in the network assigned to a position in the ID table after updating the ID tables based on the information gathered in the dissemination step. Knowing this position in the ID table allows the joiner to participate in all the necessary algorithms: partition / crash and join detection / information dissemination.

In order to allow new nodes to learn the IDs of the nodes that are already in the network, the existing nodes alternately transmit their IDs and the time slot when they arrived on channel 1. This process can be interleaved with the execution of the monitoring algorithm, i.e., odd time slots can be used for the monitoring algorithm while even time slots are reserved for getting to know all existing nodes.

4 Energy and Trade-offs

So far, we assumed that there are as many channels available as there are sets. However, our algorithm can be modified such that it works for networks with a bounded number of k channels. It can also be adapted to dissipate only a limited amount of energy e. See the technical report of this paper [8] for a detailed explanation.

5 Related Work

Many algorithms have been designed for wireless networks under varying assumptions concerning the communication model (reception range, collision detection, transmission failures, etc.). There are many problems that are non-trivial even in single-hop networks. We focus here on networks where nodes cannot distinguish collisions from noise (no-collision detection model). The ability to detect collisions can lead to an exponential speed up, e.g., as shown in [12] for leader election. Moreover we consider the energy expenditure for transmission and listening. Basic algorithms for these networks can be used as services or building blocks for more complex algorithms and applications. Among them are initialization (n nodes without IDs are assigned labels $1, \ldots, n$) [14], leader election [13,15], size approximation [3,9], alerting (all nodes are notified if an event happens at one or more nodes) [11], sorting (n values distributed among n nodes, the ith value is moved to the ith node) [10,17], selection problems like finding the minimum, maximum, median value [16] and computing the average value [13], and do-all (schedule t similar tasks among n nodes with at most f failures) [4]. Note that in contrast to our work the adversary examined in these papers cannot let nodes join or crash. Moreover we cannot apply existing size approximation algorithms to estimate the number of newly joined nodes, since they do not handle node failures and they do not give high probability results for a small number of joining nodes. Our work can be seen as continuous initialization with the extension that more information is available. New nodes can join the network later and are given a label (position in the ID table). After each round of our self-monitoring algorithm, these labels are updated and in addition all nodes know which nodes have failed. Moreover, the ID table can be used to designate a leader and all nodes are aware of the current network size. In [1], a routing problem is studied in a multi-channel, single-hop, time slotted scenario and energy is considered as well. The algorithm they propose is not suitable for our application, since it requires a preprocessing phase of $O(n)$ time slots.

One of the problems underlying the monitoring problem is the dynamic broadcast problem, where an adversary can continuosly inject packets to be delivered to all participants of the network, see [5] for (im)possibility results and algorithms (nodes are assumed not to crash in this model).

The problem we solve can be viewed as a special case of the continuous gossip problem, introduced in [7] recently: an adversary can inject rumours as well as crash and restart participating nodes at any time, yet the rumours need to reach their destination before a deadline. The authors analyze the problem in a message passing model with unbounded message size and no collisions and devise an algorithm with a guaranteed per-round message complexity. Our update items can be viewed as rumours that directly depend on the crashes and restarts and the deadlines are related to the number of crashes and restarts in a time interval.

References

1. Bakshi, A., Prasanna, V.K.: Energy-Efficient Communication in Multi-Channel Single-Hop Sensor Networks. In: Conference on Parallel and Distributed Systems, p. 403. IEEE, Los Alamitos (2004)
2. Bar-Yehuda, R., Goldreich, O., Itai, A.: Efficient Emulation of Single-Hop Radio Network with Collision Detection on Multi-Hop Radio Network with No Collision Detection. Distributed Computing 5(2), 67–71 (1991)
3. Caragiannis, I., Galdi, C., Kaklamanis, C.: Basic computations in wireless networks. In: Deng, X., Du, D.-Z. (eds.) ISAAC 2005. LNCS, vol. 3827, pp. 533–542. Springer, Heidelberg (2005)
4. Chlebus, B.S., Kowalski, D.R., Lingas, A.: Performing work in broadcast networks. Distributed Computing 18(6), 435–451 (2006)
5. Chlebus, B.S., Kowalski, D.R., Rokicki, M.A.: Maximum throughput of multiple access channels in adversarial environments. Distributed Computing 22(2), 93–116 (2009)
6. Chockler, G.V., Keidar, I., Vitenberg, R.: Group communication specifications: a comprehensive study. ACM Computing Surveys (CSUR) 33(4), 427–469 (2001)
7. Kowalski, D.R., Georgiou, C., Gilbert, S.: Meeting the deadline: On the complexity of fault-tolerant continuous gossip. In: PODC (2010)
8. Holzer, S., Pignolet, Y.A., Smula, J., Wattenhofer, R.: Monitoring Churn in Wireless Networks. Technical report, Computer Engineering and Networks Laboratory (TIK), ETH Zurich, Switzerland (2010),
   ftp://ftp.tik.ee.ethz.ch/pub/publications/TIK-Report-328.pdf
9. Kabarowski, J., Kutylowski, M., Rutkowski, W.: Adversary immune size approximation of single-hop radio networks. In: Cai, J.-Y., Cooper, S.B., Li, A. (eds.) TAMC 2006. LNCS, vol. 3959, p. 148. Springer, Heidelberg (2006)
10. Kik, M.: Merging and Merge-Sort in a Single Hop Radio Network. In: Wiedermann, J., Tel, G., Pokorný, J., Bieliková, M., Štuller, J. (eds.) SOFSEM 2006. LNCS, vol. 3831, p. 341. Springer, Heidelberg (2006)
11. Klonowski, M., Kutyłowski, M., Zatopianski, J.: Energy Efficient Alert in Single-Hop Networks of Extremely Weak Devices. In: Dolev, S. (ed.) ALGOSENSORS 2009. LNCS, vol. 5804, pp. 139–150. Springer, Heidelberg (2009)
12. Kowalski, D.R., Pelc, A.: Leader Election in Ad Hoc Radio Networks: A Keen Ear Helps. In: 36th International Colloquium on Automata, Languages and Programming, p. 533 (2009)
13. Kutyłowski, M., Letkiewicz, D.: Computing Average Value in Ad Hoc Networks. In: Rovan, B., Vojtáš, P. (eds.) MFCS 2003. LNCS, vol. 2747, pp. 511–520. Springer, Heidelberg (2003)

14. Kutyłowski, M., Rutkowski, W.: Adversary Immune Leader Election in Ad Hoc Radio Networks. In: Di Battista, G., Zwick, U. (eds.) ESA 2003. LNCS, vol. 2832, pp. 397–408. Springer, Heidelberg (2003)
15. Lavault, C., Marckert, J.F., Ravelomanana, V.: Quasi-optimal energy-efficient leader election algorithms in radio networks. Information and Computation 205(5), 679–693 (2007)
16. Singh, M., Prasanna, V.K.: Optimal energy-balanced algorithm for selection in a single hop sensor network. In: IEEE Workshop on Sensor Network Protocols and Applications (SNPA) (2003)
17. Singh, M., Prasanna, V.K.: Energy-optimal and energy-balanced sorting in a single-hop wireless sensor network. In: Pervasive Computing and Communications (PERCOM) (2003)

Lifetime Maximization of Monitoring Sensor Networks

Peter Sanders and Dennis Schieferdecker*

Karlsruhe Institute of Technology (KIT), 76128 Karlsruhe, Germany
{sanders,schieferdecker}@kit.edu

Abstract. We study the problem of maximizing the lifetime of a sensor network assigned to monitor a given area. Our main result is a linear time dual approximation algorithm that comes arbitrarily close to the optimal solution, if we additionally allow the sensing ranges to increase by a small factor. The best previous result is superlinear and has a logarithmic approximation ratio. We also provide the first proof of NP-completeness of this specific problem.

1 Introduction

Wireless sensor networks have become a prominent research topic in recent years. Their unique structure and limitations provide new and fascinating challenges. A network consists of a union of small nodes that are equipped with sensing, communication and processing capabilities. The nodes are usually only battery powered with no means of recharging. Therefore, energy is a highly limited resource and energy consumption becomes a critical factor in this context. On the other hand, the sensor nodes themselves are cheap and available in abundance. This fact is exploited to counter their inherent limitations. Wireless sensor networks can be used for a multitude of monitoring tasks. Thus, there has been a lot of research on monitoring problems.

In this paper, we consider the question of how to maximize the lifetime of a monitoring sensor network when each node has a nonrechargeable battery with limited capacity. The basic idea is to switch on only subsets of nodes at a time while the remaining nodes are in an energy saving sleep-mode. Our results apply to several variants of this question. In the *target monitoring problem*, we are given a set of points in the plane that need to be monitored, i.e., during the entire lifetime of the network and for every target t, there must be an active node with t in its sensing range. In the *area monitoring problem*, every point in a designated area must be monitored. During most of this paper we will assume a uniform fixed sensing range for all nodes. While this assumption is common in theoretical papers, it is unrealistic in practice. However, we believe that our techniques can be adapted for more general shapes of sensing areas. Moreover, sensing ranges do not come into play at all when we reinterpret the area monitoring problem as the

---

* Partially supported by the German Research Foundation (DFG) within the Research Training Group GRK 1194 "Self-organizing Sensor-Actuator-Networks".

C. Scheideler (Ed.): ALGOSENSORS 2010, LNCS 6451, pp. 134–147, 2010.

problem to regularly take samples of point-measurements at a given minimum *resolution*, i.e., every point of the monitoring area ·is at most a given distance away from a sample point. This combination of a simple geometric model and a realistic interpretation was one of the main motivations for us to look at this particular problem. Area monitoring was previously studied by Berman et al. [1,2] and a superlinear algorithm for finding efficient schedules with a logarithmic approximation ratio was presented. Our main result is a linear time dual approximation algorithm that comes within a factor $(1-\epsilon)$ of the optimum if we additionally allow the sensing range to grow by a factor $(1+\delta)$ for arbitrary constants ϵ and δ. Our focus is the approximability of this problem. Thus, we are initially content with a sequential approximation algorithm which can be later used to evaluate distributed variants.

We give more related work in Section 2, define the model in Section 3 and then present the approximation algorithm in Section 4 and discuss an adaptation to target monitoring in Section 5. Since previous NP-completeness results only apply to a variant of the target monitoring problem without geometric structure, we also provide the missing NP-completeness proof in Section 6. A conclusion and an outlook complete the paper (Section 7).

2   Related Work

There has been a lot of activity in the field of wireless sensor networks over the past years and, thus, there already exist many contributions dealing with the optimization of energy-constraint networks designed for specific tasks. Monitoring tasks are a particularly large field of applications for wireless sensor networks. Thus, determining schedules that maximize the lifetime of these networks has been the focus of a lot of work.

In [3], Cardei and Wu first classify this problem as area monitoring and target monitoring. Later in [1], Berman et al. argue that area monitoring can be reduced to target monitoring of $O(n^2)$ targets for a class of sensor models, given a network of n sensors. Thus, it is sufficient to regard only the latter problem.

Slijepcevic and Potkonjak study the problem of monitoring a set of targets in [4]. Their approach is based on disjoint sets of sensor nodes, each of which covers all of the targets. They further simplify the problem by assuming that each node has the same initial energy. Thus, in an optimal solution given these constraints, each node is used in at most one set and each set is active for the same amount of time. They state that set-k-cover is a generalization of their problem and provide a heuristic for set-k-cover which they use to solve their problem. Unfortunately, they do not provide asymptotic runtimes or approximation guarantees.

A more general model is analyzed by Cardei et al. in [5]. Here, sensor nodes are allowed to be part of more than one set but their initial battery capacity is still assumed to be equal. They propose two heuristics, one using a linear programming (LP) approach and the other being a greedy algorithm. The former has a runtime complexity of $O(n^3p^3)$ with n the number of sensor nodes and p an upper bound on the number of sets. The latter takes $O(dm^2n)$ with n the number of sensor nodes, m the number of targets and d the minimum number of nodes covering a target. They do not give approximation guarantees. Cardei et al. also provide a proof of NP-completeness, reducing from 3-SAT. This proof is subsequently cited by most works on this subject even though it only applies to the more general case with no geometric structure.

In [1,2], Berman et al. discuss the problem of area monitoring without enforcing constraints on the node sets or battery capacities as the previous authors did. They outline an efficient data structure and algorithm to transform an area monitoring task to a target monitoring task. After giving a LP formulation of the problem, they provide an approximation algorithm using the Garg-Könemann algorithm [6] as basis. Their proposed algorithm has a runtime complexity of $O(1/\epsilon^2 n \log n \cdot T)$ with n the number of sensor nodes and T the runtime of an auxiliary min set cover algorithm. The approximation guarantee is $(1+\epsilon)(1+2\log n)$. They also provide LP formulations for two further models, one only requiring partial coverage of the area and the other taking into account communication costs. Both are solvable with the same setup as their initial model.

A variation of the previous area monitoring problem is considered by Dhawan et al. in [7]. They generalize upon the initial model of Berman et al. by introducing variable sensing ranges that are directly linked to their energy consumption over time. They provide an approximation algorithm along the same line as Berman et al., introducing a new heuristic for the Garg-Könemann subroutine. Their algorithm has an $(1+\epsilon)(1+\log m)$ approximation guarantee, m being the number of targets to cover, and runs in $O(1/\epsilon^2 n \log n \cdot T)$ with n the number of sensor nodes and T the unspecified runtime of the subroutine.

The area monitoring problem introduced by Berman et al. was picked up by Gu et al. in 2007 [8]. Even though they only model target monitoring, this approach leads to the same LP formulation. They extend the model by demanding the existence of a data gathering tree with appropriate energy costs for communication. They propose a column generation approach to exactly solve the LP problem and provide an algorithm to generate good initial solutions. This is a well-known and adequate technique to manage large-scale LP problems in practice. No runtime guarantees are provided since the problem is still NP-hard.

In 2009, Luo et al. revisited the problem as one example to demonstrate their technique for solving large LPs [9]. As Gu et al. , they apply a column generation technique as exact solver. Their main contribution is a new way to generate new columns that yields a speed-up of more than one order of magnitude. Their model also offers rudimental support for incorporating connectivity costs into the energy consumption of the sensor nodes. As before, no theoretical runtime guarantees are given, only simulational values.

3   Model and Problem Definition

Sensor Network Model. This paper considers a sensor network consisting of n nodes $\{S_1, \ldots, S_n\} = \mathcal{S}$. Each node S_i, $i \in \{1, \ldots, n\}$ consists of a triple (x_i, y_i, b_i), denoting its position in the plane (x_i, y_i) and its battery capacity b_i.

Nodes are placed arbitrarily in the plane. We assume that nodes only consume energy while actively monitoring their surroundings and that energy consumption is constant over time and independent of small changes in the sensing range. We further assume that communication and processing costs are proportional to monitoring costs[1]. All quantities are normalized, i.e. sensor nodes consume one unit of energy per unit of time and battery capacity is stated in units of energy.

Covers. Let an *area* be a connected or unconnected region with a description complexity linear in $|\mathcal{S}|$. Given an area A and a sensing range R, a set of sensor nodes $C \subseteq \mathcal{S}$ is called a cover, if area A is contained in the union of disks of radius R centered at each sensor node. In particular, the set of all sensor nodes $\mathcal{S}$ is a cover if any cover exists. The set of all possible covers is called $\mathcal{C}$.

Problem Definition. Consider a sensor network $\mathcal{S}$, an area A and a sensing range R. What is the maximum time T area A can be monitored by these sensors before this becomes impossible due to node failure? In particular, we want to determine a set of m covers $\underline{C} = \{C_1, \ldots, C_m\} \subseteq \mathcal{C}$ and a corresponding set of durations $\underline{t} = \{t_1, \ldots, t_m\}$ that maximizes the lifetime $T = \sum_{j=1}^{m} t_j$ while respecting the limited battery capacities, i.e.

$$\sum_{i:S_j \in C_i} t_i \leq b_j \ \forall \ S_j \in \mathcal{S}. \tag{1}$$

We refer to this problem as *sensor network lifetime problem (SNLP)* [1].

A tuple $(\underline{C}, \underline{t})$ is also called a *schedule*. Applying a schedule implies activating each cover iteratively for the corresponding duration. If a cover is active, all of its sensor nodes are active and all other ones are sleeping.

4   Approximation Algorithm

We introduce two techniques for solving simpler variants of the original problem. First, we consider discretizing sensor positions by snapping them to a grid[2]. Secondly, we consider solving subproblems restrained to small areas of the plane. Subsequently, we combine both variants in our approximation algorithm and prove its approximation guarantee and asymptotic runtime.

A problem instance is denoted by a triple $(\mathcal{S}, A, R)$ with $\mathcal{S}$ the set of sensor nodes, A the area to be monitored and R the sensing range of each node. A solution to problem $(\mathcal{S}, A, R)$ consists of a tuple $(\underline{C}, \underline{t})$ with $\underline{C}$ a sequence of covers and $\underline{t}$ a sequence of corresponding durations, i.e. t_i denotes the duration of cover C_i. A solution is called feasible if condition (1) is fulfilled. We abbreviate the lifetime of a solution to problem $(\mathcal{S}, A, R)$ by $T\langle \mathcal{S}, A, R \rangle$. The lifetime of an optimal solution is denoted by $T_{\mathrm{opt}}\langle \mathcal{S}, A, R \rangle$, respectively.

Subsequently, we usually omit mentioning area A for brevity. We also normalize sensing ranges to 1 w.l.o.g. .

---

[1] Thus, we can incorporate communication and processing costs implicitly by using effective monitoring costs that are a linear combination of all three types of costs.

[2] A grid is a set of points $\{(\alpha \cdot i, \alpha \cdot j) | i, j \in \mathbb{Z}\}$ with $\alpha \in \mathbb{R}$ the width of the grid.

4.1   Discretizing Positions

Consider a modified problem with sensor nodes restricted to positions on a grid. Given an algorithm $\mathcal{A}$ that computes f-approximate solutions for this special problem, we can find an approximation of the original problem with a small computational overhead, if we also allow the sensing ranges to increase by a small amount. Lemma 1 summarizes this claim.

Algorithm 1.

input: parameter $\delta \in [0, 1]$, sensor nodes $\mathcal{S}$, area A, sensing range R
output: set of covers $\underline{C}$, set of corresponding durations $\underline{t}$

1. Define a grid of width $\delta/2$.
2. Move every node in $\mathcal{S}$ to the closest point on the grid $\rightarrow \tilde{\mathcal{S}}$.
3. Use algorithm $\mathcal{A}$ to solve $(\tilde{\mathcal{S}}, 1 + \delta/2) \rightarrow (\underline{C}, \underline{t})$.
4. Return $(\underline{C}, \underline{t})$.

Lemma 1. *Let $\delta \in [0, 1]$. Algorithm 1 yields a feasible solution to problem $(\mathcal{S}, 1 + \delta)$ with lifetime $T\langle \mathcal{S}, 1 + \delta \rangle \geq f \cdot T_{\mathrm{opt}}\langle \mathcal{S}, 1 \rangle$. The running time outside algorithm $\mathcal{A}$ is $O(|\mathcal{S}|)$.*

Proof. Correctness: Consider the original problem $(S, 1)$. Moving all nodes in S to the closest point on a grid of width $\delta/2$ yields $\tilde{S}$. Each node is shifted by at most $\frac{\sqrt{2}}{2} \cdot \delta/2 < \delta/2$. Note that if we additionally increase the sensing range by a factor $1 + \delta/2$, a cover with respect to $(S, 1)$ is also a cover with respect to $(\tilde{S}, 1 + \delta/2)$ as depicted in Figure 1 and proved in Corollary 1 for a single node. Thus, $T_{\mathrm{opt}}\langle \tilde{S}, 1 + \delta/2 \rangle \geq T_{\mathrm{opt}}\langle S, 1 \rangle$ and algorithm $\mathcal{A}$ computes a solution to $(\tilde{S}, 1 + \delta/2)$ with lifetime $T\langle \tilde{S}, 1 + \delta/2 \rangle \geq f \cdot T_{\mathrm{opt}}\langle \tilde{S}, 1 + \delta/2 \rangle \geq f \cdot T_{\mathrm{opt}}\langle S, 1 \rangle$. A solution to $(\tilde{S}, 1 + \delta/2)$ is also a solution to $(S, 1 + \delta)$ by the same argument as above for $(S, 1)$ and $(\tilde{S}, 1 + \delta/2)$. Thus the solution provided by algorithm $\mathcal{A}$ is also a feasible solution for $(\mathcal{S}, 1 + \delta)$ with lifetime $T\langle \mathcal{S}, 1 + \delta \rangle \geq f \cdot T_{\mathrm{opt}}\langle \mathcal{S}, 1 \rangle$.

Computational Overhead: $O(|\mathcal{S}|)$ is the time required to relocate all sensor nodes to their closest grid point. □

Corollary 1. *Consider a circle C with center $\underline{x} = (x, y)$ and radius r covering area A and circle D with center $\underline{x} + \underline{dx}$, $\underline{dx} = (dx, dy)$ and radius $r + |\underline{dx}|$. Then, D also covers A.*

Proof. For each point $\underline{p} = (x_p, y_p)$ in A holds $|\underline{p} - \underline{x}| \leq r$. According to the triangle inequality $|\underline{p} - (\underline{x} + \underline{dx})| \leq |\underline{p} - \underline{x}| + |\underline{dx}| \leq r + |\underline{dx}|$, and thus, no point $\underline{p}$ in A is further away from $\underline{x} + \underline{dx}$ than $r + |\underline{dx}|$. □

Note that this approach assumes that small changes in sensing range R have no impact on the energy consumption of the sensor nodes. Also note that the applied approach of rounding continuous values to some discrete numbers is a common technique found in many other approximation schemes.

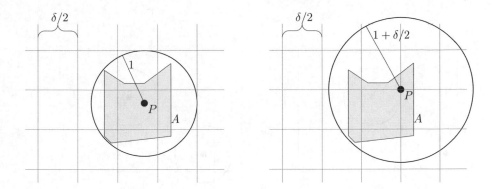

Fig. 1. *Left.* Sensor node P with sensing range 1 covers area A. A grid of width $\delta/2$ is plotted. *Right.* Sensor node P has been moved to a grid position and its sensing range increased to $1 + \delta/2$. It still covers area A.

4.2   Area Partitioning

Consider the original problem $(\mathcal{S}, A, 1)$ and a partition of the plane into axis-aligned squares of width k. If we confine our problem to a single square T of this partition, we only have to consider covering area $A \cap T$ with the subset of sensor nodes in $\mathcal{S}$ that lie within T or less than one sensing range outside.

Given an algorithm $\mathcal{A}$ that computes f-approximate solutions for problems restricted to small squared areas, we can compute a solution for each square of the partition and combine them to a solution of the whole problem[3]. Unfortunately, such a solution does not have to be feasible. It is possible that a sensor node has to be considered for the coverage of more than one square and, thus, the node might require more than its available capacity to fulfill its assignments.

Now, consider a set of k partitions $\underline{\mathcal{I}} = \{\mathcal{T}^i\}$ with $i \in \{0, \ldots, k-1\} = \mathbb{Z}_k$. All partitions consist of axis-aligned squares of width k. Partition $\mathcal{T}^{i+1}$ is generated from partition $\mathcal{T}^i$ by translation to the top and to the right by 1 for $i \in \mathbb{Z}_k$ (see Figure 2). Observe that a sensor node has to be considered for the coverage of at most 4 squares. Also, the case of more than 1 square only occurs in at most two partitions as shown in Figure 2.

A solution $(\underline{C}^i, \underline{t}^i)$ of problem $(\mathcal{S}, 1)$ constructed from the solutions of each square of partition $\mathcal{T}^i$, $i \in \mathbb{Z}_k$ as described above, satisfies the two conditions

$$T\langle \mathcal{S}, 1 \rangle^i = \sum_{j : C_j^i \in \underline{C}^i} t_j^i \geq f \cdot T_{\mathrm{opt}}\langle \mathcal{S}, 1 \rangle, \tag{2}$$

$$\forall S_n \in \mathcal{S} : \sum_{j : S_n \in C_j^i} t_j^i \leq \begin{cases} 4 \cdot b_n & \text{node } S_n \text{ needed by more than one square,} \\ 1 \cdot b_n & \text{otherwise.} \end{cases} \tag{3}$$

---

[3] The schedules of all squares can be executed concurrently and independently. A node is active if the schedule of any square requires it to be active.

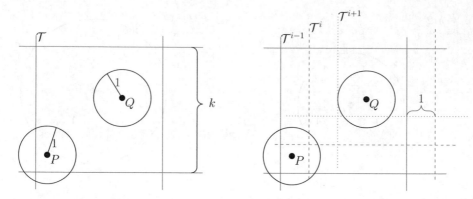

Fig. 2. *Left.* One partition $\mathcal{T}$ is depicted. Sensor node P has to be considered for the coverage of 4 squares, i.e. the circle around P with radius equal to one sensing range overlaps 4 squares. *Right.* Three subsequent partitions $\mathcal{T}^{i-1}$, $\mathcal{T}^i$ and $\mathcal{T}^{i+1}$ are shown. In partitions $\mathcal{T}^{i-1}$ and $\mathcal{T}^i$ node P overlaps 4 squares and Q only one. In partition $\mathcal{T}^{i+1}$ P overlaps only one square and Q two squares.

The lifetime $T\langle \mathcal{S}, 1\rangle^i$ of each solution is the sum over the durations $t^i_j \in \underline{t}^i$ of its covers $C^i_j \in \underline{C}^i$. It is optimal up to a factor of f. Similarly, the active time of each sensor node $S_n \in S$ is the sum over the durations $t^i_j \in \underline{t}^i$ of each cover $C^i_j \in \underline{C}^i$ with $S_n \in C^i_j$, i.e. of the covers containing node S_n. Its active time is at most 4 times its battery capacity.

Now, we can compute k (infeasible) solutions $(\underline{C}^i, \underline{t}^i)$ of problem $(\mathcal{S}, 1)$ with respect to each partition $\mathcal{T}^i$, $i \in \mathbb{Z}_k$ by combining the solutions of algorithm $\mathcal{A}$ for each square of the respective partition as described above. We obtain a feasible solution by concatenating these solutions and scaling the durations of each cover by a constant c, i.e. $(\cup_{i\in\mathbb{Z}_k}\underline{C}^i, c\cdot\cup_{i\in\mathbb{Z}_k}\underline{t}^i)$. Here, $c\cdot\cup_{i\in\mathbb{Z}_k}\underline{t}^i$ denotes a union of all $\underline{t}^i$ with each element $t^i_j \in \underline{t}^i$ multiplied by c. Lemma 2 summarizes this claim.

Lemma 2. *Let $k = \lceil 10/\epsilon \rceil$ with $\epsilon \in (0,1]$. Given an (infeasible) solution $(\underline{C}^i, \underline{t}^i)$ of problem $(\mathcal{S}, 1)$ with respect to each partition $\mathcal{T}^i, i \in \mathbb{Z}_k$ that has lifetime $T\langle \mathcal{S}, 1\rangle^i \geq f \cdot T_{\mathrm{opt}}\langle \mathcal{S}, 1\rangle$, a union of the solutions of all partitions as defined above and with $c = (1-\epsilon)/k$ is a feasible solution to problem $(\mathcal{S}, 1)$ with lifetime $T\langle \mathcal{S}, 1\rangle \geq f \cdot (1-\epsilon) \cdot T_{\mathrm{opt}}\langle \mathcal{S}, 1\rangle$.*

Proof. Lifetime: The lifetime $T\langle \mathcal{S}, 1\rangle$ of the union is the sum of the lifetimes $T\langle \mathcal{S}, 1\rangle^i$ for each partition $\mathcal{T}^i$, scaled by $(1-\epsilon)/k$. This sum is bounded by

$$T\langle \mathcal{S}, 1\rangle = \frac{1-\epsilon}{k} \sum_{i\in\mathbb{Z}_k} T\langle \mathcal{S}, 1\rangle^i \geq \frac{1-\epsilon}{k} \sum_{i\in\mathbb{Z}_k} f\cdot T_{\mathrm{opt}}\langle \mathcal{S}, 1\rangle = f\cdot(1-\epsilon)\cdot T_{\mathrm{opt}}\langle \mathcal{S}, 1\rangle$$

as claimed in the lemma. The inequality follows by Equation (2).

Feasibility: Each sensor node $S_n \in \mathcal{S}$ is active for the sum of the durations t^i_j of all covers $C^i_j \in \underline{C}^i$ with $S_n \in C^i_j$ over all partitions $\mathcal{T}^i$ with $i \in \mathbb{Z}_k$. This sum is bounded by

$$\frac{1-\epsilon}{k} \sum_{i \in \mathbb{Z}_k} \sum_{j:S_n \in C_j^i} t_j^i \leq \frac{1-\epsilon}{k}\left((k-2)\cdot 1 + 2\cdot 4\right)\cdot b_n \leq b_n.$$

The first inequality follows by Equation (3) and the fact that a sensor node is only required for the coverage of more than one square in at most two partitions. The second inequality follows due to our choice of k. Thus, the active time of each sensor node S_n is bound by b_n and, therefore, the solution is feasible. □

A similar approach, using shifting partitions to devise a polynomial approximation scheme for numerous NP-complete geometric covering and packing problems, has first been proposed by Hochbaum and Maas in [10].

4.3 Full Method

After introducing these two techniques, we now present our approximation algorithm. The general approach is depicted by Algorithm 2.

We assume the availability of an algorithm $\mathcal{A}$ that computes f-approximate solutions for problem instances $(\mathcal{S}, 1)$ confined to a small squared area and with sensor nodes restricted to positions on a grid with a runtime complexity of $g_{\mathcal{A}}(|\mathcal{S}|)$. Note that this algorithm combines the restrictions of both algorithms assumed in the previous sections.

Now, consider a general problem $(\mathcal{S}, 1)$. We construct a feasible solution $(\underline{C}, \underline{t})$ similar to Section 4.2 by using algorithm $\mathcal{A}$ to compute solutions for squares of partitions of the plane and combining them. But since algorithm $\mathcal{A}$ also requires the sensor nodes to lie on a grid, we can only compute these solutions, if we allow the sensing ranges to grow by a small amount, similar to Section 4.1. The whole algorithm yields a solution that comes arbitrarily close to the optimal solution if we additionally allow the sensing ranges to increase by a small factor and runs in pseudo-linear time. Theorem 1 summarizes these claims.

Algorithm 2. Approximation Algorithm

input: parameter $\delta \in [0,1], \epsilon \in (0,1]$, sensor nodes $\mathcal{S}$, area A, sensing range R
output: set of covers $\underline{C}$, set of corresponding durations $\underline{t}$

1. Define a grid of width $\delta/2$.
2. Move every node in $\mathcal{S}$ to the closest point on the grid $\to \tilde{\mathcal{S}}$.
3. Define k partitions $\mathcal{T}^i$ of the plane into axis-aligned squares of width k with $\mathcal{T}^{i+1}$ generated from partition $\mathcal{T}^i$ by translation to the top and to the right by 1 for $i \in \mathbb{Z}_k$.
4. For each partition $\mathcal{T}^i$,
   - use algorithm $\mathcal{A}$ to solve $(\tilde{\mathcal{S}}, 1+\delta/2)$ confined to each square of $\mathcal{T}^i$,
   - combine these partial solutions $\to (\underline{C}^i, \underline{t}^i)$
5. Unite the k solutions to $(\underline{C}, \underline{t}) = (\cup_{i \in \mathbb{Z}_k}\underline{C}^i, (1-\epsilon)/k \cdot \cup_{i \in \mathbb{Z}_k}\underline{t}^i)$.
6. Return $(\underline{C}, \underline{t})$.

Theorem 1. *Let $\delta \in [0, 1]$ and $k = \lceil 10/\epsilon \rceil$ with $\epsilon \in (0, 1]$. Algorithm 2 computes a feasible solution $(\underline{C}, \underline{t})$ of problem $(\mathcal{S}, 1 + \delta)$ with lifetime*

$$T\langle \mathcal{S}, 1 + \delta \rangle \geq (1 - \epsilon) \cdot f \cdot T_{\mathrm{opt}}\langle \mathcal{S}, 1 \rangle.$$

The runtime complexity of Algorithm 2 is pseudo-polynomially bounded by

$$O\Big(|\mathcal{S}| + 1/\epsilon|\mathcal{S}| \cdot g_{\mathcal{A}}(O(1/\delta^2\epsilon^2))\Big) = O(|\mathcal{S}|).$$

Proof. *Feasibility*: The feasibility of solution $(\underline{C}, \underline{t})$ follows directly from the proof of correctness in Lemma 1 and the proof of feasibility in Lemma 2. The latter states that the combination of feasible solutions to small squares results in a feasible solution. According to the former, a solution to each square is feasible even if sensor nodes are relocated to grid positions. Thus, $(\underline{C}, \underline{t})$ is feasible.

Approximation Guarantee: By applying a grid discretization, we obtain an approximation guarantee $T\langle \mathcal{S}, 1 + \delta \rangle \geq f \cdot T_{\mathrm{opt}}\langle \mathcal{S}, 1 \rangle$ for the solution of each square according to Lemma 1. As stated by Equation (2), the same approximation guarantee holds for each solution $(\underline{C}^i, \underline{t}^i)$ of $(\mathcal{S}, 1 + \delta)$ with $(\underline{C}^i, \underline{t}^i)$ obtained by combining the solutions of all squares of partition T^i, $i \in \mathbb{Z}_k$. Combining these k solutions as described above, yields an additional factor $(1 - \epsilon)$ in the approximation guarantee according to Lemma 2. The claimed lifetime follows.

Runtime: According to Lemma 1, there is an additive overhead of $O(|\mathcal{S}|)$ when using a grid discretization. The solution for each square can be found in $g_{\mathcal{A}}(O(1/\delta^2\epsilon^2))$ since each square only contains $O(1/\delta^2\epsilon^2)$ distinct grid points and, thus, at most as many sensor nodes. The number of sensor nodes to be considered for covering each square is higher by at most a constant factor since only nodes closer to the square than one sensing range have to be considered in addition. There are k partitions and in each partition there are at most $4|\mathcal{S}|$ squares to be considered since, according to Section 4.2, each sensor node is required for the cover of at most 4 squares in each partition. Thus, solutions for $k \cdot O(4|\mathcal{S}|) = O(1/\epsilon|\mathcal{S}|)$ squares have to be found.   □

Note that if δ, ϵ are constant, the input of algorithm $\mathcal{A}$ is of constant size. Thus, any implementation of algorithm $\mathcal{A}$ would only contribute a constant factor to the runtime of Algorithm 2 with respect to $|\mathcal{S}|$. Naturally, one would try to use an efficient implementation or one with a good approximation ratio f. For example, even an exact solver could be used.

Refinement. We can refine the runtime complexity of Algorithm 2 if area A is connected. $|S|$ disks of radius $1 + \delta$ can span at most $2r|S|/k = O(\epsilon(1 + \delta)|S|)$ squares of width k if they have to be connected. Thus, the number of squares to be considered in each partition is restricted accordingly. Note that this arrangement requires A to be an axis-aligned rectangular area of infinitesimal small width.

If area A is good-natured as specified below, we can further reduce the number of squares to be considered in each partition. According to [11], at least $2/\sqrt{27}r^2$

disks of radius r are required to cover an area of size 1. Thus, $|\mathcal{S}|$ disks of radius $1+\delta$ cover at most $O(\epsilon^2(1+\delta)^2|\mathcal{S}|)$ squares of size k^2. This estimation holds true if the length of the border of A times $1+\delta$ is much smaller than the area occupied by A. Note that area A does not have to be connected for this assessment.

If we can assess the lifetime of the sensor network, the runtime complexity can be further improved. With T_{lower} a lower bound on the lifetime of the sensor network and b_{max} the maximum capacity over all sensor nodes, $\lceil T_{lower}/b_{max} \rceil$ denotes the minimum number of sensor nodes required to cover any position for the complete lifetime of the network. This reduces that number of nodes that can be active in each partition to at most $1/\lceil b_{max}/T_{lower} \rceil |\mathcal{S}|$, if a cover exists. Since the number of relevant squares depends on the number of sensor nodes, it is reduced accordingly.

Also note that several of the numerical constants can be further optimized. The width of the grid can be reduced to $\delta/\sqrt{2}$ and the the minimum width of a square to $k = \lceil 6\frac{1-\epsilon}{\epsilon} \rceil$ without having to change the given statements. The range of parameter δ remains strict unless partitions are constructed differently. The range of parameter ϵ is strict.

Finally, different partitions of area A can be used to improve the runtime. For example, using a hexagonal partitioning scheme results in only $k = \lceil 4\frac{1-\epsilon}{\epsilon} \rceil$ partitions that have to be computed, but each hexagon covers about $\sqrt{3}$ times more space than one square.

5 Adaptation to Target Monitoring

Berman et al. stated in [1,2] that the area monitoring problem can be reduced to a target monitoring problem for convex sensing ranges. Thus, many subsequent studies only concern themselves with target monitoring. Our approximation algorithm was originally designed for the problem of monitoring an arbitrary area, but it can be easily adapted to monitor a set of discrete targets.

In principle, Algorithm 2 is already sufficient for this task. We only have to replace algorithm $\mathcal{A}$ by another one that solves the target monitoring problem on a squared area with sensor nodes placed on a grid. However, the runtime of this algorithm also depends on the number of targets. This can be resolved by also discretizing target positions. Multiple targets occupying the same position can be regarded as one for the purpose of covering. If we relocate them to the same grid positions as the sensor nodes, there are at most $O(1/\delta^2\epsilon^2)$ targets in each square. Thus, the runtime of the approximation algorithm no longer depends on the number of targets.

Note that for our statements to remain correct, all sensing ranges have to be doubled, i.e. $T_{opt}\langle \mathcal{S}, 1 + \delta \rangle$ has to be replaced by $T_{opt}\langle \mathcal{S}, 1 + 2\delta \rangle$ and solving $(\tilde{\mathcal{S}}, 1 + \delta/2)$ by solving $(\tilde{\mathcal{S}}, 1 + \delta)$. This approach is required since now both, sensor nodes and targets, are relocated. It is depicted in Figure 3 analogical to Figure 1 for the area monitoring case.

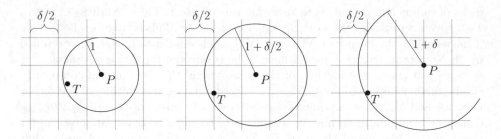

Fig. 3. *Left.* Sensor node P with sensing range 1 covers target T. Both are located in arbitrary positions. A grid of width $\delta/2$ is plotted. *Middle.* Target T has been moved to a grid position. The sensing range of sensor node P has to be increased to $1 + \delta/2$ to still cover T. *Right.* Sensor node P has also been moved to a grid position and its sensing range increased by an additional $\delta/2$ to $1 + \delta$. It still covers target T.

6 Proof of NP-Completeness

In this section, we provide a proof of NP-completeness of SNLP by exploiting certain properties of linear programs (LPs). We are convinced that this novel proof is necessary since the currently accepted proof by Cardei et al. in [5] does not take into account the geometric structure of the problem. By this omission a much more difficult problem was considered.

We first introduce a geometric problem and prove its NP-completeness. Then, we formulate SNLP as linear program and prove that it is equally hard to solve than a related LP problem. Finally, we show that the related problem and the geometric problem are equivalent.

Theorem 2. *The Minimum Dominating Set (MDS) problem on unit disk graphs is NP-hard [12]. The same is true for weighted MDS on unit disk graphs.*

Lemma 3. *Given a unit disk graph $G = (V, E)$ and a unit disk embedding of V, a set $D \subseteq V$ is a dominating set iff the the set of unit disks centered at D is a cover of V.*

Proof. First, let the set of unit disks centered at D be a cover of V. Thus, there is at least one node $d \in D$ for each node $v \in V$ within a distance of at most 1. By definition of the unit disk graph, there exists an edge (d, v) or $d \equiv v$. Therefore, D is a dominating set of G.

Now, let D be a dominating set of G. Thus, every node $v \in V$ is either in D or neighboring to a node $d \in D$. By definition of the unit disk graph, the distance between v and d is at most 1 in the latter case. Therefore, the set of unit disks centered at D covers N. □

Definition 1. Minimum-Cost Geometric Disc Coverage (MCGDC). *Given a set of points P in the plane and a set of unit disks U with associated costs $c_{1,\dots,|U|}$. Can all points in P be covered by a subset $D \subseteq U$ with total cost $\sum_{i \in D} c_i \leq C$?*

Theorem 3. *MCGDC is NP-complete.*

Proof. NP-hardness is proved by reduction of the decision variant of weighted MDS. Nodes V of the MDS input graph $G = (V, E)$ become centers of the unit disks U in MCGDC and are also used as point set P. Then, the geometric cover of U computed by MCGDC is also a dominating set of V, as shown by Lemma 3. Since costs in MCGDC correspond to weights in MDS, a solution of MCGDC is also a solution of the decision variant of weighted MDS. NP-completeness follows trivially.   □

Definition 2. Linear Programs. *SNLP can be formulated as linear program* $T_{\mathrm{opt}}\langle \mathcal{S}, 1 \rangle = \max\{\underline{1} \cdot \underline{t} | \mathbf{M}\underline{t} \leq \underline{b}\}$ *with* $\underline{1} = (1, \ldots, 1) \in \mathbb{R}^{|\mathcal{S}|}$ *and* $\mathbf{M}_{i,j} = 1$ *iff* $S_i \in C_j$, $\mathbf{M}_{i,j} = 0$ *otherwise. Note that each column of matrix* $\mathbf{M}$ *corresponds to a cover* $C_j \in \mathcal{C}$.

The dual linear program $\min\{\underline{b} \cdot \underline{w} | \mathbf{M}^{\mathrm{T}}\underline{w} \geq \underline{1}\}$ *can be read as finding minimal costs for all sensor nodes so that the cost of each cover is at least 1. We interpret the elements of* $\underline{w} = (w_1, \ldots, w_{|\mathcal{S}|})$ *as costs for using the respective nodes, i.e.* w_i *is the cost of node* $S_i \in \mathcal{S}$.

Definition 3. Separation Problem. *Given an LP, verify whether a candidate solution meets all constraints of the LP, and if not, provide a counter-example.*

Theorem 4. *The separation problem associated with an LP is polynomially solvable iff the corresponding LP is polynomially solvable [13].*

Lemma 4. *The separation problem associated with the dual of SNLP is equivalent to MCGDC.*

Proof. The separation problem associated with the dual of SNLP can be formulated as follows: Given a candidate solution consisting of sensor nodes $\mathcal{S}$ and associated weights $\underline{w}$, decide whether there exists a cover of area A using nodes with a total cost of less than 1. If true, the candidate solution does not fulfill all constraints. Since covering an area is equal to covering a set of points [1,2], this problem is equal to MCGDC with costs $c_i = w_i$ and $C = 1$.   □

Theorem 5. *The Sensor Network Lifetime Problem (SNLP) is NP-complete.*

Proof. Theorem 3 states that MCGDC is NP-complete. Since MCGDC and the separation problem associated with the dual of SNLP are equivalent (Lemma 4), the latter is also NP-complete. Thus, the dual of SNLP is also NP-complete by Theorem 4. Since a solution of the dual problem of an LP can be transformed into a solution of the LP in polynomial time [14], SNLP is NP-complete.   □

This concludes the proof of NP-completeness of SNLP. Note again that this proof incorporates the geometric structure of the problem unlike the proof by Cardei et al. in [5]. Neglecting this structure, they only proved the NP-completeness of a much more general problem.

7   Conclusion

Even though our theoretical results are very strong, they only mark a first step. There are still many ways to enhance the underlying model, e.g. considering non-uniform sensing ranges is of great interest to us. Thus, we are currently looking into basing our algorithm more firmly in the field of computational geometry. By proving its approximation and runtime guarantees for general low-dimensional metrics, the inclusion of obstacles and variable sensing ranges into our model should become easy. Also, a generalization to higher dimensions and angular dependent sensing ranges would be possible, as well as removing the dependence on squared partitions which would provide more flexibility.

Furthermore, we intend to implement and to experimentally evaluate our approximation algorithm using an exact solver based on column generation as algorithm $\mathcal{A}$ for computing the small subproblems. This task will most likely encompass several interesting aspects of the field of algorithm engineering.

Since we are considering a sensor network, a distributed implementation of our algorithm is a natural extension. Its structure is already well-suited for a parallel implementation with the partition of the considered area into independent squares. This could be taken even further, e.g. with all sensor nodes organizing themselves independently into these partitions. Overall, we are very interested in looking into distributed variants of our approximation algorithm.

Finally, we hope that our novel proof of NP-completeness will be spread in the community and, henceforth, be referenced as correct proof for the area monitoring problem (SNLP).

Acknowledgements. We would like to thank Sanjeev Arora and David Steurer for providing key ideas of this work and for the enlightening insight into approximation algorithms and computational geometry they provided.

References

1. Berman, P., Calinescu, G., Shah, C., Zelikovsky, A.: Power efficient monitoring management in sensor networks. In: Proceedings of the Wireless Communications and Networking Conference 2004, vol. 4, pp. 2329–2334. IEEE Computer Society Press, Los Alamitos (March 2004)
2. Berman, P., Calinescu, G., Shah, C., Zelikovsky, A.: Efficient energy management in sensor networks. In: Pan, Y., Xiao, Y. (eds.) Ad Hoc and Sensor Networks. Wireless Networks and Mobile Computing, vol. 2, pp. 71–90. Nova Science Publisher, Bombay (2005)
3. Cardei, M., Wu, W.: Energy-efficient coverage problems in wireless ad-hoc sensor networks. Computer Communications 29(4), 413–420 (2006)
4. Slijepcevic, S., Potkonjak, M.: Power efficient organization of wireless sensor networks. In: Proceedings of the IEEE International Conference on Communications 2001, pp. 472–476 (June 2001)
5. Cardei, M., Thai, M.T., Li, Y., Wu, W.: Energy-Efficient Target Coverage in Wireless Sensor Networks. In: Proceedings of the 24th Annual Joint Conference of the IEEE Computer and Communications Societies (Infocom), vol. 4, pp. 1976–1984. IEEE Computer Society Press, Los Alamitos (2005)

6. Garg, N., Könemann, J.: Faster and Simpler Algorithms for Multicommodity Flow and other Fractional Packing Problems. In: Proceedings of the 39th Annual IEEE Symposium on Foundations of Computer Science (FOCS 1998), pp. 300–309. IEEE Computer Society, Los Alamitos (1998)
7. Dhawan, A., Vu, C.T., Zelikovsky, A., Li, Y., Prasad, S.K.: Maximum Lifetime of Sensor Networks with Adjustable Sensing Range. In: Proceedings of the International Workshop on Self-Assembling Wireless Networks. IEEE Computer Society, Los Alamitos (2006)
8. Gu, Y., Liu, H., Zhao, B.: Joint Scheduling and Routing for Lifetime Elongation in Surveillance Sensor Networks. In: Proceedings of the 2nd IEEE Asia-Pacific Service Computing Conference (APSCC), pp. 304–311 (2007)
9. Luo, J., Girard, A., Rosenberg, C.: Efficient Algorithms to Solve a Class of Resource Allocation Problems in Large Wireless Networks. In: 7th International Symposium on Modeling and Optimization in Mobile, Ad Hoc, and Wireless Networks, WiOpt (June 2009)
10. Hochbaum, D.S., Maass, W.: Approximation schemes for covering and packing problems in image processing and VLSI. Journal of the ACM 32(1), 130–136 (1985)
11. Williams, R.: The Geometrical Foundation of Natural Structure: A Source Book of Design. The Dover Publications, New York (June 1979)
12. Masuyama, S., Ibaraki, T., Hasegawa, T.: The Computational Complexity of the m-Center Problems on the Plane. IEICE Transactions Japan E64(2), 57–64 (1981)
13. Grötschel, M., Lovász, L., Schrijver, A.: The ellipsoid method and its consequences in combinatorial optimization. Combinatorica 1(2), 169–197 (1981)
14. Dantzig, G.B.: Linear Programming and Extensions. Princeton University Press, Princeton (1963)

MSDR-D Network Localization Algorithm

Kevin Coogan[1], Varun Khare[1], Stephen G. Kobourov[1], and Bastian Katz[2]

[1] Department of Computer Science
University of Arizona
{kpcoogan,vkhare,kobourov}@cs.arizona.edu
[2] Faculty of Informatics
Universität Karlsruhe (TH)
katz@ira.uka.de

Abstract. We present a distributed multi-scale dead-reckoning (MSDR-D) algorithm for network localization that utilizes local distance and angular information for nearby sensors. The algorithm is anchor-free and does not require particular network topology, rigidity of the underlying communication graph, or high average connectivity. The algorithm scales well to large and sparse networks with complex topologies and outperforms previous algorithms when the noise levels are high. The algorithm is simple to implement and is available, along with source code, executables, and experimental results, at http://msdr-d.cs.arizona.edu/.

1   Introduction

Wireless sensor networks are widely studied and have numerous applications, such as environmental monitoring and mapping [1]. In most applications, determining the location of the sensors in a sensor network is an important problem. Manual configuration is infeasible in large-scale networks and relying on location hardware such as a GPS in each sensor can be expensive in terms of cost, size, or energy. Relying on a fraction of location-aware sensors (also called *anchors* or *seeds*) offers a good cost/accuracy tradeoff. However, GPS-like devices are ineffective inside buildings, under thick tree canopies and underground, making anchor-based methods unsuitable. With this in mind we consider localizing a network of anchor-free sensors in areas with non-trivial (e.g., non-simple, non-convex) underlying topologies. We assume that the sensors are distributed randomly and have distance (*range*) and angle information about their immediate neighbors, but no initial knowledge of their location. Distance information in sensor networks can be computed by measuring either round trip times or signal strength. Sensors equipped with multiple antennae, such as UCLA's Medusa [19], can be used to compute angle information by providing a counter-clockwise ordering of neighbors, as well as an approximation of the angle between adjacent neighbors. It is typical to assume the values of range and angle measurements approximate a Gaussian distribution centered around the actual value. Our force-directed MSDR-D algorithm uses these two measurements in a distributed fashion to efficiently compute sensor locations without relying on strong assumptions, such as high average degree or rigidity of the underlying graph, use of anchors, simple underlying topologies, etc.

C. Scheideler (Ed.): ALGOSENSORS 2010, LNCS 6451, pp. 148–160, 2010.
© Springer-Verlag Berlin Heidelberg 2010

1.1 Related Work

Many different algorithms for sensor network localization have been proposed, relying on nearly as many different assumptions. While certainly failing to mention all relevant previous work, here we try to briefly survey earlier work on anchor-free, range-based, force-directed methods. Using the classical multidimensional scaling technique, MDS-MAP [21] is a centralized anchor-free algorithm which depends only on the range data and works well when sensor nodes are uniformly distributed. MDS-MAP does not work well on irregularly-shaped networks where the shortest path distance between pairs of sensor nodes correlates poorly with their actual Euclidean distance. MDS-MAP(P) [20] is a distributed version which stitches together small patches obtained via MDS-MAP. It uses a computationally expensive refinement step to avoid accumulation of errors in the incremental stitching process. Costa *et al.* [3] use local refinements to improve the stitching of local MDS maps but rely on a non-trivial fraction of anchor nodes.

Priyantha *et al.* [17] propose a distributed anchor-free layout technique based on force-directed methods, while Gotsman and Koren [12] utilize a distributed majorization technique. However, neither approach makes use of angular information, and both make the simplifying assumption that sensors are distributed in convex polygonal areas. Of these approaches that do utilize angle information, most assume that some number of the sensors in the graph know their positions *a priori*, either by way of GPS [6,16,18,19] or by manual input [10].

A similar spring-embedder based algorithm is used as part of the VFA sensor deployment algorithm [22]. VFA assumes random placement of some sensors across a region, and then uses a distributed algorithm to determine placement of new sensors for optimal coverage given range information. Fekete *et al.* [8] and Kröller *et al.* [15] use a combination of stochastic, topological, and geometric ideas for determining the topology of the region and its boundary. However, this approach assumes average node degrees in the hundreds to achieve its results, whereas we reply on average node degrees that are an order of magnitude smaller.

Vivaldi [4] and similar systems for predicting network latency [5] use a force-directed style algorithm in a distributed manner to estimate round trip times in a network, without probing all pairs of nodes to measure distances. However, Vivaldi embeds node locations in 2-D space in order to approximate round trip times, without regard for their actual locations. In our setting we would like to embed the nodes so that the embedding approximates the actual locations of the sensors.

The multi-scale dead-reckoning (MSDR) algorithm [7] is a centralized anchor-free force-directed localization algorithm that uses range and angular information. Instead of shortest paths between pairs of nodes, MSDR computes dead-reckoning paths, based on range and angular data, to avoid the accumulation of errors in non-uniform topologies (i.e., topologies where the shortest path in the underlying graph does not correlate with the Euclidean distance). Katz and Wagner [14] describe a force-directed approach that uses angular information similar to [7] in a distributed fashion. Their approach, while distributed, uses a hierarchical grouping of nodes that requires "global" exchange of information prior to the localization of any node, thus incurring high communication and storage overhead. Specifically, a hierarchy with all nodes in the graph must be built in a centralized fashion and stored in all nodes before the actual localization can begin.

1.2 Our Contribution

We present MSDR-D, a new sensor network localization algorithm that is fully distributed. Our algorithm employs a force-directed method that computes dead-reckoning
distances between nodes in the network, while relying on only local range and angular information. These distance measurements are more accurate than shortest path
distances, which becomes crucial in non-convex and non-simple network topologies.
MSDR-D also scales well to large and sparse networks and is robust to the accumulation of errors due to its multi-scale nature and low communication overhead. MSDR-D
is a truly distributed algorithm, in the sense that instructions are given to each node and
result in a localization of the entire graph with no global information (e.g., a representation of the entire underlying network, a communication hierarchy, centralized server)
required at any stage. MSDR-D outperforms earlier algorithms especially with noisy
input data. Most importantly, the algorithm employs no broadcast messages, and uses a
constant number of local messages and constant memory per node.

2 Distributed MSDR Algorithm

Our algorithm is a distributed version of the multi-scale dead-reckoning (MSDR) al-
gorithm of Forrester *et al.* [7], which is in turn a force-directed placement algorithm.
Therefore, we begin with a brief review of force-directed algorithms in general, and of
MSDR in particular.

2.1 Force Directed Algorithms

In its full generality, the sensor network localization problem can be thought of as that of
calculating a graph layout. Force-directed algorithms, also known as spring-embedders,
calculate a graph layout by defining an objective function which maps each layout into a
number in $\mathcal{R}^+$ representing the energy of the layout. This function is defined so that low
energies correspond to good layouts, that is, layouts in which adjacent nodes are near
each other and non-adjacent nodes are well spaced. A force-directed algorithm proceeds
by repeatedly calculating forces acting on each node and moving nodes around in search
of a (often local) minimum of the energy function. The forces acting on a node can be a
combination of attractive forces between neighbors and repulsive forces between non-
adjacent nodes as in the Fruchterman-Reingold algorithm [9]. Alternatively the forces
can be based on graph theoretic distances, determined by the length of the shortest paths
between them, as in the Kamada-Kawai algorithm [13]. The force exerted on node v in
graph G in the Kamada-Kawai algorithm is calculated as follows:

$$F(v) = \sum_{\forall u \neq v} \left(\frac{d(u, v)^2}{\mathrm{dist}_G(u, v)^2 \cdot \mathrm{IdealLength}^2} - 1 \right) (\mathrm{pos}[u] - \mathrm{pos}[v]),$$

where $d(u, v)$ is the current Euclidean distance between nodes u and v, $\mathrm{dist}_G(u, v)$
is the length of the shortest path between nodes u and v, IdealLength is a constant
corresponding to the desired distance between a pair of adjacent vertices (determined
by the size of the graph and the drawing area), and $\mathrm{pos}[u]$ and $\mathrm{pos}[v]$ are the positions

Fig. 1. Typical results illustrating localizations of a U-shaped network using only range information (from [7]). The network on the left contains pairs of nodes whose graph distances are not well correlated with their Euclidean distances (especially pairs of nodes at opposite ends of the U) transforming the U into a W or a Z.

of nodes u and v in the current layout. The energy of the current layout is obtained by summing the forces acting on all nodes in the graph.

In simple, convex topologies the graph distance, computed as shortest path between two nodes, correlates well with the Euclidean distance between them. However, this is not true for more complicated topologies where a long path between two nodes does not necessarily imply they are physically far from each other (e.g., nodes at opposite ends of a U-shaped network); see Fig. 1. With the help of angular information about neighboring edges along the path between a pair of nodes we can overcome this problem as shown by the MSDR algorithm.

2.2 MSDR

MSDR is a force-directed algorithm which computes the placement of nodes in few phases involving only subsets of nodes. It uses a modified force calculation which takes into account edge lengths and angles between adjacent edges. MSDR consists of two main stages: in the first stage a graph filtration is computed in a bottom-up fashion and in the second stage the filtration is used in the top-down manner to place the nodes in the graph.

The first stage constructs the graph filtration $\mathcal{V} = \{\mathcal{V}_0, \mathcal{V}_1, \ldots, \mathcal{V}_m\}$. The set initial set $\mathcal{V}_0$ contains all the nodes in the graph. Set $\mathcal{V}_1$ is a maximal independent set and contains nodes at 2^1 hops from each other. In general, set $\mathcal{V}_i$ contains nodes that are at least 2^i hops away from each other, and $\mathcal{V}_i \subset \mathcal{V}_{i-1}$. When complete, there are $m + 1$ total filtration sets such that $\mathcal{V}_m \subset \mathcal{V}_{m-1} \subset \ldots \mathcal{V}_2 \subset \mathcal{V}_1 \subset \mathcal{V}_0$, with the smallest set containing exactly 3 nodes.

The second stage of the MSDR algorithm consists of m phases of force-directed calculations, used to compute node locations, one filtration set at a time, starting with the smallest set $\mathcal{V}_m$. It is easy to see that the number of phases m is at most logarithmic in the size of the network, or more precisely at most logarithmic in the diameter of the network, as nodes at filtration level i are at distance at least 2^i from each other.

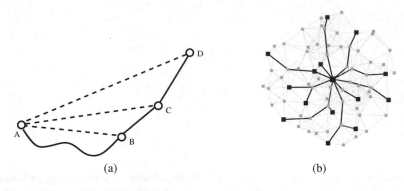

(a)   (b)

Fig. 2. (a) Computing $\text{dist}_{DR}(A, D)$, given a path between them with intermediate nodes B and C, where the dead reckoning distance between adjacent nodes is equal to the distance between them (from range data) using the law of cosines: $\text{dist}_{DR}(A, C) = \sqrt{\text{dist}^2_{DR}(A, B) + \text{dist}^2_{DR}(B, C) - 2\text{dist}_{DR}(A, B) * \text{dist}_{DR}(B, C) * cos(\widehat{ABC})}$ and similarly $\text{dist}_{DR}(A, D)$ once we have $\text{dist}_{DR}(A, C)$. (b) A combination of neighbors and far away nodes are used to fit a locally obtained map in the larger network.

In order to run the force-directed algorithm on the nodes in the smallest filtration set $\mathcal{V}_m$, distances between the 3 nodes in this set are needed. A breadth first search from each node is used to find a path to the other two nodes. Once a path has been found, the local distance and angle information at each step is used in a "dead-reckoning" fashion to calculate the distance to each of the other nodes.

Deduced reckoning (or dead reckoning) is an ancient method for estimating the current position of a moving object, assuming knowledge of the direction and distance traveled from a previously known position. Given a path between two nodes, along with the lengths of the edges and the angles between adjacent edges, we can calculate the dead reckoning location of one node with respect to the other using the law of cosines; see Fig. 2(a). Thus, we can replace the shortest path distance with the dead reckoning distance in the force-directed calculation, by adding only local calculation and communication overhead (only immediate neighbors in the sensor network need to communicate) to propagate the information. The main advantage of dead reckoning distances is that they correlate well with Euclidean distances for both simple and complex topologies (non-simple, non-convex, etc.).

In phase i, nodes that are in $\mathcal{V}_{i-1}$, but not in $\mathcal{V}_i$ are localized. For each new node, breadth first search is used to find its distance to a small number of nodes that have already been placed. After each phase, a local force-directed refinement to the placements is applied. In this way new nodes receive an initial placement in the graph, and already placed nodes have their positions refined. The process continues in this "multi-scale" fashion until the nodes in $\mathcal{V}_0$ (i.e., all the nodes) have been placed. Note that the dead-reckoning forces used to calculate node displacements are given by:

$$F_{DR}(v) = \sum_{\forall u \neq v} \left(\frac{\text{d}(u, v)^2}{\text{dist}_{DR}(u, v)^2 \cdot \text{idealLength}^2} - 1 \right) (\text{pos}[u] - \text{pos}[v]),$$

where $\text{dist}_{DR}(u, v)$ is the dead-reckoning distance between nodes u and v, computed from the edge lengths and angles between adjacent nodes along the u-v path.

MSDR creates very good anchor-free localizations, performing much better than earlier algorithms when the underlying network topologies are non-simple, or non-convex. The algorithm scales to large and sparse networks as it is resilient to noise and accumulation of errors. The main disadvantage of the MSDR algorithm is that it is inherently centralized, thus forcing prohibitively high communication overhead if implemented in distributed fashion. Katz and Wagner [14] use a distributed, hierarchical reduction technique in an effort to decentralize the inherently centralized force-directed algorithm. In the first of two phases of this algorithm, a global overlay hierarchy is computed in an inherently centralized way and stored in each node. The second phase utilizes the hierarchy in a distributed localization of the sensor nodes. The algorithm begins with each node exchanging information with its 3-hop neighborhood and running a local force-directed localization. Only a fraction of the nodes, a maximal independent set, then defines an overlay network, connecting pairs of nodes having distance at most 3 in the original graph. Using estimated distances and directions from local solutions as the input, the same step is recursively applied on the overlay network, until the overlay network finally consists of a single node. This node then is localized as the origin and all nodes in the network are assigned positions in a top-down fashion. Given a localization for a node in some level's overlay network, close "dominated" nodes from the next lower level network are positioned using the local solution of the already localized node in the respective overlay level. Unlike iterative approaches that "glue" together local solutions, this approach benefits from the stress minimization on different scales, preventing cumulative localization errors especially in very large networks.

2.3 MSDR-D

Both of the above force-directed algorithms [7,14] result in very accurate localizations but they are far from perfect when implemented in distributed fashion. The main disadvantage of these approaches is the reliance on a centralized server which computes the localization and the corresponding prohibitively high communication overhead. Specifically, the Katz and Wagner algorithm [14] builds and stores a hierarchy for the entire graph before the localization, which leads to the high communication and storage overhead. In our approach we overcome such problems due to the truly distributed nature of our algorithm, albeit at the expense of somewhat reduced quality of the localization.

MSDR-D Overview: MSDR-D begins with a single arbitrarily chosen root node and then localizes the network in a "bottom up" manner. The root node calculates a neighborhood of nearby nodes (including itself) that it will localize. We call this neighborhood the root's k-neighborhood, where k refers to the maximum number of hops from the root to any node in the neighborhood and is typically a small constant like 2 or 3. To this neighborhood, the root adds a small number of "far-away" nodes that are used to improve the global localization. Using these two types of nodes, the root performs a local MSDR force-directed localization that utilizes distance and angle information, and assigns a position to each node in its k-neighborhood. Finally, the root examines its k-neighborhood, and selects nodes adjacent to, but outside, the neighborhood to be root nodes for the next iteration.

In the next iteration, all selected nodes become root nodes and build their own neighborhoods. Since these new roots are on the edge of the old neighborhood, it is expected that a fraction of the nodes in the new k neighborhoods will have already been placed. The distance and angle information for these nodes is used to perform the localization, but their positions never change. Once a node is placed, it is considered fixed. It is this overlap with previous iterations along with the far-away nodes that allows for the "stitching together" of local results. The iterations of localizing neighborhoods and selecting new roots continues until all nodes in the graph have been placed.

The k-neighborhood: Since our MSDR-D algorithm relies on the notion of localizing nodes that are "close" to the root, we need to define precisely what this means. We use the idea of a k-hop neighborhood, where a root node's k-hop neighborhood is all the nodes that can be reached from the root in no more than k hops. Note that here we do not take into consideration actual distances, but count immediate neighbors as nodes that are one hop away. We assume, for the purposes of the localization, that all nodes in the neighborhood know the distances (from the sensor range data) to all other nodes in the neighborhood. Typically, small value of k will result in small neighborhoods that can be localized well with respect to each other, but not with respect to nodes in the graph outside the neighborhood. Conversely, large values of k take into account more graph information, but require more work and communication to calculate the forces for all the nodes in the neighborhood. In our implementation k is an input parameter typically set to 2 or 3.

Far-away nodes: We would like to use as much graph information as possible to place the nodes at each iteration, but we do not want to suffer the communication, computation, and memory penalties of increasing k too much. Instead, we use a few "far-away" nodes as a substitute of a much larger neighborhood; see Fig. 2(b). The idea is to randomly select some constant number of nodes that are too far away from the root to be in its k-neighborhood, and incorporate their information into the localization. The information from these nodes improves the localization steps by aligning the local placements with the overall shape of the network. To select these nodes we use a simple random-walk algorithm starting with a border node (a node with non-neighborhood nodes as immediate neighbors). The number of steps in the walk is chosen at random between 1 and some constant smaller that the diameter of the network. At each step a random neigbor is selected and a message is passed, containing the current path and dead reckoning distance to the root. After the last step, the information is propagated back to the root node along the stored path and the last node is added to the neighborhood as a far-away node. In our implementation the number of far-away nodes is an input parameter typically set to 9 or 10.

Pseudocode: Algorithm 1 summarizes the MSDR-D algorithm that is executed at each individual sensor node. Each node is assumed to be waiting for a message from elsewhere in the network. Two kinds of messages can arrive: one that wants to assign a location to the node, and another that orders the node to become a root, and perform its own localization. Note that once a node has a location in the graph, it ignores all following messages.

In line 6 of the pseudocode, "myLocation" refers to the location of the node receiving the message. In line 11 of the pseudocode, "$k + 1$ hop neighbors" are the border nodes (nodes at graph distance $k+1$ from the current root node). These nodes are not assigned locations by the root and are candidates to be root nodes in the next iteration.

Algorithm 1. MSDR-D Distributed Localization Algorithm

```
 1: Handle Message:: Location loc
 2: if myLocation == null then
 3:     myLocation = loc
 4: end if
 5: Handle Message:: Start Localization
 6: if myLocation==null then
 7:     Create neighborhood of k-hop neighbors and farAway nodes
 8:     Calculate angle and distance information from neighbors
 9:     Localize
10:     Distribute coordinates to k-hop neighbors
11:     Ping k+1 hop neighbors to Start Localization
12: end if
```

3   Experiments and Results

In this section, we describe our methodology for experimentation, the generation of our simulated sensor networks, and the metrics we use to compare results to other experiments. Of the previous algorithms that utilize range and angular information, most assume that some number of the sensors in the graph know their positions *a priori*, either by way of GPS [6,16,18,19] or by manual input [10]. Such assumptions make it significantly easier to localize than in our setting, where we have no a priori positions. Further, some of the earlier algorithms assume an underlying network protocol, only report results on small graphs, or do not make source code available. We directly compare MSDR-D to two previous algorithms [7,14] which make the same assumptions (use of distance and angular information, no reliance on anchors or special network protocols).

3.1   Experimental Setup

We use simulated networks of sensors that are distributed across a variety of underlying shapes, leading to different network topologies. Input parameters that control the network type include the number of sensor nodes, the average node degree, shape of the area in which to distribute the nodes, and range and angle errors. We vary the number of sensor nodes from 50 to 1000. The average node degree is typically between 6-12. We use several standard shapes to evaluate the performance of the algorithm, including square, star, square donut (square with a hole in the center), and U-shape; see Fig. 3. Range errors vary from 0 to 50% and angle error varies from $0°$ to $25°$. Note that an angle error of $20°$, which may sound too accurate, means that a neighbor is sensed anywhere $20°$ to the left or $20°$ to the right of its true location (which corresponds to a sector of angle $40°$ or 1/9 of the total 360). Both kinds of errors are drawn from a Gaussian distribution.

Fig. 3. Localization of networks (1000 nodes, degree 8, range error 20%, angle error $10°$) with non-convex and non-simple topologies: input above, MSRD-D results below

Once the shape of the underlying network has been chosen, sensor nodes are distributed at random, so as to achieve the desired average degree. When small average degrees are desired, the network might become disconnected; we ignore these cases and only consider connected networks. This leads to a more regularly connected networks, akin to grid-with-perturbation networks [2].

3.2 Evaluation Metrics

There is a large number of different metrics used to evaluate the performance of sensor localization algorithms. Different assumptions (anchored or anchor-free, range-based or range-free, static or mobile) and different goals (resilience to errors, scalability in the number of sensor nodes, applicability in non-simple topologies) lead to different metrics that best capture the particular setup. For anchored networks it is often enough to measure the average distance between the location of a node, $loc[u]$, and its true position, $pos[u]$, over all nodes in the network: Error $= (\sum_{\forall u} |pos[u] - loc[u]|)/n$. However, such a metric assumes that some of the nodes are anchors, and the final layout has been aligned so as to match the true network using affine transformations (rotation, translation, scaling) [20,21].

The *global energy ratio* used by Priyantha *et al.* [17] and the *average relative deviation* (ARD) used by Gotsman and Koren [12] are employed in an anchor-free setting and consider the distances between the $O(n^2)$ pairs of nodes in the network. The two metrics are similar and appropriate for comparing layouts obtained by different anchor-free algorithms for graphs of the same size. However, both metrics fail to compare the quality of the localizations across different graph sizes, as they are total rather than scaled sum-of-squares type measurements.

The Frobenius metric [11] has been used to evaluate the performance of anchor-free localization algorithms [7,14] and is well-suited to compare the quality of the localizations across different graph sizes. The Frobenius metric is a scaled sum-of-squares and can be used to measure the global quality of the localization, by considering all pairs of distances between nodes in the network:

$$FROB = \sqrt{\frac{1}{n^2} \sum_{i=1}^{n} \sum_{j=1}^{n} (\hat{d}_{ij} - d_{ij})^2}.$$

4 Results

Here we compare the MSDR-D algorithm to the MSDR and the Katz-Wagner algorithms. The results in Figure 4 show the performance of the three algorithms across four shapes when varying the size of the network from 50 to 1000 nodes and using range and angle data with little noise. All three algorithms scale well as the number of

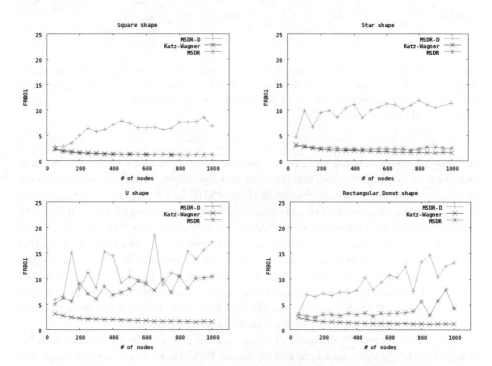

Fig. 4. Comparison between MSDR, Katz-Wagner, and MSDR-D measured by Frobenius error across square-shape, star-shape, U-shape and donut-shape with 50 to 1000 nodes. There were ten trials per shape, using networks with average node degree 8, range error of 20%, angle error of 10°, k-neighbor value of 3, and far away value of 10.

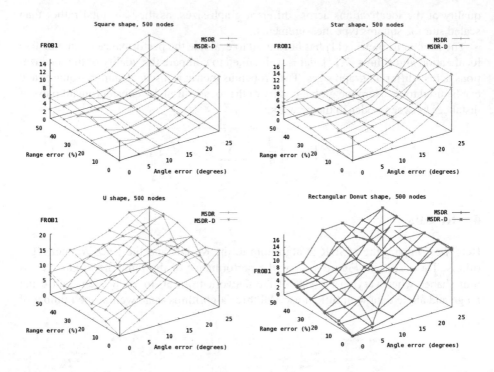

Fig. 5. Comparison between MSDR and MSDR-D measured by Frobenius error across square-shape, star-shape, U-shape and donut-shape with 500 nodes. There were ten trials per shape, using networks with average node degree 8, range error of 0-50%, angle error of $0°$-$25°$, k-neighbor value of 3 and far away value of 10.

nodes in the sensor network increases. When the noise level is low MSDR-D produces localizations with higher errors that the other two algorithms. However, even though the errors are higher, the localizations obtained by MSDR-D are still very good as seen in Fig. 3. More importantly, MSDR-D is truly distributed algorithm and does not incur the high communication and memory overhead of the other two, which require $O(n \log n)$ broadcast messages and $O(n)$ size memory per sensor node. The MSDR-D algorithm limits the memory needs at each sensor node since it gathers information for only k-neighborhood and far away nodes. As communication at a global scale is avoided, no routing information needs to be maintained at the nodes. The dramatic reduction in communication and memory usage for MSDR-D do come with a price, namely a loss in localization accuracy, when compared to the other two algorithms.

In Figure 5 we consider the quality of localizations produced by MSDR and MSDR-D under varying angle and range errors. Recall that MSDR considers the angle and distance information between all pairs of sensor nodes. The large number of forces used to localize individual nodes results in an large error in the final localized position. MSDR-D only considers small neighborhood graphs of fixed sizes and hence limits the number of forces used in the localization. This explains the higher quality localizations obtained by MSDR-D when the noise levels increase. For high noise levels MSDR-D outperforms the centralized MSDR algorithm. This is especially pronounced for non-convex network topologies such as the U-shape and the star.

5 Conclusion

We presented a new distributed algorithm, MSDR-D, that localizes sensor networks with non-trivial topologies, using only noisy range and angular information. MSDR-D uses a combination of nearby nodes and randomly selected far-away nodes from outside the neighborhood to place local nodes in a way that is accurate locally and fits well with the overall shape of the network. The algorithm scales well as the number of nodes in the network increases. With increasing data noise, MSDR-D outperforms its predecessors. Most importantly, unlike earlier force-directed, anchor-free algorithms, MSDR-D is a truly distributed algorithm that employs no broadcast messages. The algorithm is simple to implement and is available, along with source code, executables, and experimental results, at `http://msdr-d.cs.arizona.edu/`.

References

1. Akyildiz, I.F., Weilian, S., Sankarasubramaniam, Y., Cayirci, E.E.: A survey on sensor networks. IEEE Communications Magazine 40(8), 102–114 (2002)
2. Bruck, J., Gao, J., Jiang, A.A.: Localization and routing in sensor networks by local angle information. In: MobiHoc 2005, pp. 181–192 (2005)
3. Costa, J.A., Patwari, N., Hero III, A.O.: Distributed weighted-multidimensional scaling for node localization in sensor networks. ACM Trans. on Sensor Networks 2(1), 39–64 (2006)
4. Dabek, F., Cox, R., Kaashoek, F., Morris, R.: Vivaldi: A decentralized network coordinate system. In: ACM Conference on Applications, Technologies, Architectures, and Protocols for Computer Communications, pp. 15–26 (2004)
5. de Launois, C., Uhlig, S., Bonaventure, O.: Scalable route selection for ipv6 multi-homed sites. In: Boutaba, R., Almeroth, K.C., Puigjaner, R., Shen, S., Black, J.P. (eds.) NETWORKING 2005. LNCS, vol. 3462, pp. 1357–1361. Springer, Heidelberg (2005)
6. Doherty, L., Pister, K., Ghaoui, L.E.: Convex optimization methods for sensor node position estimation. In: INFOCOM 2001, pp. 1655–1663 (2001)
7. Efrat, A., Erten, C., Forrester, D., Iyer, A., Kobourov, S.: Force-directed approaches to sensor localization. In: ALENEX 2006, pp. 108–118 (2006)
8. Fekete, S.P., Kröller, A., Pfisterer, D., Fischer, S., Buschmann, C.: Neighborhood-based topology recognition in sensor networks. In: Nikoletseas, S.E., Rolim, J.D.P. (eds.) ALGOSENSORS 2004. LNCS, vol. 3121, pp. 123–136. Springer, Heidelberg (2004)
9. Fruchterman, T., Reingold, E.: Graph drawing by force-directed placement. Software – Practice and Experience 21(11), 1129–1164 (1991)
10. Galstyan, A., Krishnamachari, B., Lerman, K., Pattem, S.: Distributed online localization in sensor networks using a moving target. In: IPSN 2004, pp. 61–70 (2004)
11. Golub, G.H., Van Loan, C.F.: Matrix Computations. Johns Hopkins Press, Baltimore (1996)
12. Gotsman, C., Koren, Y.: Distributed graph layout for sensor networks. In: 12th Symposium on Graph Drawing (GD), pp. 273–284 (2004)
13. Kamada, T., Kawai, S.: An algorithm for drawing general undirected graphs. Information Processing Letters 31, 7–15 (1989)

14. Katz, B., Wagner, D.: Multi-scale Anchor-free Distributed Positioning in Sensor Networks. In: WTASA 2007 (2007)
15. Kröller, A., Fekete, S.P., Pfisterer, D., Fischer, S.: Deterministic boundary recognition and topology extraction for large sensor networks. In: SODA 2006, pp. 1000–1009 (2006)
16. Niculescu, D., Nath, B.: Ad hoc positioning system (APS) using AOA. In: INFOCOM 2003, pp. 1734–1743 (2003)
17. Priyantha, N.B., Balakrishnan, H., Demaine, E., Teller, S.: Anchor-free distributed localization in sensor networks. In: SenSys 2003, pp. 340–341 (2003)
18. Reichenbach, F., Salomon, R., Timmermann, D.: Distributed obstacle localization in large wireless sensor networks. In: IWCMC 2006, pp. 1317–1322 (2006)
19. Savvides, A., Han, C., Srivastava, M.: Dynamic Fine-Grained localization in Ad-Hoc networks of sensors. In: MOBICOM 2001, pp. 166–179 (2001)
20. Shang, Y., Ruml, W.: Improved mds-based localization. In: Proceedings of IEEE INFOCOM 2004, pp. 2640–2651 (2004)
21. Shang, Y., Ruml, W., Zhang, Y., Fromherz, M.P.J.: Localization from mere connectivity. In: Proceedings of MobiHoc 2003, pp. 201–212 (2003)
22. Zou, Y., Chakrabarty, K.: Sensor deployment and target localization in distributed sensor networks. Trans. on Embedded Computing Sys. 3(1), 61–91 (2004)

Virtual Raw Anchor Coordinates: A New Localization Paradigm*

Florian Huc, Aubin Jarry, Pierre Leone, and José Rolim

Computer Science Department
University of Geneva
Battelle A, route de Drize 7
1227 Carouge, Switzerland
firstname.name@unige.ch

Abstract. A wide range of applications in wireless sensor networks rely on the location information of the sensing nodes. However, traditional localization techniques are dependent on hardware that is sometimes unavailable (e.g. GPS), or on sophisticated virtual localization calculus which have a costly overhead.

Instead of actually localizing nodes in the physical two-dimensional Euclidean space, we use directly the raw distance to a set of anchors to produce multi-dimensional coordinates. We prove that the image of the physical two-dimensional Euclidean space is a two-dimensional surface, and we show that it is possible to adapt geographic routing strategies on this surface, simply, efficiently and successfully.

1 Introduction

Localization plays an important role in wireless sensor networks. Indeed, if the identity of each sensor is used in the MAC layer to differentiate the neighbors of each node, what is important at the application level is the locations inside the monitored area, not individual sensors. Indeed, many applications need topological information for internal interventions such as tracking, or for external interventions such as the shipment of supplies or rescue team intervention. As such, information is retrieved from specific locations; communications are sent between locations; and network actions take place at specific locations, be it the movement of sensors (if they are so equipped) sleep schedule reconfigurations, or generally reprogramming to adapt to a new situation in the network. From the point of view of sensors, topology awareness enables them to know in which area of the network they are, and to appreciate the distance to and from particular areas of interest. Since sensors generally do not have routing tables that are costly to maintain, it also allows the use of the topological properties of the network for routing. This is generally referred to as geographic routing. Of the many efficient geographic routing algorithms that have been devised, we cite GFG/GPSR [5,12] and OAFR [15] which use greedy routing and face routing on

---

* Work partially funded by project FRONTS 215270.

a planarized connectivity graph. When authorizing the use of a bit of memory at each node, early obstacle detection algorithms have been proposed [11,19].

In order to obtain coordinates, the nodes may rely on interferometry [17] or on an external source of knowledge, such as a GPS or Galileo unit, pressure or magnetic field measurements, and so on. Coordinates may be also manually assigned by men, robots or unmanned aerial vehicles (UAV). This dependency on hardware or on external intervention entails a lot of drawbacks for wireless sensor networks. First of all, hardware devices have a monetary cost, take up space and weight, and consume energy, all of which are critical resources when designing miniaturized motes that will be dispatched in the thousands. Secondly, external intervention is not self-contained and thus may not be available. As an illustration, GPS systems are not available underground, inside parts of buildings, under sea, in case of satellite failure or if sensors are deployed on a planet not equipped with satellites.

In order to reduce the dependency on external positioning, only a handful of sensors – usually called anchors – may be positioned at start, whereas regular sensors have access to relative spatial information using optional hardware (angle measurements, distance measurements by time difference of arrival between sound and radio signals, etc.) or using their access to the wireless medium: distances may be measured with the strength of received signals, or more simply, by hop-count. A nice introduction on the various positioning methods for networks may be found in [21]. Positioning methods can be classified into three main types, whether one achieves absolute positioning, relative positioning or only local positioning. In absolute positioning, the coordinate system has a global coherence within the system but also with respect to exterior coordinates. Relative positioning is only coherent within the network, whereas local positioning just asks for local coherence. In [16], three localization algorithms are compared, namely Ad-hoc positioning, Robust positioning, and N-hop multilateration. These three algorithms have a common three phase structure: they first determine node to anchor distances, then compute node positions, and optionally refine the positions through an iterative procedure. Some authors improved accuracy by using angles measurement [6,25,26].

Dependency on external intervention or hardware is further reduced by having no sensor with extra capabilities or information. Some authors thus propose to compute virtual coordinates instead of real ones. Indeed, many algorithms do not need actual two dimensional coordinates, but the relative position of the nodes. In [3,4] the authors call this problem the training problem and propose an algorithm allowing the sensors (which are asynchronous) to estimate their distance to a central sink. This algorithm needs the sink to be able to emit to all the nodes of the network, and its output is a partition of the network in rings. If the sink is also equipped by directional antennas, it is also feasible to partition the networks in slices. Hence the authors propose to use the ring number and the slice number of each nodes as coordinates. Other papers [7,18,23,24] propose to compute virtual coordinates from the distance between nearby nodes and have the advantage of not needing anchors. Still this approach may lead to unsolvable issues if the network is not dense enough. To avoid this, in [23], the authors use a mobile unit to assist in measuring the distance between nodes. It also helps to improve accuracy. For these papers, the key point is to obtain sufficient data on inter node distances. In [14], the authors study the problem of computing missing inter-nodes distances from known ones. They propose an algorithm, which given distances from all nodes to some anchors, recompute the unknown distances with an arbitrary precision. They also discuss complexity and non approximability issues.

Virtual coordinates have also been discussed in other contexts. In the context of peer-to-peer networks embedded in the Internet, Hotz proposed in [9] to use the distance to anchors as virtual coordinates while using only triangle inequalities to estimate distances. Following this trend, Ng and Zhang proposed in [20] to first compute coordinates for the anchors (called landmarks in their paper) by using linear system resolution tools, and then to compute locally coordinates for the nodes (by solving smaller linear systems). Not only were the experimental results quite good, it was theoretically proved in [14] that provided that the anchors were randomly selected, in a sufficiently large number, and provided that the distance between anchors was respected in the new coordinate system, the distortion of distances in the new coordinate system could be arbitrarily low. In the context of air navigation, Farell et all [8] considered the idea of using distances rather than coordinates and proposed that collision avoidance and other time-critical algorithms used GPS pseudo-ranged rather than derived coordinates. In this paper, we discard any preprocessing technique and propose to directly use raw distance information. We study routing algorithms using directly the distance to the anchors as coordinates, as first proposed in [10], without computing from them 2-dimensional coordinates. In Section 2 we precisely describe how the idea is implemented, in Section 3 we analyze how a message sent towards a destination performs in the new coordinate system, and we present some simulation results in Section 4.

2   Implementation

Current localization methods rely on raw information computed externally from normal sensing nodes (exact location of some anchors), and on raw information computed locally in normal sensing nodes (distance to anchors, angle measurements). In this paper, we do use the information about the distance to some anchors, but we completely discard any physical information that the anchors might have. This gives much more flexibility in the way sensor networks are deployed: anchors might be external entities, as planes or robots; anchors might be specialized nodes whose only purpose is to emit a strong signal, or they might be randomly chosen sensors which advertise their distance to the other nodes.

We build a multi-dimensional coordinate system using directly the raw information, i.e. the distance to the anchors. Given a node at location X, we define the multi-dimensional coordinates $f(X)$ of this node as its distance to the anchors at location $A_1, A_2, \ldots A_n$:

$$f : X \rightarrow \begin{pmatrix} d(X, A_1) \\ d(X, A_2) \\ \dots \\ d(X, A_n) \end{pmatrix}.$$

We call this function the anchor coordinates function, and we call these multi-dimensional coordinates the anchor coordinates. Whereas any distance function, such as hop count, may be used [10], in section 3 we pay a special attention to the properties of f when d is the Euclidean distance.

In the next subsection we discuss the computation costs that are specific to using multi-dimensional coordinates. We then go into the details of greedy routing implementation, and into the details of rotating multi-dimensional vectors.

2.1 Computation Cost

While saving on initialization overhead, multi-dimensional routing causes some additional computation costs when sending messages compared to traditional two-dimensional routing. Here is a break-down of various vector operations:

Operation	n-dimensional	2-dimensional
$\vec{u} + \vec{v}$	n additions	2 additions
$k\,\vec{u}$	n multiplications	2 multiplications
$\vec{u} \cdot \vec{v}$	n multiplications $n - 1$ additions	2 multiplications 1 addition
$\dfrac{\vec{u}}{\|\vec{u}\|}$	1 sqrt extraction 1 inversion $2n$ multiplications $n - 1$ additions	1 sqrt extraction 1 inversion 2 multiplications 1 addition

Note that additions and multiplications typically use 1 CPU cycle, whereas the expensive operations (square root extraction, inversion) stay the same in multi-dimensional routing as in traditional two-dimensional routing. We also point out that these computation costs are not communication costs and are lower in terms of energy consumption by some order of magnitude.

2.2 Greedy Routing

Greedy routing is the most basic geographic routing algorithm. It consists in following the direction to the destination. This basic strategy is widely used as a default mode in most geographic routing protocols. When a node at location X which wants to send a message towards a final destination at location D, three implementations of greedy routing are routinely used:

1. *(canonical)* for each neighbor location X', compute the distance $d(X', D)$ and send the message to the neighbor which is closest to D. Alternatively, compute $\overrightarrow{X'D} \cdot \overrightarrow{X'D}$ instead of $d(X', D)$.

2. for each neighbor location X', compute the scalar product $\overrightarrow{XX'} \cdot \overrightarrow{XD}$ and select the neighbor with the best result.
3. for each neighbor location X', compute the scalar product $\frac{\overrightarrow{XX'}}{||\overrightarrow{XX'}||} \cdot \overrightarrow{XD}$ and select the neighbor with the best result.

These three implementations are valid for any number of coordinates.

2.3 Rotation

When greedy strategies fail, a number of two-dimensional routing algorithms fall back on more sophisticated routing modes that use rotations or angle computations [5,12,22]. When using two dimensions, a rotation is typically defined by $rot_\alpha : (x,y) \rightarrow (x\cos\alpha + y\sin\alpha, y\cos\alpha - x\sin\alpha)$. We can't define such a rotation in n dimensions ($n \geq 3$). However, if we assume that our sensors were on a two-dimensional physical plane in the first place, then they are distributed over a two-dimensional surface in the multi-dimensional space (more on this in section 3). We do the following:

1. compute an orthonormal basis $(\overrightarrow{i}, \overrightarrow{j})$ of the tangent plane in $f(X)$ (see section 3).
2. express vectors $\overrightarrow{u}$ as $x_u \overrightarrow{i} + y_u \overrightarrow{j} + \overrightarrow{\epsilon_u}$ by computing $x_u = \overrightarrow{u} \cdot \overrightarrow{i}$ and $y_u = \overrightarrow{u} \cdot \overrightarrow{j}$. We assume that $\overrightarrow{u}$ is close to the tangent plane in $f(X)$, which means that we ignore in fact $\overrightarrow{\epsilon_u}$.

Rotations are then normally carried out on the tangent plane. The sensitive part is to compute $(\overrightarrow{i}, \overrightarrow{j})$ and to make sure that the orientation of the surface is preserved when routing the message (taking the surface upside-down has the undesirable effect of negating angles). Given a node at location X, a destination at D, and a basis $(\overrightarrow{i_{old}}, \overrightarrow{j_{old}})$ inherited from a previous node, we do the following:

1. choose two neighbors at position X_1 and X_2
   - either arbitrarily (low quality, inexpensive)
   - or such that $\frac{|\overrightarrow{XX_1} \cdot \overrightarrow{XX_2}|}{||\overrightarrow{XX_1}||||\overrightarrow{XX_2}||}$ is minimal (i.e. choose $\overrightarrow{XX_1}$ and $\overrightarrow{XX_2}$ as orthogonal as possible)
2. compute $\overrightarrow{i} = \frac{\overrightarrow{XX_1}}{||\overrightarrow{XX_1}||}$
3. compute $\overrightarrow{u} = \overrightarrow{XX_2} - (\overrightarrow{i} \cdot \overrightarrow{XX_2}) \overrightarrow{i}$
4. compute $\overrightarrow{v} = \frac{\overrightarrow{u}}{||\overrightarrow{u}||}$
5. compute $\sigma = (\overrightarrow{i} \cdot \overrightarrow{i_{old}})(\overrightarrow{v} \cdot \overrightarrow{j_{old}}) - (\overrightarrow{i} \cdot \overrightarrow{j_{old}})(\overrightarrow{v} \cdot \overrightarrow{i_{old}})$.
6. if $\sigma \geq 0$ then set $\overrightarrow{j} = \overrightarrow{v}$, else set $\overrightarrow{j} = -\overrightarrow{v}$.

Note that many algorithms using angles use normalized vectors. Therefore, most of the normalization cost when computing the basis $(\overrightarrow{i}, \overrightarrow{j})$ is not an additional cost of multi-dimensional routing.

2.4   Cross Link Detection Protocol

Many geographic routing algorithms rely on a planarized version of the communication graph, and various techniques exist to compute that graph. A common assumption is that the network forms a Unit Disc Graph or an approximation of it, which enables the computation of Gabriel Graphs (see for instance [2]). It also has been argued that this assumption is unrealistic [13], and anyhow, the utilization of virtual coordinates can distort the length of communication links in such a way that UDG properties are not preserved. We chose to adapt CLDP [13], a distributed planarization algorithm where no assumption is made on the communication graph. CLDP works in a distributed manner: it tests each link uv by computing a circuit from one node to the other and looking if a link of the circuit crosses uv. If this is the case, one of the crossing links is deleted. Links are tested until no crossing is detected.

When a network is embedded in a k dimensional space with $k \geq 3$, its links will generally not cross each other, but this has no bearing on whether the communication graph is planar or not[1]. Therefore, in order to implement CLDP using our virtual coordinates we have to understand the crossing of links according to some projection on a surface. In particular, given a 2 dimensional plane, we can assess the planarity of the communication graph by projecting the links of the network into to this plane. We implemented CLDP using virtual raw anchor coordinates as follows (when testing an edge uv):

1. Compute a plane P approximately tangent to the surface $f(\mathbb{R}^2)$ at v. P is computed by choosing a third node among the neighbors of v.
2. Create a circuit from v to u using the right hand rule in the projected image of the network on P.
3. If the projection of the circuit on P intersects the projection of uv on P, delete uv.

2.5   Greedy Perimeter Stateless Routing

GFG/GPSR, initially proposed in [5,12], is a geographic routing algorithm which guarantees a 100% message delivery. Its default mode is to use greedy routing. However it has a secondary mode which allows messages to get out of a local minimum. This secondary mode uses a planarized version of the communication graph. In this planarized graph, an obstacle inducing a local minimum is also a face. The secondary mode of GFG/GPSR is then the following: the local minimum is called the entry point, and the message is routed along the face corresponding to the obstacle using the right hand rule until it reaches a node closer to the destination than the entry point. Greedy mode routing is then resumed. Greedy mode routing implementation with multidimensional coordinates is straightforward (see Subsection 2.2). The implementation of the secondary mode is done as follows:

---

[1] For instance any graph can be represented in a 3 dimensional space without any edge intersection.

1. Compute a plane P tangent to the surface at the entry point.
2. Choose the next node using the right hand rule in the projection of the planarized network on P.
3. If the next node is closer to the destination than the entry point, resume greedy routing.

It is also possible to compute a new tangent plane at each step, and preserve a coherent orientation between tangent planes (so that the right hand rule has a meaning), as done for the implementation of GRIC in [10]. The simulations results in Section 4 were done with a single tangent plane per secondary mode, but using multiple tangent planes nevertheless yielded nearly identical results.

3 Algebraic Analysis

In the plane with Euclidean distance, any node has a pair of physical coordinates $X = (x, y)$. We denote by $A_i = (x_i, y_i)$ the physical coordinates of the ith anchor. The anchor coordinates function is a function from $\mathbb{R}^2 \to \mathbb{R}^n$ defined by

$$f : (x, y) \to \begin{pmatrix} \sqrt{(x - x_1)^2 + (y - y_1)^2} \\ \sqrt{(x - x_2)^2 + (y - y_2)^2} \\ \dots \\ \sqrt{(x - x_n)^2 + (y - y_n)^2} \end{pmatrix}.$$

Since the functions $f_i : (x, y) \to \sqrt{(x - x_i)^2 + (y - y_i)^2}$ are continuous and C^∞ except in (x_i, y_i), we show that with three or more anchors that are not on the same line, the image $f(\mathbb{R}^2)$ in $\mathbb{R}^n$ is a *continuous surface* (claim 3.1). Figure 1 represents the image of f, when there are three anchors at location $(0, 0)$, $(0, 1)$ and $(1, 0)$.

First, we describe in subsection 3.1 the vector spaces that are tangent to $f(\mathbb{R}^2)$. Next, we express in subsection 3.2 what is the physical direction of messages that use the greedy strategy with virtual coordinates. This physical direction produces a curve that approximates the paths followed by messages. We discuss in subsection 3.3 what are the convergence conditions on $f(\mathbb{R}^2)$ under which the curve ends at the destination, and prove a bound on the length of this curve. Finally, we study in subsection 3.4 how the placement of anchors affect the convergence conditions and how we can guarantee that they are met.

3.1 Tangent Space

At any point $f(x, y)$, the surface $f(\mathbb{R}^2)$ has a tangent vector space spanned by the two vectors $\frac{\partial f}{\partial x}(x, y)$ and $\frac{\partial f}{\partial y}(x, y)$. We have

$$\frac{\partial f}{\partial x}(x, y) = \begin{pmatrix} \frac{x - x_1}{\sqrt{(x-x_1)^2+(y-y_1)^2}} \\ \frac{x - x_2}{\sqrt{(x-x_2)^2+(y-y_2)^2}} \\ \dots \\ \frac{x - x_n}{\sqrt{(x-x_n)^2+(y-y_n)^2}} \end{pmatrix} \quad \text{and} \quad \frac{\partial f}{\partial y}(x, y) = \begin{pmatrix} \frac{y - y_1}{\sqrt{(x-x_1)^2+(y-y_1)^2}} \\ \frac{y - y_2}{\sqrt{(x-x_2)^2+(y-y_2)^2}} \\ \dots \\ \frac{y - y_n}{\sqrt{(x-x_n)^2+(y-y_n)^2}} \end{pmatrix}.$$

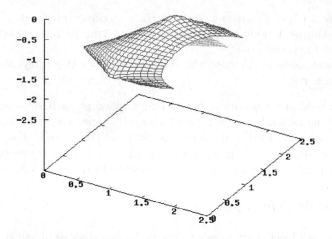

Fig. 1. Representation of the distance to three anchors

Claim. The vector space that is tangent to the surface $f(\mathbb{R}^2)$ in $f(X)$ is two-dimensional if and only if the node X and the anchors $A_1, A_2, \ldots, A_n$ are not situated on a single line in the physical space.

Proof. The tangent vector space is two-dimensional if and only if $\frac{\partial f}{\partial x}(x,y)$ and $\frac{\partial f}{\partial y}(x,y)$ are not collinear. Conversely $\frac{\partial f}{\partial x}(x,y)$ and $\frac{\partial f}{\partial y}(x,y)$ are collinear if and only if there is $\alpha \in [0, 2\pi[$ such that $\frac{\partial f}{\partial x}(x,y)\cos\alpha + \frac{\partial f}{\partial y}(x,y)\sin\alpha = 0$. By changing the physical coordinates into $u = x\cos\alpha + y\sin\alpha$ and $v = y\cos\alpha - x\sin\alpha$ (we also set $u_i = x_i\cos\alpha + y_i\sin\alpha$ and $v_i = y_i\cos\alpha - x_i\sin\alpha$), we express the tangent vector space with the two vectors

$$\frac{\partial f}{\partial u}(X) = \begin{pmatrix} \frac{u-u_1}{\sqrt{(u-u_1)^2+(v-v_1)^2}} \\ \frac{u-u_2}{\sqrt{(u-u_2)^2+(v-v_2)^2}} \\ \cdots \\ \frac{u-u_n}{\sqrt{(u-u_n)^2+(v-v_n)^2}} \end{pmatrix} \quad \text{and} \quad \frac{\partial f}{\partial v}(X) = \begin{pmatrix} \frac{v-v_1}{\sqrt{(u-u_1)^2+(v-v_1)^2}} \\ \frac{v-v_2}{\sqrt{(u-u_2)^2+(v-v_2)^2}} \\ \cdots \\ \frac{v-v_n}{\sqrt{(u-u_n)^2+(v-v_n)^2}} \end{pmatrix}.$$

Therefore, we have $\frac{\partial f}{\partial u}(X) = 0$ if and only if for all $i \in \{1 \ldots n\}, u = u_i$.

When the two vectors $\frac{\partial f}{\partial x}(x,y)$ and $\frac{\partial f}{\partial y}(x,y)$ are not collinear, then the Jacobian matrix

$$J_f(X) = J_f(x,y) = \begin{pmatrix} \frac{x-x_1}{\sqrt{(x-x_1)^2+(y-y_1)^2}} & \frac{y-y_1}{\sqrt{(x-x_1)^2+(y-y_1)^2}} \\ \frac{x-x_2}{\sqrt{(x-x_2)^2+(y-y_2)^2}} & \frac{y-y_2}{\sqrt{(x-x_2)^2+(y-y_2)^2}} \\ \cdots & \cdots \\ \frac{x-x_n}{\sqrt{(x-x_n)^2+(y-y_n)^2}} & \frac{y-y_n}{\sqrt{(x-x_n)^2+(y-y_n)^2}} \end{pmatrix}$$

defines a morphism of the physical plane into the vector space tangent to $f(\mathbb{R}^2)$ at $f(x, y)$. Given a node at position X in the physical space and its neighbors at position $X_1, X_2, \ldots, X_\delta$, it is not unreasonable to assume that for all i, $f(X_i)$ is close to the Taylor expansion $f(X) + J_f(X)(\overrightarrow{XX_i})$ in the affine space tangent to $f(\mathbb{R}^2)$ in $f(X)$.

3.2 Directional Vector

In a greedy routing strategy using virtual coordinates, the neighbor X' of choice will be a maximum for some scalar product $\overrightarrow{f(X)f(X')} \cdot \overrightarrow{f(X)f(D)}$.

Claim. Given two physical positions $X, D \in \mathbb{R}^2$, the function $s_X : \mathbb{R}^2 \to \mathbb{R}$ such that for any vector $\overrightarrow{XX'} \in \mathbb{R}^2$, $s_X(\overrightarrow{XX'})$ is the scalar product of $J_f(X)(\overrightarrow{XX'})$ by $\overrightarrow{f(X)f(D)}$ is a linear form that can be expressed as

$$\overrightarrow{XX'} \to \overrightarrow{XX'} \cdot \sum_i \alpha_i \overrightarrow{XA_i}$$

where $\alpha_i = \frac{d(X, A_i) - d(D, A_i)}{d(X, A_i)}$.

Proof. The transformation $\overrightarrow{XX'} \to J_f(X)(\overrightarrow{XX'})$ is a linear function. Since the scalar product by $\overrightarrow{f(X)f(D)}$ is a linear form, s_X is also a linear form. We may decompose the vector $\overrightarrow{f(X)f(D)}$ into $\sum_i (d(D, A_i) - d(X, A_i)) \mathbf{1}_i$ where $\mathbf{1}_i$ is the multi-dimensional vector with 1 as its ith coordinate and zeroes everywhere else. In this manner, $s_X = \sum_i s_{X,i}$ where

$$s_{X,i}(\overrightarrow{XX'}) = (d(D, A_i) - d(X, A_i)) J_f(X)(\overrightarrow{XX'}) \cdot \mathbf{1}_i$$

$$J_f(X)(\overrightarrow{XX'}) \cdot \mathbf{1}_i = \frac{(x - x_i)(x' - x) + (y - y_i)(y' - y)}{\sqrt{(x - x_i)^2 + (y - y_i)^2}}.$$

Thus $s_{X,i}$ can be expressed as

$$\overrightarrow{XX'} \to \overrightarrow{XX'} \cdot \frac{d(X, A_i) - d(D, A_i)}{d(X, A_i)} \overrightarrow{XA_i}.$$

Given a node at physical location X and a destination $D \in \mathbb{R}^2$, we call *apparent destination* related to D in X the location

$$D' = X + \sum_i \alpha_i \overrightarrow{XA_i} = X + \sum_i \frac{d(X, A_i) - d(D, A_i)}{d(X, A_i)} \overrightarrow{XA_i}.$$

3.3   Virtual Consistency

We say that the anchor coordinate system is virtually consistent at distance r for a physical destination $D \in \mathbb{R}^2$, if at every point $X \neq D$ such that $f(X)$ is in a closed metric ball of center $f(D)$ and radius r, $s_X \neq 0$. Note that $s_x = 0$ if and only if the multi-dimensional vector $\overrightarrow{f(X)f(D)}$ is orthogonal to the vector space tangent to $f(\mathbb{R}^2)$ in $f(X)$. It is also equivalent to state that the anchor coordinate system is virtually consistent at distance r for a physical destination $D \in \mathbb{R}^2$, if no closed metric ball centered on $f(D)$ and of radius $0 < r' \leq r$ is tangent to $f(\mathbb{R}^2)$.

Claim. If the anchor coordinate system is virtually consistent at distance r for a physical destination $D \in \mathbb{R}^2$, then there is $\lambda \in \mathbb{R}^+$ such that for any point X_0 with $f(X_0)$ in a closed metric ball of center $f(D)$ and radius r we have a curve $c[0, 1] \in \mathbb{R}^2$ that verifies:

- $c : [0, 1] \to \mathbb{R}^2$ is a derivable function,
- $c(0) = X_0$ and $c(1) = D$,
- At any point $t \in [0, 1[$, the vector $\frac{\partial c}{\partial t}(t)$ is collinear with the vector $\overrightarrow{c(t)D_t'}$ where D_t' is the apparent destination related to D in $c(t)$.
- $\int_0^1 ||\frac{\partial c}{\partial(t)}|| dt \leq \lambda d(X_0, D)$.

Proof. Let k be the largest positive number such that for any point $X = (x, y)$ with $f(X)$ in a closed metric ball of center $f(D)$ and radius r, the orthogonal projection of $\overrightarrow{f(X)f(D)}$ on the vector space defined by the two vectors $\frac{\partial f}{\partial x}(x, y)$ and $\frac{\partial f}{\partial y}(x, y)$ has a norm greater than or equal to $kd(X, D)$. Since f is a continuous function, the set of physical positions X such that $d(f(X), f(D)) \leq r$ is compact subset of $\mathbb{R}^2$. Therefore, if k was equal to zero, then there would be a point $X \neq D$ in the ball such that $\overrightarrow{XD}$ is orthogonal to the surface $f(\mathbb{R}^2)$, which we excluded in our assumptions.

Let $c : [0, 1] \to \mathbb{R}^2$ be the function defined by $c(0) = X_0$ and such that $\frac{\partial (f \circ c)}{\partial t}(t)$ is the orthogonal projection of $\frac{k^{-2} d(f(X_0), f(D))}{d((f \circ c)(t), f(D))} \overrightarrow{(f \circ c)(t)f(D)}$ on the vector space defined by the two vectors $\frac{\partial f}{\partial x}(c(t))$ and $\frac{\partial f}{\partial y}(c(t))$. Since

$$\frac{\partial (f \circ c)}{\partial t}(t) \cdot \frac{\overrightarrow{(f \circ c)(t)f(D)}}{||\overrightarrow{(f \circ c)(t)f(D)}||} \geq k||\frac{\partial (f \circ c)}{\partial t}(t)||$$

we can see that

$$\frac{\partial d((f \circ c)t), f(D))}{\partial t}(t) \geq d(f(X_0), f(D))$$

which implies that $c(1) = D$. The norm of $\frac{\partial c}{\partial t}(t)$ is smaller than or equal to $||(J_f(c(t)))^{-1}|| d(f(X_0), f(D))$, which means that

$$\int_0^1 ||\frac{\partial c}{\partial(t)}||dt \leq \max_{t\in[0,1]} ||(J_f(c(t)))^{-1}||d(f(X_0, f(D)))$$

$$\int_0^1 ||\frac{\partial c}{\partial(t)}||dt \leq \sqrt{n} \max_{t\in[0,1]} ||(J_f(c(t)))^{-1}||d(X_0, D).$$

3.4 Physical Consistency

We say that the anchor coordinate system is physically consistent at position X for the destination D if $\overrightarrow{XD'} \cdot \overrightarrow{XD} > 0$, where D' is the apparent destination related to D' in X. Observe that if the anchor coordinate system is physically consistent for the destination D in a ball $\mathcal{B}$ around D, then it is virtually consistent at distance r for the physical destination D, where r is the radius of the biggest multi-dimensional ball Ω such that $\Omega \cap f(\mathbb{R}^2) \subset f(\mathcal{B})$.

To study the physical consistency of the system at position X for the destination D, we split the physical plane in four parts P_1, P_2, P_3, P_4 with $P_1 = \{X'|\overrightarrow{XX'} \cdot \overrightarrow{XD} \leq 0\}$, $P_2 = \{X'|\overrightarrow{XX'} \cdot \overrightarrow{XD} > 0$ and $d(X, X') < d(X, D)\}$, $P_3 = \{X'|\overrightarrow{DX'} \cdot \overrightarrow{DX} > 0$ and $d(X, X') \geq d(X, D)\}$, $P_4 = \{X'|\overrightarrow{DX'} \cdot \overrightarrow{DX} \leq 0\}$. Since the apparent destination D' is defined by

$$D' = X + \sum_i \frac{d(X, A_i) - d(D, A_i)}{d(X, A_i)} \overrightarrow{XA_i}$$

we see as illustrated in Figure 2 that only the anchors in P_2 give a negative contribution to $\overrightarrow{XD'} \cdot \overrightarrow{XD}$.

If anchors are randomly distributed in the network, the negative contribution will most probably be small enough for the system to be consistent, unless P_1 and P_4 are almost void of nodes, which happens when X and D are located on opposite borders of the network (so that all the anchors are between them). This situation did not occur in the experiments we carried out. Nevertheless, physical inconsistency may be avoided by selecting anchors when the destination D of a message originating from X_0 is far away:

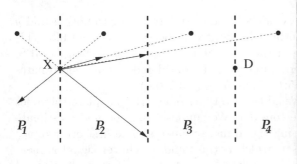
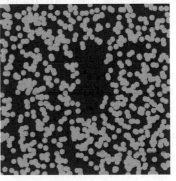

Fig. 2. Contribution of anchors in P_1, P_2, P_3, P_4 **Fig. 3.** Experimental settings

1. by default, use all the anchors.
2. compute $l_A = \max_{i \in \{1,..,n\}} \max(d(D, A_i), d(X_0, A_i))$. l_A gives an idea of the diameter of the network.
3. for each node X along the path of the message
   (a) compute $l_X = \max_{i \in \{1,...,n\}} |d(X, D) - d(X, A_i)| = ||f(D) - f(X)||_\infty$. l_X is smaller than $d(X, D)$.
   (b) if using all the anchors and if $l_X > \frac{2l_A}{3}$ then use only the anchors A_i such that $d(D, A_i) < \frac{l_A}{3}$.
   (c) if using a subset of anchors and if $l_X < \frac{l_A}{2}$ then use all the anchors.

In this way, physical inconsistency can be completely avoided in the network, at the cost of using a different coordinate system when $d(X, D)$ is comparable to the diameter of the network.

4 Experiments

4.1 Settings

We implemented CLDP and GFG/GPSR with multiple coordinates on Algo-Sensim [1] to compare the use of virtual coordinates versus real coordinates. To run our simulations, we considered a 15×15 square zone with a rectangular obstacle in the middle (cf Figure 3). We considered a density ranging from 10 to 30 which corresponds to 750-2250 nodes with a circular communication range of 1. We made simulation on one hundred different networks for each settings, over a duration of 1000 steps. At each step, one message (defined by its source and its destination) is generated.

Concerning the coordinates, we made the experiments under two scenarios : without errors and with errors. In each of them we considered three cases: the nodes know their Euclidean coordinates, the nodes know their distances to four anchors positioned at the four corners of the network or the nodes know their distance to six anchors positioned at random in the network.

4.2 Errors on Coordinates

For the Euclidean coordinates, we added an uncorrelated error to both x and y coordinates whose value is uniformly distributed in-between -0.5 and 0.5. This error represents the incertitude of the positioning using devices such as GPS. Hence a node X with exact coordinates (x, y) is considered to have coordinates $(x + b_1, y + b_2)$ where $b_1 \in (-0.5; 0.5)$ and $b_2 \in (-0.5; 0.5)$.

For the virtual coordinates, we added two types of error. To explain them, let us first describe the scenario we consider. We suppose that the nodes estimate their distance to the anchors using signal measurements. The first error represents the node's calibration offset, which is the same whichever signal is measured. To represent this, we chose a multiplicative factor uniformly distributed in-between 0.95 and 1.05. We chose a single value per node and each exact distance to anchors is multiplied by this value. A second error representing signal distortion is chosen uniformly distributed in-between -0.5 and 0.5 for each coordinate. A value is chosen independently for each coordinate. Hence if a node X has exact distances $(d_i)_1^n$ to anchors $(A_i)_1^n$, we choose $n + 1$ random variables, $a \in (0.95; 1, 05)$ and $b_i \in (-0.5; 0.5)$ $1 \le i \le n$, and the virtual coordinates of X are $(a \cdot d_i + b_i)_1^n$.

4.3   Experimental Results

We compare the efficiency of using virtual coordinates and Euclidean coordinates. We outline three different experimental results: first, the stretch of computed path (Fig. 4(a), where the stretch is the length of the computed path divided by the length of the shortest path), then the number of times the algorithm CLDP checks each link before the graph is planar (Fig. 4(c)) and finally the number of delivered messages (Fig. 4(b)).

The results of Figure 4 show that the efficiency of using virtual coordinates is the same as the efficiency of using Euclidean coordinates when we use four

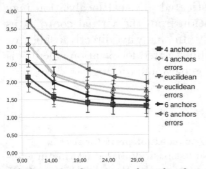

(a) Stretch of computed paths depending on density

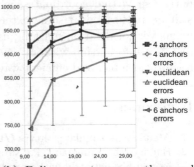

(b) Delivery rates per thousand messages, depending on density

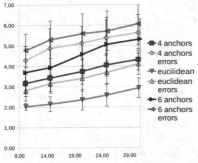

(c) Average number of times CLDP checks each edge, depending on density

Fig. 4.

anchors placed at the corners. Interestingly, the use of virtual coordinates makes the routing more resilient to errors. The delivery rates are comparable in both settings. When we use six anchors positioned at random in the network, the stretch and the delivery rate are slightly worse. This decrease in efficiency could be explained by the fact that some anchors are positioned in between sources and destinations, thus forcing the message to take a detour (cf Section 3.4, where anchors in P_2 and P_3 penalize the routing). This situation illustrates the trade-off of positioning the anchors at random, which is otherwise a great operational advantage.

5   Conclusion

Geographic routing is an essential component in connecting sensor networks. Foregoing the previously necessary localization phase where physical Cartesian coordinates are produced is an important step into making networks more robust and totally independent from external hardware. Sensor network applications that use localization information exclusively inside the network may transparently use virtual coordinates, whereas sophisticated physical localization may still be performed at some external base station from the virtual coordinates whenever localization must be used externally. In this way, directly using raw distance information without any costly or sophisticated localization calculus is a simple, viable, and efficient way to perform geographic routing.

References

1. AlgoSensim simulator, http://tcs.unige.ch/code/algosensim/overview
2. Barriere, L., Fraignaud, P., Narayanan, L.: Robust position based routing in wireless ad hoc networks with unstable transmission ranges. In: Proc. DialM, pp. 19–27 (2001)
3. Barsi, F., Bertossi, A., Sorbelli, F.B., Ciotti, R., Olariu, S., Pinotti, M.: Asynchronous Training in Wireless Sensor Networks. In: Kutyłowski, M., Cichoń, J., Kubiak, P. (eds.) ALGOSENSORS 2007. LNCS, vol. 4837, pp. 46–57. Springer, Heidelberg (2007)
4. Barsi, F., Navarra, A., Pinotti, M., Lavault, C., Ravelomanana, V., Olariu, S., Bertossi, A.: Efficient binary schemes for training heterogeneous sensor and actor networks. In: Proc. HeterSanet 2008, pp. 17–24 (2008)
5. Bose, P., Morin, P., Stojmenovic, I., Urrutia, J.: Routing with guaranteed delivery in ad hoc wireless networks. Wireless Networks 7(6), 609–616 (2001)
6. Bruck, J., Gao, J., Jiang, A.: Localization and routing in sensor networks by local angle information. In: Proc. MOBIHOC 2005, pp. 181–192 (2005)
7. Caruso, A., Chessa, S., De, S., Urpi, A.: GPS free coordinate assignment and routing in wireless sensor networks. In: Proc. INFOCOM 2005, pp. 150–160 (2005)
8. Farrell, J., Conkey, E.M., Stephens, C.: Send measurements, not coordinates. Navigation 46(3), 203–215 (1999)
9. Hotz, S.: Routing information organization to support scalable interdomain routing with heterogeneous path requirements PhD Thesis. University of Southern California, Los Angeles, CA (1996)

10. Huc, F., Jarry, A.: Vrac: Virtual routing with raw anchor coordinates in sensor networks. In: Proc. WONS 2010, pp. 106–112 (2010)
11. Huc, F., Jarry, A., Leone, P., Moraru, L., Nikoletseas, S., Rolim, J.: Early obstacle detection and avoidance for all to all traffic pattern in wireless sensor networks. In: Dolev, S. (ed.) ALGOSENSORS 2009. LNCS, vol. 5804, pp. 102–115. Springer, Heidelberg (2009)
12. Karp, B., Kung, H.: GPSR: greedy perimeter stateless routing for wireless networks. In: Proc. MOBICOM 2000, pp. 243–254 (2000)
13. Kim, Y., Govindan, R., Karp, B., Shenker, S.: Geographic routing made practical. In: Proc. NSDI 2005, pp. 217–230 (2005)
14. Kleinberg, J., Slivkins, A., Wexler, T.: Triangulation and embedding using small sets of beacons. In: Proc. FOCS 2004, pp. 444–453 (2004)
15. Kuhn, F., Wattenhofer, R., Zollinger, A.: An algorithmic approach to geographic routing in ad hoc and sensor networks. IEEE/ACM Transactions on Networking 16(1), 51–62 (2008)
16. Langendoen, K., Reijers, N.: Distributed localization in wireless sensor networks: a quantitative comparison. Computer Networks 43(4), 499–518 (2003)
17. Maroti, M., Völgyesi, P., Dora, S., Kusy, B., Nadas, A., Ledeczi, A., Balogh, G., Molnar, K.: Radio interferometric geolocation. In: Proc. SenSys 2005, pp. 1–12 (2005)
18. Moore, D., Leonard, J., Rus, D., Teller, S.: Robust distributed network localization with noisy range measurements. In: Proc. SENSYS 2004, pp. 50–61 (2004)
19. Moraru, L., Leone, P., Nikoletseas, S., Rolim, J.: Geographic Routing with Early Obstacles Detection and Avoidance in Dense Wireless Sensor Networks. In: Proc. AdHocNets 2008, pp. 148–161 (2008)
20. Ng, T., Zhang, H.: Predicting Internet network distance with coordinates-based approaches. In: Proc. INFOCOM 2002, pp. 170–179 (2002)
21. Niculescu, D.: Positioning in ad hoc sensor networks. IEEE Network, 24–29 (2004)
22. Powell, O., Nikoletseas, S.: Simple and efficient geographic routing around obstacles for wireless sensor networks. In: Demetrescu, C. (ed.) WEA 2007. LNCS, vol. 4525, pp. 161–174. Springer, Heidelberg (2007)
23. Priyantha, N.B., Balakrishnan, H., Demaine, E.D., Teller, S.: Mobile-assisted localization in wireless sensor networks. In: Proc. INFOCOM 2005, Miami, Florida, pp. 172–183 (2005)
24. Rao, A., Papadimitriou, C.H., Shenker, S., Stoica, I.: Geographic routing without location information. In: Proc. MOBICOM 2003, pp. 96–108 (2003)
25. Saad, C., Benslimane, A., König, J.: AT-DIST: A Distributed Method for Localization with high accuracy in Sensor Networks. Technical Report lirmm-00270283, lirmm (2008)
26. Stefano, G.D., Petricola, A.: A distributed AOA based localization algorithm for wireless sensor networks. Journal of Computers 3(4), 1–8 (2008)

Self-localization Based on Ambient Signals

Thomas Janson, Christian Schindelhauer, and Johannes Wendeberg

Computer Networks and Telematics, University of Freiburg, Germany
{janson,schindel,wendeber}@informatik.uni-freiburg.de

Abstract. We present an approach for the localization of passive nodes in a communication network using ambient radio or sound signals. In our settings the communication nodes have unknown positions. They are synchronized but do not emit signals for localization and exchange only the time points when environmental signals are received, the time differences of arrival (TDOA). The signals occur at unknown positions and times, but can be distinguished. Since no anchors are available, the goal is to determine the relative positions of all communication nodes and the environmental signals.

The Ellipsoid TDOA method introduces a closed form solution assuming the signals originate from far distances. The TDOA characterize an ellipse from which the distances and angles between three network nodes can be inferred.

The approach is tested in numerous simulations and in indoor and outdoor settings where the relative positions of mobile devices are determined utilizing only the sound produced by assistants with noisemakers.

1 Introduction

The increasing mobility of computing devices like smart phones, PDAs, laptops, and tablet computers is a motivation to revisit the localization problem from a fresh perspective.

The usual approach is to include special hardware like GPS receivers, which adds extra monetary cost and power consumption. However, in shielded areas and for small distances such location hardware cannot solve the problem. This is in particular the case for sensor networks in houses or tunnels. Then, the standard approach is to use anchor points in the communication network and calculate the positions by the time of arrival (TOA), time difference of arrival (TDOA) or by the received signal strength indication (RSSI) of radio signals.

Our approach starts with the following idea. Suppose we have a number of devices with microphones in a room which are connected by a communication network, e.g. mobile phones or laptop computers. Now, somebody walks through the room snapping fingers. Solely based on the time when these sound signals are received, all distances and angles between network nodes are computed.

The practicability of our approach can easily be seen. Since most modern computing devices like laptops and smart phones are equipped with everything we need (microphone, wireless LAN) the software can be run without any cost

C. Scheideler (Ed.): ALGOSENSORS 2010, LNCS 6451, pp. 176–188, 2010.

or effort. Sound sources are widely available in crowded areas like market places or in an open air concert. The noises of the people might already be sufficient to be localized.

Or consider localization in a wireless sensor network which has been a time consuming task. Our scheme enables the experimenter to automatize positioning of sensor nodes equipped with microphones just by producing some sharp sound signals before or after a field test to determine the locations of the sensors.

Our software might be extended to use with radio signals instead of sound signals. This will require special hardware to detect time points of radio signals which have to be more precise due to the speed of light. Given such hardware it is possible to compute the relative positions of network nodes like notebook computers, mobile phones, tablet computers or PDAs by using ambient radio signals coming from WLAN base stations, radio or TV broadcast, TV satellites or lightnings. Of course such a localization method must be combined with anchors which give absolute locations.

The special quality of our approach is that we do not have to know the positions of the signal sources. We compute them as well. As a consequence, we can make use of any signal for localization. Even encrypted GPS signal from an unknown positioned satellite or just the signal of a mobile phone of a by-passer will function as an information source. This clearly separates our approach from prevalent approaches which use the information of time of flight, i.e. time of arrival (TOA) or direction of arrival (DOA).

1.1   Related Work

Localization with *known* receiver or sender positions has been a broad and intensive research topic with a variety of approaches. A popular application is GSM localization of mobile phones. Various techniques exist, including angle/direction of arrival (AOA/DOA), time of arrival (TOA, "time of flight"), and time difference of arrival (TDOA) [1]. U-TDOA is a provider-side GSM multilateration technique that needs at least three synchronized base stations. As a client-side implementation needs special hardware, it is hardly prevalent in common mobile phones. Instead, many approaches introduce a distance function based on the received signal strength indication (RSSI). Stable results in the range of meters can be achieved by fingerprinting using a map of base stations [2].

Similar is localization using the RSSI function of WiFi signals. Methods include Bayesian inference [3], semidefinite programming for convex constraint functions [4][5] a combination of WiFi and ultra sound for TOA measurements like the Cricket system [6] or combinations of methods [7].

RSSI evaluation usually comes with difficulties for indoor localization due to the unpredictability of signal propagation [8]. We focus on TDOA analysis in our approach. For TDOA localization of sound and RF signals there is a basic scheme of four or more known sensors locating one signal source. This is solved in closed form [9][10] or with iterative methods [11]. TDOA determination can be done by cross correlation of pairs of signals. An optimal shift between signals is calculated, corresponding to the angle of the signal [12][13]. However, we use signals with a characteristic peak.

Moses et al. [14] use DOA and TDOA information to solve the problem of *unknown* sender and receiver positions. Though sounding similar to our problem, both problem settings differ fundamentally. The additional DOA information enables the authors to apply some sort of "bootstrapping": Initial starting points can be found to solve the problem incrementally.

Raykar et al. locate unknown receivers with onboard audio emitters by time of flight information [15]. Lim et al. locate mobile devices using the RSSI information of unknown WiFi access points [16] given some anchor points in space.

To our knowledge our problem setting of unknown sender and receiver positions with no further information but TDOA has never been addressed so far.

1.2 Problem Setting

Given a communication network of n synchronized nodes $\mathbf{M}_1, \ldots, \mathbf{M}_n$, where $\mathbf{M}_i \in \mathbb{R}^2$ denotes the unknown position in two-dimensional Euclidean space. Now m sound (or radio) signals are produced at unknown time points $t_{\mathbf{S}_1}, \ldots, t_{\mathbf{S}_m}$ and at unknown locations $\mathbf{S}_1, \ldots, \mathbf{S}_m \in \mathbb{R}^2$. Each signal $\mathbf{S}_j$ arrives at receiver $\mathbf{M}_i$ at time $t_{\mathbf{M}_i, \mathbf{S}_j}$ which is the only input given in this problem setting. We can measure this time up to an error margin which we assume to be Gaussian distributed. We assume that the signals propagate in a straight line from the sources to the receivers with the constant signal speed c and that they are distinguishable.

The problem is to compute all the distances and angles between receivers, solely from the times when environmental signals are received. Of course then, the signal directions can be computed from this information. The mathematical constraints can be described using the signal velocity c, the time $t_{\mathbf{S}_j}$ of signal creation and the time $t_{\mathbf{M}_i, \mathbf{S}_j}$ when the signal is received at $\mathbf{M}_i$:

$$c\left(t_{\mathbf{S}_j} - t_{\mathbf{M}_i, \mathbf{S}_j}\right) = |\mathbf{S}_j - \mathbf{M}_i|_2 \qquad (1)$$

where $|\mathbf{S} - \mathbf{M}|_2$ denotes the Euclidean distance in two-dimensional space.

By squaring the equations of form (1) we yield a quadratic equation system which can be written in quadratic form. Depending on the number of signals and receivers this system is under-defined, well-defined or even over-defined. It can be rewritten as an optimization problem where a polynomial function of degree four needs to be minimized. There is only small hope for an efficient solution for such problems in general.

Our solution considers the case where the signal sources are so far from the receivers that the time difference at two receivers depends only on the angle between the signal beam and the line between the two receivers. The Ellipsoid TDOA method is an elegant closed form solution for three receivers in the two-dimensional space. The solution is tested in numerical simulations of sound sources with realistic distributions of gaussian error.

Finally, we show how our algorithm performs in real-world indoor and outdoor experiments. Here, we generate series of signals at random positions on circles around the computers by clanking a bottle or two wooden planks. This is the sole information we need to compute the relative distances of the computers.

2 Ellipsoid TDOA Method for Distant Sources

We consider the case where the signal origins are very far from the receivers. Under this assumption we develop an approximative approach to reveal distances and angles between a fixed number of three receivers in two-dimensional space. In this special case a smaller number of sound signals is sufficient to compute the relative locations than in the general case. Furthermore, the solution of the problem can be expressed in a closed form.

Once the receiver triangle ABC has been reconstructed we determine the direction of the signal origins.

2.1 TDOA Ellipse

For three receivers A, B, C in the plane and a distant source S the discrete signal is received by the receivers at time points t_A, t_B and t_C, see Fig. 1. Define

$$\Delta t_1 = t_B - t_A \tag{2}$$
$$\Delta t_2 = t_C - t_A \tag{3}$$

where Δt_1 and Δt_2 are the time differences of arrival (TDOA) between A and B, resp. A and C. For $\alpha = \angle_{CAB}$ and using the assumption of infinite distant signal origins we state:

$$x := \Delta t_1 = d_1 \cos{(\gamma - \alpha/2)} \tag{4}$$
$$y := \Delta t_2 = d_2 \cos{(\gamma + \alpha/2)} \tag{5}$$

where γ denotes the direction of $\mathbf{s}$ with respect to the bisection of α. Combining the equations we derive the following ellipse equation:

$$x^2 \frac{1}{d_1^2} + y^2 \frac{1}{d_2^2} + xy \frac{-2\cos\alpha}{d_1 d_2} = \underbrace{\frac{1}{2} - \frac{1}{2}\cos 2\alpha}_{\sin^2\alpha} \tag{6}$$

Normalization by division by $\sin^2\alpha$ (under the assumption $\alpha \notin \{0, \pi\}$, i.e. A, B, C are collinear) leads to the ellipse parameters

$$a = \frac{1}{d_1^2 \sin^2\alpha}, \qquad b = \frac{1}{d_2^2 \sin^2\alpha}, \qquad c = \frac{-2\cos\alpha}{d_1 d_2 \sin^2\alpha}$$

for $ax^2 + by^2 + cxy = 1$.

Ellipsoid TDOA localization requires at least three pairs of time differences $(\Delta t_1, \Delta t_2)$ from different distant signal origins. From these points we compute the ellipse equation with parameters a, b, c, see Fig. 2. Then, we use the above equations to compute d_1, d_2, α which can be done by the following equations:

$$d_1 = 2\sqrt{\frac{b}{4ab - c^2}}, \qquad d_2 = 2\sqrt{\frac{a}{4ab - c^2}}, \qquad \alpha = \arccos \frac{-c}{2\sqrt{ab}}$$

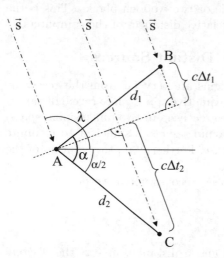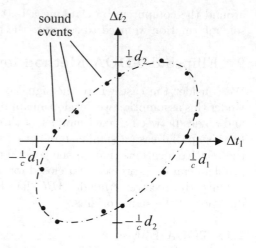

Fig. 1. Three receivers A, B, C and a signal on the horizon with direction **s**

Fig. 2. Multiple distant signal sources with time difference pairs $(\Delta t_1, \Delta t_2)$ in two dimensions form an ellipse

2.2   Linear Regression

Three ambient signals are sufficient to find the ellipse for two dimensions. Since ambient radio or sound signals are no scarce resource the additional signals can be used to overcome the inaccuracies caused by imprecise time measurements and other error sources. Given a sufficient number of $m \geq 3$ signal sources that form a set of (x, y)-tuples we obtain a system of linear equations

$$ax_i^2 + by_i^2 + cx_iy_i = 1 \tag{7}$$

where $1 \leq i \leq m$. We use linear regression to reconstruct the parameters of this ellipse. In matrix notation this is:

$$\underbrace{\begin{pmatrix} x_1^2 & y_1^2 & x_1y_1 \\ \vdots & \vdots & \vdots \\ x_m^2 & y_m^2 & x_my_m \end{pmatrix}}_{\mathbf{Q}} \underbrace{\begin{pmatrix} a \\ b \\ c \end{pmatrix}}_{\mathbf{x}} = \mathbf{1} \tag{8}$$

If $m > 3$ we use the least squares method and solve for the ellipse parameters:

$$\left(\mathbf{Q}^T\mathbf{Q}\right)\mathbf{x} = \mathbf{Q}^T\mathbf{1} \quad \Rightarrow \quad \mathbf{x} = \left(\mathbf{Q}^T\mathbf{Q}\right)^{-1}\left(\mathbf{Q}^T\mathbf{1}\right) \tag{9}$$

If $m = 3$ we solve $\mathbf{x} = \mathbf{Q}^{-1}\mathbf{1}$. For $m < 3$ the system is under-determined and cannot be solved uniquely.

Then, we use the equations of the previous subsection to compute the geometry of the triangle ABC. Since the assumption of infinitely far senders is not realistic this approach results in an approximative solution of the problem.

However, this is the best one can offer if only three signal sources are available, since the problem for three general signal positions is under-defined. Later on, we present simulations which indicate that the approximation behaves well if the signals are a small constant factor farer than the longest edge of the receiver triangle.

2.3   Simulation

We have tested the accuracy of this approximation algorithm with a computer algebra system. A simulation cycle consists of a number of sound sources arbitrarily arranged on a circle with a fixed radius around the origin. Three microphones A, B and C are positioned on a circle with a fixed radius of about 2.3 m forming a triangle with an edge length of 4 m. The sound sources are received by the microphones at time points t_A, t_B and t_C depending on the distance and the speed of sound. A probabilistic Gaussian error model has been added to each timestamp to simulate measurement errors.

For a set of different radii up to 20 m a series of 1,000 tests with 8 sound sources is run. The distance results d_1 and d_2 and the angle α between A and B are subtracted from the real values, which are read from the triangle properties. Failed runs occur if the approximated quadratic equation does not describe an ellipse. For successful runs we calculated the average and the standard deviation of the distance and angle differences.

The results show a systematic under-estimation of the distances between microphones for short ranges which improves after the perimeter of the microphones has been left at about 5 m (Fig. 3). The angle errors show high variance within the perimeter of the microphones which stabilizes quickly upon leaving it, at a range of 5 m (Fig. 4). Failing localizations occur especially if the sound source radius is equal to the microphone radius with up to 4%, but the rate drops quickly to below 1% (Fig. 5).

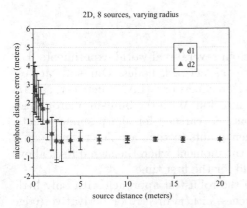
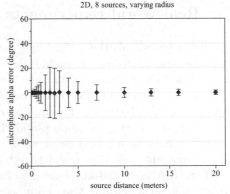

Fig. 3. Increasing sound source distances above 4 m result in distance errors below 0.1 m

Fig. 4. Increasing sound source distances above 4 m result in angle approximation errors below 2°

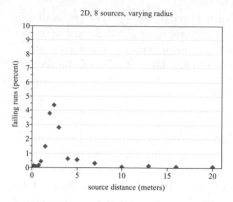

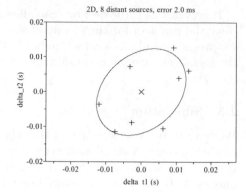

Fig. 5. After reaching a maximum at a sound source distance of 2.5 m the failure rate drops below 1 % for greater distances

Fig. 6. Eight signals with Gaussian error of $\sigma = 2$ ms were received. The elliptical form is hardly recognizable due to this high error.

A stress test was run to observe the behavior of the approximation in case of runtime variances. Distant sound sources were assumed (radius of 1,000 m) and the gaussian runtime error was increased up to a standard deviation of 2.0 ms. For comparison: In 1.0 ms a sound wave travels about 34 cm. Results show a slight over-estimation of the microphone distances and a moderate increase in angular variance. Failures increase to about 5 %. However, a Gaussian distributed error of 2 ms ranges inside the limits of nearly 3 m, which is a lot for a scenario with an edge length of 4 m. The time differences of this magnitude, drawn as x/y-plot, are hardly recognizable as an ellipse any more (Fig. 6). In our real-world experiments we observed runtime errors with a standard deviation of about 0.2 ms, which is way below the errors we induced here.

3   Real-World Experiments

We have tested this theoretical approach in several real-world experiments. For this we use a network of mobile devices as network nodes. Our software establishes UDP communication via local area network (LAN) between several devices and assures precise time synchronization. With the built-in microphones we record sound signals. The audio track is searched for sharp sound events, like clapping or finger snapping and their points in time are determined. As a peculiar mark for a sound event we use the moment when the signal rises above a environment noise dependent threshold for the first time.

Threshold comparisons showed to be the robustest approach with only little drawbacks in precision. Maximum searches, either directly or derivative (edge detection) showed to be slightly more precise but prove to be ambiguous with fatal results in cases when hosts chose different maxima.

The detected signals are exchanged between the nodes. With this information given each node can compute the relative locations using the algorithm described before.

3.1   Time Synchronisation

Common TDOA localization requires precise synchronization among receivers. While unsynchronized localization is generally possible, time synchronization reduces the number of required sound events. To get a global time reference the nodes elect a master based on priority IDs and synchronize to the master clock. The synchronization is achieved with a series of pings between master and all other nodes to get a good estimation of the round trip time (RTT) to the master. The exchanged reference timestamps are filtered for high RTT (outliers), which results from network jitter, and corrected by 1/2 RTT, assuming the network packet took the same runtime in both directions.

Our experiments pointed out that clock drift correction is essential even with the utilized high precision event timer (HPET). Although running with accurately constant speed, drift rates between different clocks of 0.03% were observed, which is too high for our purposes, if untreated. Both time offset and clock drift between client and master are obtained by linear regression of the timestamp set. The precision we achieve is within 0.1 ms in a wireless LAN with an RTT of about 10 ms and within 0.01 ms in a wired LAN with an RTT of about 1 ms.

3.2   Experiments

The first real-world test was situated in a large lecture hall with a size of $17\,m \times 13\,m$ at the University of Freiburg. We arranged 3 laptops A, B, and C in a small triangle residing on a circle with radius 2.3 m and connected them with an ethernet based LAN switch for communication. The triangle was placed in a corner of the hall to test far distant sound sources up to 16 m. To examine the measurement results we noted down the positions of the laptop microphones with a precision of 2 cm and the sound sources with a precision of 10 cm. The distances between the laptops were $d_{AB} = 4.30\,m$, $d_{AC} = 4.14\,m$ and $d_{BC} = 3.47\,m$, which results in $\angle_{CAB} = 48.6°$.

In the experiment, we generated several sound events with an empty glass bottle and a spoon on concentric circles with varying radii around the laptop triangle. The audio signals were recorded with the built-in microphones to detect timestamps for the sound events. The Ellipsoid TDOA method was executed with the timestamps of a single radius as the only input to compute the distances between the microphones. Implausible sound signals with a time difference of more than 20 ms (corresponding to 6 m) were filtered. This is to be done automatically in the future.

The evaluation showed a good convergence of the microphone distance approximations d_1 and d_2 at circle radii of 4 m and above (Fig. 9). Errors fall below 0.5 m. Angle α resides at about 58°, which is an over-estimation of 10°

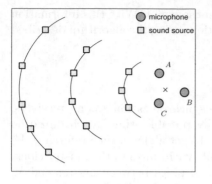

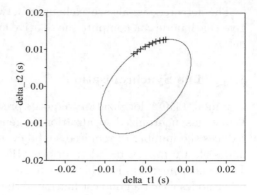

Fig. 7. Series of random signals on concentric circles with varying radii around the computers

Fig. 8. Time differences from the approximation experiment as x/y-plot. Sound signals from a distance of 13 m arrive from only one direction.

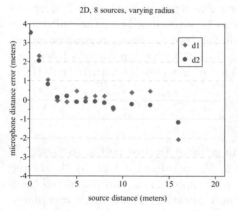

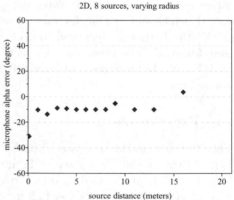

Fig. 9. Distance errors of d_1 and d_2 for the indoor experiment. Errors decrease quickly except for an outlier at 16 m.

Fig. 10. Angle error of α for the indoor experiment. Angle errors decrease except for a slight over-estimation of about 10°.

(Fig. 8). With increasing sound signal distance results degrade, which we attribute to the narrowing sector of sound origins. Due to limited room size they come from only one direction, thus making it harder to describe an ellipse, see Fig. 8. This seems to be a drawback of the technique. Obviously we need signals from different angles to reconstruct the ellipse properly.

A second experiment was performed outdoors. We expected to find more realistic conditions like wind noise, birdsong, and the nearby rapid transit system. On the other hand there would be space to generate sound events from all directions, facilitating the ellipse regression. Eight nodes, consisting of four laptops and four Apple iPhones with our software running were placed randomly on a green area of the campus in an area of $30\,\text{m} \times 30\,\text{m}$. Their positions were measured precisely to within $20\,\text{cm}$. A WLAN access point established communication between nodes for synchronization and timestamp exchange.

A series of sound events was produced by an assistant circling the experiment perimeter in varying distances. He generated clearly audible sound signals by clapping two wooden planks. We obtained a series of 50 sounds of which none were filtered.

The Ellipsoid TDOA method was applied to all combinations of three nodes with a total of $n(n-1)(n-2) = 336$ combinations. From every Ellipsoid method run only the two distance measures d_1 and d_2 were used while angle α was discarded. Symmetric duplicates were removed, which resulted in 12 measures for each of the 28 node pairs. The measures belonging to the same node pair were averaged. They form a complete graph of known node distances.

By optimization we calculated the relative positions (x_i, y_i) of the microphones from the node distances d_{ij}:

$$\min_{x,y} \left(\sum_{i=1}^{n} \sum_{j=i+1}^{n} (x_i - x_j)^2 + (y_i - y_j)^2 - d_{ij}^2 \right)$$

The resulting point set was mapped onto the real-world positions by a congruent rotation and translation. This was done by calculating the SVD (Singular Value Decomposition) of the point set correlation which provides an optimal transformation to minimize distances of associated points in the least squares sense.

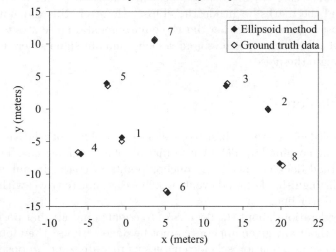

Fig. 11. Relative positions of the microphones mapped onto the ground truth data. The average distance from ground truth is $38\,\text{cm}$ (standard deviation: $14\,\text{cm}$).

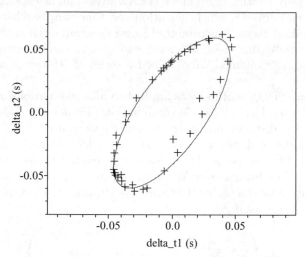

Fig. 12. Ellipse of time differences for the nodes (1), (3) and (8) with the distances $d_{(1)(3)}$ and $d_{(1)(8)}$. Nearby sound events deform the ellipse, instead of residing on the ellipse border (*lower right sector*).

The average distance from ground truth after mapping was 38 cm with a standard deviation of 14 cm. Fig. 11 shows the mapped point set and the real-world positions. Fig. 12 depicts the ellipse for node (1), (3) and (8) as an example. For the distant sound signals the marks reside on the ellipse. Only when the assistant came closer to the microphones the infinite distance assumption was violated and the marks lie inside the ellipse. However, this did not affect the robust ellipse regression. Neither did the environmental noise affect our results, as they have no influence on the sound velocity and our signals were loud enough to predominate the noise.

4   Conclusion

To our knowledge, we are the first to consider the problem of relative localization of nodes using nothing but TDOA information of ambient signals. The Ellipsoid TDOA method does not need any anchor points in space. In our method, we only need distinguishable sound events which we assume to travel with a constant speed on a direct line.

Our considerations about the degrees of freedom point out that position reconstruction without any given anchors cannot be done with less than four receivers. However, the approximation scheme enables us to state some propositions about the receiver positions and the direction of the signal sources even with three receivers.

The technique requires a minimum number of three signals in two-dimensional space. However, it directly benefits from an increased number of signal events. These are cheaply available in many environments. Then, our technique becomes very robust, even for noisy data.

Simulation and real-world tests suggest that our assumption of infinitely remote signal sources is not far-fetched. The parallax decreases quickly, as soon as we are outside the receiver perimeter. This allows us to use the approximation even in close-ranged scenarios.

The approximation scheme fails if receiver positions collapse on a line or a plane. In this case, the time differences form a line of which no ellipse can be extracted. However, this singular case can be detected and treated particularly.

In some cases of noisy data we found a slight, systematic over-estimation of receiver distances and angles. For the stress test runs this resulted in higher variance. Visual analysis of the time differences showed that the resulting ellipse does not fit the corpus of the noisy data properly. This seems to be a result of deficient ellipse regression.

4.1   Future Work

It is very obvious that time synchronization is hard to achieve for radio signals due to the much higher speed of light. The Ellipsoid TDOA method can be extended to work without time synchronization between computers. Then, the minimum number of sound signals increases from three to five. However, sound signals are not a scarce resource.

We have also seen some room for improvement in the approximation of the TDOA ellipse. While our regression minimizes the error "in some least squares sense" [17], there are more sophisticated techniques available like *geometric fit* proposed by Gander et al. [17].

Further research will involve the use of non-discrete continuous signals, e.g. voices, traffic noise or analogous radio signals. By testing for best overlaps of such signals it should be possible to compute a time difference analogously to sharp signals. This would dramatically increase the information basis of the algorithm.

References

1. Drane, C., Macnaughtan, M., Scott, C.: Positioning GSM Telephones. IEEE Communications Magazine 36, 46–54 (1998)
2. Otsason, V., Varshavsky, A., LaMarca, A., de Lara, E.: Accurate GSM Indoor Localization. In: Beigl, M., Intille, S.S., Rekimoto, J., Tokuda, H. (eds.) UbiComp 2005. LNCS, vol. 3660, pp. 141–158. Springer, Heidelberg (2005)
3. Sichitiu, M.L., Ramadurai, V.: Localization of Wireless Sensor Networks with a Mobile Beacon. In: Proceedings of the First IEEE Conference on Mobile Ad-hoc and Sensor Systems, pp. 174–183 (2004)
4. Biswas, P., Ye, Y.: Semidefinite Programming for Ad Hoc Wireless Sensor Network Localization. In: IPSN 2004: Proceedings of the 3rd International Symposium on Information Processing in Sensor Networks, pp. 46–54. ACM, New York (2004)

5. El Ghaoui, L., Doherty, L., Pister, K.S.J.: Convex position estimation in wireless sensor networks. In: Proceedings of Twentieth Annual Joint Conference of the IEEE Computer and Communications Societies, INFOCOM 2001, vol. 3, pp. 1655–1663. IEEE, Los Alamitos (2001)
6. Priyantha, N.B., Chakraborty, A., Balakrishnan, H.: The Cricket Location-Support System. In: MobiCom 2000: Proceedings of the 6th annual international conference on Mobile computing and networking, pp. 32–43 (2000)
7. Wang, Z., Zekavat, S.(R.).A.: A Novel Semidistributed Localization Via Multinode TOA-DOA Fusion. IEEE Transactions on Vehicular Technology 58(7), 3426–3435 (2009)
8. Ferris, B., Hähnel, D., Fox, D.: Gaussian Processes for Signal Strength-Based Location Estimation. In: Proceedings of Robotics: Science and Systems Conference, RSS (2006)
9. Yang, L., Ho, K.C.: An Approximately Efficient TDOA Localization Algorithm in Closed-Form for Locating Multiple Disjoint Sources With Erroneous Sensor Positions. IEEE Transactions on Signal Processing 57, 4598–4615 (2009)
10. Gillette, M.D., Silverman, H.F.: A Linear Closed-Form Algorithm for Source Localization From Time-Differences of Arrival. IEEE Signal Processing Letters 15, 1–4 (2008)
11. Carevic, D.: Automatic Estimation of Multiple Target Positions and Velocities Using Passive TDOA Measurements of Transients. IEEE Transactions on Signal Processing 55, 424–436 (2007)
12. Rui, Y., Florencio, D.: New direct approaches to robust sound source localization. In: Proc. of IEEE ICME 2003, pp. 6–9. IEEE, Los Alamitos (2003)
13. Valin, J.-M., Michaud, F., Rouat, J., Létourneau, D.: Robust Sound Source Localization Using a Microphone Array on a Mobile Robot. In: Proceedings International Conference on Intelligent Robots and Systems (IROS), pp. 1228–1233 (2003)
14. Moses, R.L., Krishnamurthy, D., Patterson, R.M.: A Self-Localization Method for Wireless Sensor Networks. EURASIP Journal on Advances in Signal Processing, 348–358 (2003)
15. Raykar, V.C., Kozintsev, I., Lienhart, R.: Position calibration of audio sensors and actuators in a distributed computing platform. In: Proceedings of the Eleventh ACM International Conference on Multimedia, p. 581. ACM, New York (2003)
16. Lim, H., Kung, L.-C., Hou, J.C., Luo, H.: Zero-configuration indoor localization over IEEE 802.11 wireless infrastructure. Wirel. Netw. 16(2), 405–420 (2010)
17. Gander, W., Golub, G.H., Strebel, R.: Least-Square Fitting of Circles and Ellipses. BIT Numerical Mathematics 34(4), 558–578 (1994)

Author Index

Printing: Mercedes-Druck, Berlin
Binding: Stein+Lehmann, Berlin